MORE PRAISE FOR THE WORLD OF SHAMANISM

"…Eminently useful and inspiring. A brilliant integrative work that pushes the frontiers of consciousness in insightful, practical, and powerful ways."

—Angeles Arrien, Ph.D., Cultural Anthropologist,
author of *The Four-Fold Way* and *The Second Half of Life*

"…Unique in bringing together the full range of anthropological, psychological, and psychiatric literature on this vital subject. It does so with admirable scholarship yet still manages to be sensitive and clear."

—Christie W. Kiefer, Ph.D., Professor Emeritus of Anthropology,
University of California at San Francisco

ABOUT THE AUTHOR

Roger Walsh came from Australia as a Fulbright Scholar to the United States, where he is professor of psychiatry, philosophy, and anthropology, and adjunct professor of religious studies at the University of California at Irvine. His writings and research have received over two dozen national and international awards and honors, while his teaching has received one national and six university awards. His publications include *Paths Beyond Ego: The Transpersonal Vision, Higher Wisdom: Eminent Elders Explore the Continuing Impact of Psychedelics,* and *Essential Spirituality: The Seven Central Practices.*

TO WRITE TO THE AUTHOR

If you wish to contact the author or would like more information about this book, please write to the author in care of Llewellyn Worldwide and we will forward your request. Both the author and publisher appreciate hearing from you and learning of your enjoyment of this book and how it has helped you. Llewellyn Worldwide cannot guarantee that every letter written to the author can be answered, but all will be forwarded. Please write to:

Roger Walsh, M.D., Ph.D.
℅ Llewellyn Worldwide
2143 Wooddale Drive
Woodbury, Minnesota 55125-2989

Please enclose a self-addressed stamped envelope for reply,
or $1.00 to cover costs. If outside U.S.A., enclose
international postal reply coupon.

Many of Llewellyn's authors have websites with additional information and resources. For more information, please visit our website at http://www.llewellyn.com

THE WORLD OF
SHAMANISM

NEW VIEWS OF AN ANCIENT TRADITION

ROGER WALSH, M.D., Ph.D.

Llewellyn Publications
Woodbury, Minnesota

First Edition
Sixth Printing, 2012

Book design by Donna Burch
Cover art © Digital Stock & Photodisc
Cover design by Gavin Dayton Duffy
Edited by Jane Hilken
Llewellyn is a registered trademark of Llewellyn Worldwide Ltd.

Acknowledgment is gratefully made for permission to reproduce the following:
    American Museum of Natural History: *A Koryak woman shaman with drum*, p. 190.
    Sherana Harriette Frances: *Psychedelic session—death and rebirth*, pp. 76–84.
    Natural Museum of Denmark: (1) *Aua and his wife*, p. 51, and (2) *Igjugarjuk*, p. 65.

Library of Congress Cataloging-in-Publication Data for *The World of Shamanism* is on file at the Library of Congress.
ISBN: 978-0-7387-0575-0

Llewellyn Publications
A Division of Llewellyn Worldwide Ltd.
2143 Wooddale Drive
Woodbury, Minnesota 55125-2989
www.llewellyn.com

Printed in the United States of America

This book is dedicated to three people who have done so much
to bring the best of shamanism to the West:

Michael Harner
What Vivekananda did for Hinduism and D. T. Suzuki for Zen,
Michael Harner has done for shamanism; namely,
brought the practices and potentials of this tradition to the awareness of the West.

Sandra Harner
By mastering both shamanism and psychology, Sandra Harner exemplifies one of the central
opportunities of our time: the opportunity of integrating diverse sources of wisdom
to more effectively heal and serve.

Angeles Arrien
By so ably embodying and expressing her tradition,
Angeles Arrien inspires and awakens those graced by her presence.

———————

And to five people whose work helped create new fields
and made new understandings of shamanism possible:

Huston Smith
Scholar and sage who so ably explains and embodies the depths of the great religions.

Charles Tart
Who pioneered the investigation of states of consciousness.

Stan Grof
Whose groundbreaking research revealed the farther reaches of mind.

Ken Wilber
Whose integral vision is the most encompassing intellectual framework of our time,
and a healing gift to a fragmented world.

———————

and
Frances Vaughan
Awakener of intuition and gift to us all.

CONTENTS

PART V

The Shaman's Universe

PART VI

Shamanic Techniques

CONTENTS

ACKNOWLEDGMENTS

I would like to express my deep appreciation to the many people who offered assistance with the writing of *The World of Shamanism*. Exceptionally valuable feedback came from Timothy White and Ken Wilber.

Other people who contributed to this project in various ways include William Andrew, Allyn Brodsky, Etzel Cardena, Marlene Dobkin de Rios, Steve Donovan, Betty Sue Flowers, Gordon Globus, Maria Globus, Tom Hurley, Stan Krippner, John Levy, Michael Murphy, Patrick Ophals, Don Sandner, Bruce Scotton, Deane Shapiro, Huston and Kendra Smith, John White, and Michael Winkelman. Members of a Psychiatry Residents Seminar at the University of California at Irvine who gave valuable feedback include Gary Bravo, Melissa Derfler, Charles Grob, Diane Harris, Barbara Kaston, Mitch Liester, Jim Mc-Quade, Pat Poyourow, Susan Seitz, Ken Steinhoff, and Nathan Thuma.

Special thanks to several people who were exceptionally generous with their time, feedback, and assistance. These include Angeles Arrien, Kent Carroll, Michael Harner, Arthur Hastings, Chris Kiefer, Charles Tart, and, as always, Frances Vaughan. Bonnie L'Allier provided her usual excellent administrative and secretarial support, ably assisted by Hann Wang.

PART I

WHO, WHERE, WHEN, AND WHAT IS A SHAMAN?

Reality is more complex than we would like.
If we insist upon it making sense,
We will find ourselves despairing.
Reality cannot be neatly packaged....
Reality is all that is, and this is often at odds
With what we imagine it should be.

—*Rabbi Yannai, an early Jewish sage*[332]

CHAPTER 1

Why Shamanism and Why Now?

The old gods are dead or dying and people everywhere are searching…
—*Joseph Campbell*

The world of shamanism is awakening. After long being demonized by clergy, diagnosed by psychiatrists, and dismissed by academics, interest in shamanism is thriving.

How could this be? How could a tradition many times older than the pyramids survive in an era of space ships and superconductors? How could humankind's most ancient healing discipline coexist with modern medicine? And how could spiritual practices that preceded the Bible, Buddha, and Lao Tsu by thousands of years become popular in our Western scientific culture?

Yet such is the case. Once there was serious concern that these ancient practices might be lost forever. Now academic texts pour from printing presses, and there are waiting lists for workshops offering introductions to these "archaic techniques of ecstasy." What has happened, and why? This explosion of Western interest reflects many factors. Some are cultural, some academic, while others reflect the nature of shamanism and its techniques.

THE OPENING OF THE WESTERN MIND

One factor is that Western culture has changed. In our global village, with cultures sloshing into one another, there is widespread interest in non-Western healing and spiritual practices such as yoga and meditation. This love affair with spiritual practices now encompasses traditions from all parts of our shrinking globe. Jewish Kaballah, Christian contemplation, Sufi zikr, and Hindu and Taoist yoga all have their Western devotees. It was surely only a matter of time before this newfound fascination would encompass shamanism.

Another powerful and controversial factor in the opening of the Western mind was psychedelics. Their widespread use in the sixties unleashed experiences of such intensity and impact that they shook the very foundations of society. Suddenly millions of people found themselves blasted into types of experiences and states of consciousness that were, quite literally, beyond their wildest dreams. A Pandora's box of heavens and hells, highs and lows, trivia and transcendence poured into minds and societies utterly unprepared for any of them. For perhaps the first time in 2,000 years since the Greek Eleusinian mysteries, a significant proportion of a Western culture experienced powerful alternate states of consciousness.

Some of these states were obviously painful and pathological, and they filled blaring newspaper headlines. Yet others were clearly transcendent states that demonstrated to an unsuspecting world the remarkable plasticity of consciousness and the extraordinary range of alternate states available to us. What to make of these states and the drugs that induce them is still an unresolved puzzle for the Western world. However, it was surely inevitable that they would fuel fascination with tribal practitioners who use them in systematic, sacred ways for spirituality and healing.

THE OPENING OF THE ACADEMIC MIND

Anthropologists have studied shamanism since the birth of their discipline. As we will see, some of those studies were initially ethnocentric and dismissive, but over time became more sympathetic and balanced. Most research was done from a safe academic distance as observers rather than as practitioners. However, beginning in the 1960s, something novel happened; something that would change certain anthropologists, their profession, and their culture in ways none of them could have guessed.

Some anthropologists—such as Barbara Tedlock, Michael Harner, and Larry Peters, together with a few psychologists such as Bradford Keeney—began not just to observe but to learn and practice shamanism themselves. In doing so they began to appreciate the power of its practices, the impact of its experiences, and the potentials of altered states in ways they had not even suspected. For some of them, shamanism went from being an interesting academic study to a compelling personal practice, a practice they sought to share. They did this not only through academic reports but also through popular writings and workshops. This choice immediately consigned them to academic controversy, since a mere whiff of popularization is enough to make many academics sniff in suspicion. So powerful has Michael Harner's impact been, that he is widely credited with being the prime mover behind the Western popularity of shamanic practices and the birth of so-called "core shamanism" and "neoshamanism." Personal accounts of his transformation from traditional academic to nontraditional shaman can be found in books such as *The Way of the Shaman*[152] and *Higher Wisdom*.[396]

Academia both leads and follows popular trends. Therefore, it was only a matter of time before anthropologists began to sit up, puzzle, and worry over the rising tide of neoshamanism. That puzzlement continues to this day, and we will return to it later. But one clear effect was a born-again interest in researching shamanism.

Other intellectual fields were also affected not only by shamanism but also by the waves of interest in topics such as meditation, yoga, spirituality, and consciousness. Transpersonal psychology was the first new field specifically devoted to the study of such phenomena, and it rapidly spawned transpersonal anthropology and sociology.[399] The term *transpersonal* was chosen to reflect the central importance of experiences in which the sense of self or identity extends beyond (*trans*) the personality or personal to encompass wider aspects of community, culture, and even cosmos. Such experiences have been highly valued across cultures and centuries. Other fields, such as consciousness studies, the anthropology of consciousness, and research on dreams, visualization, and meditation quickly followed. Consciousness and consciousness-altering disciplines had finally attained academic respectability, and in turn they fostered further interest in shamanism.

There was another academic event, and a very curious one at that, which sparked interest in shamanism. Beginning in 1968, a young anthropology graduate student at the University of California at Los Angeles (UCLA) published a wildly popular series of books claiming to report his years of intensive training under a Yaqui Indian "man of knowledge."[46–48; 67] The student was Carlos Castaneda, soon to be one of the world's most famous, or infamous, anthropologists. The early books received much acclaim, both popular and professional, and a thesis based on his "research" was awarded a Ph.D. The award has been called UCLA's worst mistake, because as successive books flowed from the presses, they became increasingly improbable, and their authenticity was definitively skewered by Richard DeMille[66; 67] in his books *Castaneda's Journey* and *The Don Juan Papers*. This minor difficulty did little to diminish their popularity, and they continued to provide valued teaching stories for thousands of readers.[397] They also continued to inspire interest in shamanism, even though the world and practices Castaneda portrayed have precious little in common with it.

Castaneda remained a reclusive and enigmatic figure till the end. I had the opportunity of meeting him twice, and I even took the training offered by his "witches"—the women who were supposedly his fellow sorcerers and students.[74] I found Castaneda to be a powerful and charismatic figure, but the witches' training offered a curious mélange of body movements that had virtually nothing to do with shamanism.

THE AVAILABILITY OF SHAMANIC TECHNIQUES

A final factor contributing to its popularity concerns the availability and nature of some shamanic practices. Interested Westerners no longer have to climb Nepalese mountains or brave Amazon jungles, although surprising numbers do. Most, however, happily settle for a comfortable, nearby hotel where they can enroll in one of the many available neoshamanic workshops.

The speed of some shamanic techniques helps. Disciplines such as meditation or yoga may be powerful but can require weeks or months of practice to induce palpable effects. Not so for shamanism. Some people with no prior training can walk into a workshop and, within minutes of listening to shamanic drumming, experience meaningful visions and insights.

Of course, initial workshop experiences are very different from traditional mastery that can require many years of arduous training and testing. In fact, there is debate about whether brief workshops for Westerners should even be called "shamanic training." Nevertheless, the net result of these cultural, academic, and shamanic currents is that the West's newfound fascination with shamanism continues to grow.

CHAPTER 2

Why *The World of Shamanism?*

A new intellectual understanding of reality is an important catalyst…. Many of the transpersonal experiences that are potentially of great therapeutic value involve such a basic challenge to the individual's world view that he or she will have serious difficulty in letting them happen unless properly intellectually prepared.

—Stan Grof[130]

Most scientific studies of shamanism have been by anthropologists. This is hardly surprising, for it is the anthropologists who have braved everything from arctic winters to tropical jungles to observe native shamans at work. However, several other disciplines, and especially psychology, can complement and enrich anthropological contributions. And, of course, the study of shamanism also has much to contribute to psychology.

PSYCHOLOGY'S "CONTRIBUTIONS"

Unfortunately, psychology's past contributions have been decidedly mixed. Many studies are now outdated, while others have been flawed by superficial interpretations, insufficient anthropological data, and lack of personal experience of shamanic practices. So while psychology can offer valuable insights, it has also produced notable misunderstandings, some of which distorted our view of shamanism for decades.

One source of these misunderstandings was Freudian psychoanalysis. Long the dominant school of Western psychiatry, it fostered a distinctly negative view of shamanism and most things religious. Freud took a dim view of religions, usually regarding them as defense mechanisms at best or psychopathology at worst. Transcendent experiences—even the most profound and ecstatic—were all too often regarded as pathological regressions of near-psychotic proportions. Mystical experiences were diagnosed as "neurotic regressions to union with the breast," while enlightenment was dismissed as a regression to intrauterine stages.[399] Even saints and sages were chopped down to neurotic size.

Not surprisingly, shamanism often fared badly at the hands of psychoanalytically minded researchers. Since shamans may exhibit periods of bizarre behavior, enter altered states of consciousness, have visions, and claim to commune with spirits, they were all too often dismissed as disturbed. As we will see, schizophrenia, hysteria, and epilepsy were common diagnoses, in spite of considerable evidence to the contrary. The unfortunate result was often a tragic insensitivity to the deeper, positive aspects of this tradition.

Is there any reason to think that psychological explanations might be better now? Yes, because Western psychology has advanced significantly. The field is no longer tightly wedded to psychoanalysis, psychoanalysis has softened its stance toward religion, and schools have emerged that are sympathetic to religious experience—for example, humanistic, transpersonal, and Jungian psychologies.

New research fields have also emerged. Studies of psychosomatic healing, consciousness, dreaming, meditation, mystical experiences, and placebo effects all throw new light on shamanic practices. In addition, a small but growing number of psychologists and psychiatrists have undertaken shamanic or core shamanic training themselves. Western psychology is now better equipped to appreciate religious practices in general and shamanism in particular.

THE BIG PICTURE

The World of Shamanism has several aims. The first is to introduce shamanic practices and the second is to examine them in the light of modern research to assess how, when, and why they work.

A third goal is to evaluate extreme claims about shamans. On one hand, many early researchers diagnosed and dismissed them as merely neurotic or psychotic, charlatans or con men. On the other hand, popular writers sometimes portray them as superhuman saints or sages. Careful examination explodes both myths.

The World of Shamanism also aims to examine shamanism from a larger perspective, a perspective that is historical, cross-cultural, and inter-religious. For the first time in history we have access to virtually all the world's religious, healing, and consciousness-altering disciplines. Consciousness-altering disciplines are practices—such as shamanism, yoga, or contemplation—that can induce beneficial states of consciousness. Examples of such states include deep concentration, calm, and equanimity; the first of these consciousness traditions was shamanism.

Now that we have information about many such traditions from around the world, we can compare them. These comparisons allow us to recognize important similarities between shamanism and other traditions, as well as equally important differences. For example, there are obvious similarities between the shaman's life and training and "the hero's journey"—the archetypal life pattern displayed by heroes from diverse times. Yet there are also crucial differences, such as their types of insight or states of consciousness. These differences will become clear when we map shamanic states of consciousness precisely.

Comparisons such as these also illuminate how consciousness-altering disciplines have evolved across the centuries, and how this evolution has both reflected and fostered the evolution of human consciousness and religious experiences. Then we can see where shamanism fits within this vast evolutionary panorama. We will do this by using the largest and most comprehensive intellectual framework currently available: an integral vision.

A PERSONAL PERSPECTIVE

My own professional background is primarily in medicine, psychiatry, and psychology. In addition, I have long been interested, both personally and professionally, in transformative practices ranging from psychotherapy to diverse contemplative and spiritual disciplines. Some three decades of practical and intellectual exploration have given me a deep appreciation for the power and profundity of these disciplines and their ability to foster healing, exceptional abilities, and spiritual awakening. And I say this as a person who was a confirmed skeptic of all things spiritual, until I tried the practices for myself.

Shamanism is one such discipline. However, while I have been fortunate to meet and learn from traditional shamans, I have not done systematic fieldwork. Likewise, while I have participated in core shamanism workshops and have benefited from many shamanic techniques, I am not traditionally trained. I therefore draw gratefully on the field research of others, while hopefully contributing a perspective informed by an unusual combination of professional training, research experience, and personal practice in several relevant areas.

Hopefully, one valuable aspect of this perspective is its interdisciplinary scope. My intellectual and contemplative interests have been wide-ranging, and I am forever curious about the ways in which different disciplines can inform one another. Consequently, one goal for this book is to explore the implications of recent advances in diverse fields—for example, psychosomatic medicine, psychology, meditation, and comparative religion—for understanding shamanism.

One intellectual orientation of mine is toward what might be called "assumptive minimalism." That is, I prefer to make as few assumptions as possible when examining a topic. For example, I don't simply presuppose that shamans have the healing or parapsychological abilities that they claim, but neither do I simply accept certain mainstream dismissals of such claims. Rather, I am much more interested in waiting to see what the actual evidence is and am therefore content to remain agnostic if necessary. This attitude tends to upset both believers and skeptics, but hopefully it yields greater clarity in the end.

The World of Shamanism began as a revision and updating of a previous book, *The Spirit of Shamanism*. However, so many new ideas and information were added, so much revision, reorganization, and updating performed, that it soon became apparent that a new book had been born. Consequently, *The World of Shamanism* draws gratefully on its predecessor but also goes far beyond it.

CHAPTER 3

What Is a Shaman?
The Challenge of Definition

If names be not correct, language is not in accordance with the truth of things. If language be not in accordance with the truth of things, affairs cannot be carried on to success.

—Confucius[344]

What is a shaman? On this crucial point there is remarkably little agreement and "practically every scholar forms his own opinion of what constitutes shamanism."[169]

THE CHALLENGE OF DEFINITION

Challenges for Anthropologists

The French anthropologist Roberte Hamayon edited a book with a telling title: *The Concept of Shamanism: Uses and Abuses.* In it she lamented, "For more than a century the question of what shamanism really is in the final analysis has hindered all attempts to define it."[102]

In fact, the problem has become worse rather than better. The popularity of shamanic practices in the West, divorced from their traditional cultural context and goals, has created thousands of practitioners and a movement that is to be called—what? "Neoshamanism" is one term in vogue.

In addition, because of its growing popularity, the term "shaman" has become an hon-orific title. Consequently, people have rushed to apply the title to their heroes. Jungian psychologists, for example, have anointed Jung as "the closest thing we have to an authentic shaman in the modern West..."[259] Likewise, some philosophers see the influence of sha-manism behind the rise of Greek philosophy, and one declared, "It is henceforth one of the accepted anthropological truths that Socrates was the last shaman and the first philoso-pher."[139] This "accepted truth" is news to anthropologists. So one problem is that the terms *shaman* and *shamanism* are used in very different ways.

The Challenge of Language

But the problem goes deeper. This kind of definitional problem is by no means unique to shamanism. The more one looks at any religious or healing discipline, the more variation becomes apparent. There is no one kind of Christianity or Hinduism or medicine.

In fact, the deeper one looks, the more any definition of any term becomes elusive. In fact, the philosopher Jacques Derrida famously concluded that every term is an *aporia*, a problem or question that eludes any final resolution. No wonder that, in the words of *The Encyclopedia of Philosophy*, "The problems of definition are constantly recurring...no prob-lems of knowledge are less settled than those of definition..."[1]

For the philosopher Ludwig Wittgenstein,[419] "philosophy is a battle against the be-witchment of our intelligence by means of language." However, the battle has been less than fully successful. Of course, this is no surprise to mystics, who have long claimed that only contemplative, transrational intuition escapes the net of language and that, in the words of the Taoist sage, Lao Tzu,

> Existence is beyond the power of words to define:
> Terms may be used
> But none of them are absolute.[40]

So the challenge of defining shamanism, or anything else, turns out to be far deeper than we usually assume. We cannot expect absolute certainty or agreement from our terms and definitions. However, we can follow Confucius's advice and try to use them carefully and skillfully, knowing that, as the great religious scholar Huston Smith put it, "All human thought proceeds from words. As long as words are askew, thought cannot be straight."[344]

A Practical Solution

How, then, can we proceed? One practical solution is to use what is called a "stipulative" definition: a definition that does not necessarily follow previous rules or patterns of use, but does stipulate precisely how the term is being used. To do this we will trace how the terms *shaman* and *shamanism* have been used in the past, identify key features, assess their validity, and then attempt to integrate valid features into a coherent definition. Let us begin by examining the ways in which understandings and definitions of shamanism have evolved over time.

PAST DEFINITIONS

The term shamanism comes from the word *saman* of the Tungus people of Siberia, meaning "one who is excited, moved, raised." It may be derived from an ancient Indian word meaning "to heat oneself or practice austerities"[25] or from a Tungus verb meaning "to know."[169] But whatever its derivation, the term *shaman* has been widely adopted by anthropologists to refer to specific groups of healers in diverse cultures who have sometimes been called medicine men, witch doctors, sorcerers, wizards, magicians, or seers. However, these terms are too vague to serve the precise definition we are seeking.

Early anthropologists were particularly struck by the shamans' unique interactions with "spirits." Many in the tribe might claim to see or even be possessed by spirits. However, only the shamans claimed to have some degree of control over them and to be able to command, commune, and intercede with them for the benefit of the tribe. Thus Shirokogoroff, one of the earliest explorers of the Siberian Tungus people, stated:

> In all Tungus languages this term (saman) refers to persons of both sexes who have mastered spirits, who at their will can introduce these spirits into themselves and use their power over the spirits in their own interests, particularly helping other people, who suffer from the spirits.[335]

In a later chapter we will take up the surprisingly difficult challenge of deciding just what these "spirits" may be.

Whereas early explorers were most impressed by shamans' interactions with spirits, later researchers were intrigued by shamans' ability to control the states of consciousness in which these interactions occur. As Western culture became interested in altered states of consciousness (ASCs), so too researchers became interested in the widespread use of altered states in religious practices. However, as we will see, there are many possible ASCs. Therefore, the question naturally arises, "Which ones are peculiar to, or defining of, shamanism?" It turns out that there are broad and narrow kinds of definitions.

In broad definitions, the "only defining attribute is that the specialist enter into a controlled ASC on behalf of his community."[284] Such specialists could include, for example, yogis who enter samadhi or mediums who enter a trance and then claim to speak for spirits. So a broad ASC definition of shamanism would include any practitioners who enter controlled alternate states of consciousness, no matter which particular alternate states these may be.

Narrow definitions, on the other hand, specify the alternate state(s) more precisely, usually as kinds of "ecstatic" states. Mircea Eliade set the tone. Eliade was one of the twentieth century's outstanding religious scholars, and for decades his text *Shamanism: Archaic Techniques of Ecstasy* was regarded as a classic, but is now mired in controversy. In it he argued that "A first definition of this complex phenomenon, and perhaps the least hazardous, will be: shamanism = technique of ecstasy."[83]

Here ecstasy infers not bliss, but more a sense, as the *Random House Dictionary* defines it, "of being taken or moved out of one's self or one's normal state and entering a state of intensified or heightened feeling." As it turns out, this definition of ecstasy as "being taken out of one's self or one's normal state" is particularly appropriate for shamanism.

A distinctive feature of the shamanic ecstasy is the experience of "soul flight," "journeying," or "out-of-body experience." In their ecstatic state, shamans may experience themselves, their soul or spirit, flying through space and traveling to either other worlds or distant parts of this world. In Eliade's words, "The shaman specializes in a trance during which his soul is believed to leave his body and ascend to the sky or descend to the underworld."[83]

Spiritual experiences reflect the techniques used to induce them as well as the cosmology used to frame them. The shamanic cosmology often comprises a three-tiered universe of upper, middle, and lower worlds, the middle one corresponding to our earth.[152] Shamans range throughout this threefold world system in order to learn, to obtain power, or to diagnose and treat those who come for help. During these journeys, shamans may meet the animals or spirits who inhabit them, see the cause and cure of patients' illness, or intercede with friendly or demonic forces on behalf of the community.

So far we have three key features of shamanism to include in a definition:

1) Shamans can voluntarily enter altered states of consciousness.

2) In these states they may experience themselves "journeying" to other realms.

3) They use these journeys for acquiring knowledge or power and for helping people in their community.

Interaction with spirits is also frequently mentioned in definitions of shamanism. In addition, Michael Harner suggests that a key element of shamanic practices may be "contact with an ordinarily hidden reality." For him a shaman is "a man or woman who enters an altered state of consciousness at will to contact and utilize an ordinarily hidden reality in order to acquire knowledge, power, and to help other persons. The shaman has at least one, and usually more, 'spirits' in his personal service."[146]

Should these two additional elements—"contacting a hidden reality," and interaction with "spirits"—be included as essential elements of a definition of shamanism? Here we are on tricky philosophical ground. Certainly this is what shamans experience and believe they are doing. However, it is an enormous philosophical leap to assume that this is what they are actually doing. Jumping from phenomenology (experience) to ontology (claims about reality) is always risky.

The fundamental nature (or in philosophical terms, the "ontological status") of both the realms that shamans experience and the entities they meet is an open question. To the shaman they are usually interpreted as independently and fully "real." However, to a Westerner with no belief in other realms or entities, spirits and other realms would be interpreted as mere mind creations. These philosophical questions will be explored more fully in a later chapter. Suffice it to say for now that the interpretation of the nature of these phenomena depends on one's own philosophical leanings or worldview. We are therefore on safer ground while defining shamanism if we skirt these questions of philosophical interpretation as much as possible.

A SYNTHETIC DEFINITION

Putting all these elements together, what do we get?

Shamanism can be defined as a family of traditions whose practitioners focus on voluntarily entering altered states of consciousness in which they experience themselves or their spirit(s) interacting with other entities, often by traveling to other realms, in order to serve their community.

This definition covers several key features of shamanism. The reference to "a family of traditions" acknowledges that there are variations among shamanic practitioners. At the same time, the definition is precise enough to help distinguish shamanism from other traditions and practices, as well as from various psychopathologies with which it has been confused. For example, priests may lead rituals but they rarely enter altered states. On the other hand, mediums may enter altered states but do not usually journey, while Tibetan Buddhists may sometimes journey, but this is not a major focus of their practice. On the pathological side, those suffering from mental illness may enter altered states and meet "spirits," but they do so as involuntary victims.

Of course, this definition will not include every conceivable shaman nor satisfy everyone. Nor should it; no single definition can. Nevertheless, it has several strengths. First, it covers the major features said to characterize shamanism, yet is reasonably narrow and precise. This will allow us to focus our investigation on a clearly distinguished group of practices and practitioners that almost all researchers would agree are indeed shamanic.

Second, this definition focuses on practices and experiences rather than on beliefs and dogma. This is consistent with Michael Harner's claim that "shamanism is ultimately only a method, not a religion with a fixed set of dogmas."[148] Of course, shamans do hold certain relatively fixed beliefs. No person or tradition can survive without a consistent belief system.

There is a centuries-long debate over whether shamanism can properly be called a religion. To avoid becoming embroiled in this argument and also the debate over what exactly defines a religion, here I will simply sidestep the issue and refer to shamanism as a religious tradition. At other times, depending on the context, I will also refer to it as a consciousness discipline, a spiritual discipline, or a healing discipline, since it contains all these elements.

CHAPTER 4

The When and Where of Shamanism: Origins and Distribution

Man is the being who, however dimly and half-consciously, always understands,
and must understand, his own being historically.
—*William Barrett*[22]

ORIGINS

Shamanism is one of humankind's most ancient traditions, spanning perhaps tens of thousands of years. The American anthropologist Michael Brown points out that "anthropologists are fond of reminding their students that shamanism, not prostitution, is the world's oldest profession."[36] Not only is it the oldest profession but also one of the most widespread, found today in areas as scattered as Siberia and South America.

The striking similarities among shamans raise the obvious question of how these similarities emerged. Perhaps they developed spontaneously in different locations, evoked by innate human tendencies or recurrent social needs. Another possibility is that they resulted from migration from common ancestors.

Migration alone seems unlikely. Shamanism occurs among tribes with so many different languages that diffusion from a common ancestor must have begun at least 20,000 years ago.[416; 418] But would shamanic practices remain so remarkably stable in so many cultures, while language and social practices changed so drastically? Migration alone can hardly account for shamanism's far-flung distribution.

It follows that some recurring combination of social forces and innate abilities led to the repeated discovery of shamanic practices and states of consciousness in diverse times and cultures. Certainly humans seem to have an innate tendency to enter altered states, and some of those states are very specific. For example, for 2,500 years Buddhists have accessed eight highly specific states of extreme concentration called *jhanas*, while yogis have accessed similar concentrative *samadhis*.[37; 121] Clearly, the human mind tends to settle into certain specific states of consciousness if given the right conditions or practices, and this suggests an underlying neural basis.[a]

Similarly for shamanic states. These can be induced by diverse conditions, and most people can experience them to some degree[152]—all of which suggests that the mind has an inherent tendency to adopt them. Since common experiences such as isolation, fatigue, hunger, or rhythmic sound induce them, they would likely be discovered by many cultures and generations. Given that shamanic states can be meaningful and healing, the methods for inducing them would likely be transmitted across generations, supportive beliefs would develop, and shamanism would be born again.

DISTRIBUTION

Since shamanism has endured so long and spread so widely, an obvious question is why does it occur in some cultures and not in others? Cross-cultural research suggests some answers. The anthropologist Michael Winkelman compared magico-religious practices in forty-seven societies spanning almost 4,000 years from 1750 B.C. (the Babylonians) to the present.[417; 418] Remarkably, prior to Western influences, all of these cultures used altered states of consciousness for religious and healing practices.

But although shamanic practices extend to most regions of the world, they occur primarily in particular types of societies: nomadic and hunting and gathering tribes. These people have little agriculture and almost no social classes or political organization. Within these tribes the shaman plays many roles: healer, ritualist, mythologist, medium, and master of spirits. With their many roles and the power vacuum offered by a classless society, shamans exert a major influence on their people.

However, as societies evolve and become more complex, the situation changes dramatically. As societies become fixed rather than nomadic, agricultural rather than foraging, and socially and politically stratified rather than classless, then shamanism, as such, dwindles. In its place appear a variety of specialists who focus on one of the shaman's many roles. Instead of shamans we now find healers, priests, mediums, and sorcerers/witches. These specialize respectively in medical, ritual, spirit possession, and malevolent magic practices. A contemporary parallel is the waning of the medical general practitioner or G.P., together with the multiplication of medical specialists.

It is interesting to compare some of the ancient specialists with the shamanic G.P. who preceded them. Priests emerge as representatives of organized religion and are often moral and even political leaders. They lead social rituals and pray to the spiritual forces on behalf of their society. Yet unlike their shamanic ancestors, they usually have little direct experience of altered states.[167]

Shamans are often ambivalent figures, revered for their healing power yet sometimes also feared for their malevolent magic. Whereas priests inherit the shamans' beneficial religious and magical roles, sorcerers and witches are viewed as the specialists in malevolent magic, and, as such, they tend to be feared and persecuted. For example, Michael Brown found that the Aguaruna people of Peru "insist that sorcerers, when discovered, must be executed for the good of society."[36]

Mediums specialize in spirit possession. While they do not undertake journeys, they do enter ASCs in which they experience themselves receiving messages from the spirit world. Recall that some researchers use a broad definition of shamanism that includes anyone using altered states to serve their community. Such a definition fails to distinguish shamans and mediums, both of whom use altered states, though of quite different types. Since shamans are usually found in foraging societies and mediums in more complex ones, this provides a further reason to distinguish them.[30; 417]

As cultures evolve, so too do their religious practitioners. Though shamans as such largely disappear from complex societies, most of their roles and skills are retained by various specialists. However, there is one exception: journeying. None of the shaman's successors focus on journeying.

Why this practice should largely disappear is a mystery. Michael Harner attributes it to suppression of shamanic practices by organized religion; during the nineteenth century it was a criminal offense in parts of Europe to own a drum. Another factor may have been the discovery of techniques such as yoga and meditation. However, it is unclear whether these factors alone could account for the virtual absence in complex societies of a practice that was powerful enough to spread around the world, survive for thousands of years, and form the basis for humankind's most ancient and durable religious tradition.

Figure 1. The rock engravings of Les Trois Frères cave in France are among the most dramatic examples of early human art. Tens of thousands of years ago, unknown artists crawled deep underground to draw a tangle of hundreds of animals. These animals surround a lone bison-headed human figure, which may represent one of humankind's earliest shamans. (Tracing by Henri Breuil of rock engravings in Les Trois Frères cave.)

PART II

THE BIG PICTURE

Each being contains in itself the whole intelligible world.
Therefore, All is everywhere....Man as he is now has ceased to be the All.
But when he ceases to be a mere ego, he raises himself again and penetrates the whole world.

—*Plotinus* [171]

CHAPTER 5

Essential Spirituality: Central Principles and Practices of Spiritual Life

> Although there is a great number of [spiritual] practices all of them have a common purpose because all of them are methods for subduing our uncontrolled mind. Our present mind is like a wild elephant—out of control and hard to tame.
> —*Geshe Kelsang Gyatso, Tibetan Buddhist teacher*[138]

Not only do we have an unprecedented richness of information but also of spiritual disciplines. We are the first generation to have all the world's spiritual and religious traditions available to us and to be able to practice them without being burned at the stake. This remarkable situation makes it possible to identify crucial principles and practices common to different traditions.

CENTRAL PRINCIPLES

The Interdependence of Virtues

The idea that spiritual qualities depend on and support one another echoes through the wisdom literatures of both East and West. The key claim is, as Michael Murphy, a philosopher and founder of the famed Esalen Institute, summarized it, "Every virtue requires other virtues to complete it."[250]

A similar theme echoes through the East. One of the most famous of all Eastern Orthodox Christian texts, *The Philokalia*, asks, "Which virtue is the most important?" and replies "The answer to this is that the virtues are linked one to another, and follow as it were a sacred sequence, one depending on the other..."[272] In China, Confucius warned, "Possessed of courage but devoid of morality, a gentleman will make trouble while a small man will be a brigand."[207] Likewise Buddhist psychology describes in precise terms how certain positive mental qualities tend to strengthen one another, and how others—such as effort and calm—need to be in balance.[268]

There actually seem to be two distinct concepts contained in the idea of the interdependence of virtues. The first is that virtues complement one another. The second is that the cultivation of one virtue facilitates the cultivation of others.

Authentic Traditions Offer Multifaceted Disciplines

Given the interdependence of virtues, it is not surprising that authentic spiritual disciplines provide multiple techniques and practices. As such, they offer rounded psychological and spiritual training: for example, the yogas of Taoism and Hinduism, the eight-fold path of Buddhism, and certain Western contemplative traditions. Michael Murphy's book *The Future of the Body*[250] offers an excellent discussion of the strengths and weaknesses of various traditions.

The necessity of multifaceted disciplines is supported by recent psychological research on development. It is now apparent that development proceeds not in some monolithic manner in which all psychological capacities and qualities grow together, but rather in a loosely correlated way. Ken Wilber points out that the maturation of one "developmental line" or capacity, such as intellectual ability, can readily outstrip others, such as moral or emotional development. The result is uneven or lopsided development that is fraught with potential problems for the individual and sometimes for his or her society. For example, intellectual development seems to be necessary, but by no means sufficient, for moral development. Therefore, highly intelligent but morally immature people—such as Hitler and the Nazis—can act in extremely unethical ways and thereby inflict horrendous suffering on societies or even the planet.[412] The fate of our species and our planet may depend on our ability to match our intellectual and technological mastery with our emotional and moral maturity. Wise people have long recognized this kind of need, and authentic spiritual disciplines therefore offer a full complement of practices that foster maturation of many facets of personality.

The Authenticity of Spiritual Disciplines

Early researchers comparing contemplative disciplines often assumed that all of them—whether yoga or shamanism, Taoism or Sufism—resulted in the same common final experience and developmental stage.[b] However, it is now increasingly clear that while some disciplines may converge, and perhaps even display a so-called "transcendent unity of religions,"[328] different disciplines may also induce quite different experiences and also aim for different developmental levels. Recognizing this, Ken Wilber made a crucial distinction between two vital religious dimensions: *legitimacy* and *authenticity*.[407]

The *legitimacy* of a tradition refers to the degree to which it satisfies the psychological needs of a population at its current developmental level.

The *authenticity* of a discipline refers to the developmental level for which a tradition aims. That is, a tradition is said to be authentic to the extent to which it aims to foster development to higher, transpersonal stages.

To these we can add *effective authenticity*, which is a measure of the extent to which a discipline is effective in moving practitioners to the higher stages for which it aims.

However, we probably need a more nuanced view of both *authenticity* and *effective authenticity*. Given that there are many independent psychological capacities, we can not speak precisely of a person being at a single level of development. Certainly we can recognize a center of gravity or an average level of development in any individual. However, we also need to recognize that development can be uneven and that a person may be at quite distinct levels on different capacities.

Likewise, disciplines may have different effects on different capacities. That is, a particular discipline might foster some capacities more than others. For example, classical Confucianism was probably good at cultivating, and therefore highly authentic for, moral development, but was probably far less effective for concentration.

THE SEVEN CENTRAL PRACTICES

If one plumbs, investigates into, sharpens, and refines himself,
a morning will come when he will gain self-enlightenment.

—*Lu Shiang-Shan, neo-Confucian sage*[57]

There seems to be widespread agreement among the sages of the world's great religions that there are seven qualities of heart and mind and seven kinds of practices to develop them that are central to a full spiritual life.[392] These practices are essential for anyone who would live wisely, love wholeheartedly, mature fully, and contribute effectively.

Above all, these seven practices are indispensable for anyone who seeks the higher reaches of spiritual life. These higher reaches are known by many names: *enlightenment* and *liberation, salvation* and *satori, fana* and *nirvana, awakening* and *Ruah Ha-qodesh*. Different names, but all point to the highest human possibility, which, paradoxically, is simply the recognition of who we really are.

But of course that "who" turns out to be far, far more than we usually think. In fact it, and we, turn out to be not only more than we think, but more than we can think. "This Mind is the Buddha" exclaimed the great Huang Po[27] and numerous other Buddhist masters. "Here, in my own soul, the greatest of all miracles has taken place—God has returned to God,"[157] rejoiced the remarkable Christian Meister Eckhart. This is possible because in the words of one of India's greatest philosopher-sages, Sri Aurobindo: "The Self is that one, immutable, all-pervading, all-containing, self-existent reality or Brahman hidden behind our mental being into which our consciousness widens out when it is liberated from the ego…"[15]

We could multiply examples endlessly, but the general point is simple. There is widespread agreement that seven kinds of practices are central and essential for anyone who would live life to the fullest.[d] These seven practices are:

1) Living ethically, 2) Transforming emotions, 3) Redirecting motivation,
4) Training attention, 5) Refining awareness, 6) Cultivating wisdom,
and 7) Serving others.

Here, I will illustrate them with quotations from multiple religions and focus on shamanic sources in later chapters. For an expanded discussion of these practices, and exercises to make them part of your life, see my book *Essential Spirituality: The Seven Central Practices*.

LIVING ETHICALLY

Regard your neighbor's gain as your gain
And your neighbor's loss as your own loss.
—*Tai Shang Kon Ying P'ien (Taoism)*[276]

Spiritual traditions regard ethical living as an essential foundation. However, their understanding of ethics is very different from conventional views and far more psychologically astute. "Rare are those who understand virtue," sighed Confucius.[207]

Spiritual traditions view ethics not in terms of conventional morality, but rather as an essential discipline for training the mind. Contemplative introspection makes it painfully apparent that unethical behavior—behavior that aims at inflicting harm—both stems from and strengthens unhealthy, destructive motives and emotions such as greed, anger, and jealousy. In Western psychological terms, unethical behavior reinforces these destructive mental elements; in Asian terms, it stamps their "karmic imprint" on the mind, karma here being the psychological residue left by past behavior.

Conversely, ethical behavior—behavior intended to enhance the well-being of all—heals the mind. It cultivates healthy qualities—such as kindness, calm, and compassion—while inhibiting unhealthy destructive motives and emotions through a process psychologists call "reciprocal inhibition." Once this is recognized, ethics change dramatically. It becomes not something imposed from without but rather something sought from within, not a sacrifice but rather enlightened self-interest, a gift to both others and oneself. As the Buddha pointed out: "Whatever you do, you do to yourself."[42]

At first ethical training involves a struggle to reverse old habits. However, with practice it becomes increasingly effortless and spontaneous until "whatever is…thought to be necessary for sentient beings happens all the time of its own accord."[111] Confucius described this stage as one in which "I could follow the dictates of my own heart; for what I desired no longer overstepped the boundaries of right."[384] The well-known Buddhist meditation teacher Jack Kornfield describes the maturation of ethical living as follows: "At first, precepts [ethics] are a practice. Then they become a necessity, and finally they become a joy."[199]

TRANSFORMING EMOTIONS

Everything from ruler, minister, husband, wife and friends to mountains, rivers, spiritual beings, birds, animals, and plants should be truly loved in order to realize my humanity that forms one body with them, and then my clear character will be completely manifested, and I will really form one body with Heaven, Earth and the myriad things.

—Wang Yang Ming (neo-Confucian sage) [50]

There are three key components to emotional transformation.

1) Reducing problematic emotions such as fear, anger, and jealousy

2) Cultivating positive emotions such as love, joy, and compassion

3) Developing equanimity

Spiritual disciplines contain a wealth of practices for both reducing difficult emotions and for cultivating beneficial ones to remarkable levels. For example, Christian *agape*, yogi *bhakti* (transpersonal love), Buddhist *karuna* (compassion), and Confucian *jen* (humanity) reach their full flowering only when they unconditionally and unwaveringly embrace all people and even all creatures.

This is facilitated by the third component of emotional transformation: the cultivation of equanimity. Equanimity is an imperturbability that maintains mental equilibrium and allows emotions such as love and compassion to remain unwavering, even under duress. This is, for example, the Stoic's *euthymia*, the Jewish *hishtavut*, the Christian "divine apatheia," and the "contented self" of Islamic Sufism. Western psychology recognizes a weaker form of this that it calls "affect tolerance."[425] Emotional transformation presumably fosters "emotional intelligence" that research suggests is associated with exceptional personal, interpersonal, and professional success.[122] Here psychology would agree with the twelfth-century Jewish physician and teacher Maimonides that "emotions of the soul should be watched, regularly examined, and kept well balanced."[163]

REDIRECTING MOTIVATION

All you want is to be happy. All your desires, whatever they may be, are of longing for happiness. Basically, you wish yourself well....Desire by itself is not wrong. It is life itself, the urge to grow in knowledge and experience. It is the choices you make that are wrong. To imagine that some little thing—food, sex, power, fame—will make you happy is to deceive oneself. Only something as vast and deep as your real self can make you truly and lastingly happy.

—Sri Nisargadatta Maharaj (twentieth-century Hindu sage) [257]

Traditionally, redirecting motivation has two major components. The first is to reduce the compulsive power of craving; the second is to change the objects of desire.

The spiritual view of the importance of reducing craving was succinctly summarized by Mohammad with his words "the miser is the poorest of all"[9] and by the Buddha in his second and third Noble Truths. The second truth states that "the cause of suffering is craving," and the third claims that freedom from craving brings freedom from suffering. The neo-Confucian philosopher-sage Wang Yang Ming went so far as to claim that

> the learning of the great person consists entirely in getting rid of the obscuration of selfish desires...so as to restore the condition of forming one body with Heaven, Earth, and the myriad things.[50]

With spiritual practice, motivation becomes less scattered and more focused; the things desired become more subtle and more internal. There is less concern with material acquisition and more concern with metamotives, especially self-transcendence and selfless service. Traditionally this motivational shift was seen as "purification." In Western psychological terms it seems analogous to movement up Maslow's hierarchy of needs[227] and in social terms to the historian Arnold Toynbee's idea that "etherealization" occurs as cultures evolve.[80] Contemporary research agrees that psychological maturity leads to greater concern for others.[397]

TRAINING ATTENTION

Control the mind.
Attain one-pointedness.
Then the harmony of heaven
Will come down and dwell in you.
You will be radiant with life.
You will rest in Tao.
—*Chuang Tzu, Taoist philosopher*[236]

For contemplative traditions, cultivating attention and concentration is crucial. By contrast, attentional training is much misunderstood in the West. In fact, "No subject occupies a more central place in all traditional teachings; and no subject suffers more neglect, misunderstanding, and distortion in the thinking of the modern world."[326]

For a century, Western psychology made the tragic error of accepting the dismal conclusion of William James that "attention cannot be continuously sustained."[178] Yet James went further to suggest that

> the faculty of voluntarily bringing back a wandering attention over and over again is the very root of judgment, character and will. No one is *compos sui* if he have it not. An education which would improve this faculty would be the education par excellence....It is easier to define this ideal than to give practical direction for bringing it about.[176]

Here is a stark contrast between Western psychology, which says attention cannot be sustained, and contemplative disciplines, which say that attention can and *must* be sustained if we are to mature to our true potentials.

Controlling attentional wanderlust is so important because the mind tends to take on qualities of the objects to which it attends, and according to yoga, "Whatever we contemplate or place our attention on, that we become."[94] For example, thinking of an angry person inflames anger while thinking of a loving person elicits love. Here's a little experiment that will make this crystal clear:

> Take a deep breath, relax, and notice how you feel. Now visualize or think about someone you know who seems like an angry person. When you have that person in mind, notice how you feel. Let that image go, take a breath, and relax. Then visualize or think of someone who is warm and loving. Now, how do you feel? Probably very different.

Those who can control attention can therefore cultivate specific emotions and motives. Eventually they can bring their minds to such calm and stillness that awareness becomes clear and reveals our true nature. The Bible urges, "Be still and know that I am God,"[295] while the *Bhagavad Gita*, the Hindu classic, describes the results of concentration and calm as follows:

> When, through the practice of yoga,
> the mind ceases its restless movements,
> and becomes still, one realizes the Atman [Self],
> it satisfies one entirely.
> Then one knows that infinite happiness
> which can be realized by the purified heart...[290]

Chuang Tzu gave an equally beautiful description:

> When water is still it is like a mirror....
> And if water thus derives lucidity from stillness,
> How much more the faculties of mind?
> The mind of the sage being in repose
> Becomes the mirror of the universe.[117]

REFINING AWARENESS

Contemplatives of all stripes agree that our usual awareness is insensitive and impaired: fragmented by attentional instability, colored by clouding emotions, and distorted by scattered desires. Similar ideas echo through Western thought, which suggests that we mistake shadows for reality (Plato) because we see through "narrow chinks" (William Blake), a "reducing valve" (Aldous Huxley), or "through a glass darkly" (St. Paul).

The fifth practice therefore refines awareness by making perception more sensitive, more accurate, and more appreciative of the freshness and novelty of each moment. Then, according to Chuang Tzu, one "sees what the eyes sees, and does not add to it something that is not there."[238]

The antidote to this blindness is practicing clear, continuous awareness. Clear awareness heals and transforms, and the Buddha declared that "mindfulness...is helpful everywhere."[267] Contemplatives would agree with Fritz Perls, the founder of Gestalt therapy, that "awareness per se—by and of itself—can be curative."[277]

WISDOM

> Happy are those who find wisdom....
> She is more precious than jewels,
> And nothing you desire can compare with her....
> And all her paths are peace....
> Get wisdom, get insight: do not forget
>
> —*Jewish Torah*

Wisdom is deep understanding of, and practical skill in responding to, the central existential issues of life. Existential issues are those crucial and universal concerns that all of us face simply because we are human. They include finding meaning and purpose in our lives, managing relationships and aloneness, acknowledging our limits and smallness in a universe vast beyond comprehension, living in inevitable uncertainty and mystery, and dealing with suffering and death. A person who has developed deep insights into these issues, and skills for dealing with them, is wise indeed.

Wisdom is much more than knowledge, and Taoism is very clear that "he who is learned is not wise."[280] Whereas knowledge simply requires information, wisdom requires understanding it; knowledge informs us whereas wisdom transforms us; knowledge is something we have, wisdom something we must become.

Spiritual disciplines regard the cultivation of wisdom as a central goal of life. They particularly recommend the following: To seek wisdom from the company of the wise, from the study of their writings, from reflecting on the nature of life and death, and by spending time in nature, silence, and solitude. Above all, they urge us to look within ourselves, since as Lao Tzu said, "Knowledge studies others, wisdom is self-known."[40]

SERVING OTHERS: AN ALTRUISTIC LIFE

> All that one gives one gives to oneself.
> If this truth is understood,
> Who will not give to others?
> —*Ramana Maharshi*[297]

Spiritual disciplines regard altruistic service as both a means to, and an expression of, maturity. "Make it your guiding principle to do your best for others," urged Confucius, and "put service before the reward you get for it."[207] Likewise, the Buddha claimed that if we really understood the transformative power of generosity we would not want to eat a meal without sharing it.

Generous service can transform the mind. Giving inhibits qualities such as craving and jealousy, while strengthening positive emotions such as love and happiness.

In addition, what we ourselves experience reflects what we want others to experience. If we plot revenge and plan pain for others, we tend to inflame emotions such as anger and hatred in ourselves. Yet when we desire happiness for others we tend to feel it ourselves, an experience that Buddhists call "sympathetic joy." This is why practices designed to cultivate benevolent feelings—such as love, compassion, and sympathetic joy—can produce remarkably ecstatic states.

Western psychologists are reaching similar conclusions. Generous people tend to be happier and psychologically healthier and to experience a "helper's high."[251; 397] As people age, they increasingly find that it is their legacy—their contributions to the world and future generations—that gives meaning and satisfaction to their lives.[213] The so-called "paradox of pleasure" is that taking time to make others happy makes us happier than devoting all our efforts to our own pleasure.[251] Some therapists use this principle by, for example, advising clients to do something for another person each day. Abraham Maslow summarized the contemplative understanding as follows: "The best way to become a better helper is to become a better person. But one necessary aspect of becoming a better person is via helping other people."[226] Mohammad summarized this practice extremely simply with the words "be kind to all."[9]

SUMMARY

These are the seven practices that sages the world over emphasize as central and essential for a full spiritual life. Together they constitute a "technology of transcendence" for awakening our potentials and living life to the fullest. Shamans were the first to develop this art, and in the following chapters we will explore the specific ways in which shamans use it.

CHAPTER 6

What Is a Hero?
Life's Aims and Games

Only if we know that the thing which truly matters is the infinite can we avoid fixing our interests upon futilities and upon all kinds of goals which are not of real importance.

—Carl Jung

Shamans stand at the head of a long lineage of extraordinary individuals who have lived, excelled, or loved so well that ordinary mortals have regarded them with awe or jealousy or both. These are humankind's heroes, the healers, helpers, saints, or sages who exemplify our untapped potentials. Their lives have been immortalized in song, legend, and myth. Ordinary mortals have wondered and puzzled about them, venerated or even worshipped them, and often felt that they must be more than merely human, even when the heroes themselves made no such claims.

"Are you a God?" they asked the Buddha. "No," he replied.
"Are you an angel, then?" "No."
"Then what are you?"
Replied the Buddha, "I am awake."[344]

We now have accounts of the heroes of diverse times and cultures and can therefore discern the common contours of their lives. The mythologist, Joseph Campbell, did just this in his book *The Hero with a Thousand Faces*.[44] Campbell identified life themes and stages and mapped these as "the hero's journey." While there are variations according to culture, historical period, and type of hero, the general contours and crises display common themes.

Shamans may be our earliest heroes, because the stages of their quest—their challenges, training, and triumphs—demonstrate these themes. Therefore, let us step back and examine the common characteristics of humankind's greatest heroes from different centuries and cultures. From this panoramic perspective we can then identify universal goals, training, tests, and traps, as well as unique features of the shaman's path.

TYPES OF HEROES

But first, we need to supplement Joseph Campbell's scheme. For Campbell's map, brilliant as it is, does not distinguish well between different types of heroes. He collected diverse accounts (legends, myths, biographies) of all types of heroes—such as warriors, healers, saints, and gods—and distilled the adventures and stages of life that all heroes pass through. Campbell's genius lay in recognizing the unity behind diversity, the common thread that runs through these many lives, and in unifying them into a single grand story.

But this grand unification comes at a price and that price is the obscuring of differences. For while it is true that there are similarities between the journey of a saint and a warrior, there are also major differences, and Campbell tends to elevate them all to the same transcendent status.[408]

What Campbell gave us is a brilliant *horizontal* map that traces the development and life stages of the composite hero. To this we can add a *vertical* map of the different levels on which life's aims and games are played. The vertical map enables us to distinguish among different types of heroes, to separate saints from warriors and sages from power seekers. We then have a scheme that allows us to recognize the universal—the stages common to all heroes—while at the same time acknowledging the particular—the different types and levels of life goals, games, and heroes. Different types of heroes reflect different types of games. We therefore need to examine the different types of games that people in general, and heroes in particular, can play in order to decide just what type of hero the shaman is.

The word "game" is a little tricky since it is often used to imply something trivial or frivolous. However, it can also refer to something far more significant; namely, choosing to confront meaningful challenges that test and hone our abilities as we strive for cherished goals. It is in this sense that the word is being used here.

Without meaningful games we languish in boredom and meaninglessness. In his book *The Master Game*, Robert DeRopp claims: "What people really need and demand from life is not wealth, comfort or esteem, but *games worth playing*." Therefore, he advises, "Seek, above all, for a game worth playing….Having found the game, play it with intensity—play as if your life and sanity depended on it (they do depend on it)."[68]

But there are games and there are games. Some are constructive, while others are ultimately destructive to both the individual and society, no matter how initially satisfying. Robert DeRopp offers incisive analyses of various games and points out that

> life games reflect life aims and the games men choose to play indicate not only their type, but also their level of inner development….We can divide life games into "object" games and "meta" games. Object games can be thought of as games for the attainment of material things, primarily money and the objects which money can buy. Meta games are played for intangibles such as knowledge or the "salvation of the soul."[64]

Object games aim for the concrete things of the world, especially for "the physical foursome" of money, power, sex, and status. Meta-games, on the other hand, are more subtle and aim for intangibles such as truth, beauty, or knowledge.

At the summit of these meta-games DeRopp places the Master Game: the quest for enlightenment, salvation, or awakening. This is the game played by sages across cultures and centuries. It is the game of exploring and mastering not the outer but the inner world of one's own mind and consciousness. Its ultimate goal is no less than to recognize and dissolve into one's true nature and to delight in the greatest of all possible discoveries: the ecstatic realization that this nature is inseparable from the Divine.

Different traditions express this in different ways but the message is clearly the same. In the great monotheistic traditions we find:

The kingdom of heaven is within you. (Jesus, Christianity)

Those who know themselves know their Lord. (Mohammad, Islam)

He is in all, and all is in Him. (Judaism)

Centuries earlier, similar words were already pouring from ecstatic Chinese practitioners:

> Those who know completely their own nature, know heaven. (Mencius,
> Confucianism)[280]

> In the depths of the soul, one sees the Divine, the One. (The Chinese *Book of Changes*)

Indian traditions also offer the same gift, the recognition that

> Atman [individual consciousness] and Brahman [universal consciousness] are one.
> (Hinduism)

> Look within, you are the Buddha. (Buddhism)[392]

But this raises a painfully obvious question: Why do most of us sleepwalk through life oblivious of our true nature? DeRopp explains that the basic idea underlying all the great religions

> is that man is asleep, that he lives amid dreams and delusions, that he cuts himself
> off from the universal consciousness…to crawl into the narrow shell of a personal
> ego. To emerge from this narrow shell, to regain union with the universal conscious-
> ness, to pass from the darkness of the ego centered illusion into the light of the
> non-ego, this was the real aim of the *Religion Game* as defined by the great teachers;
> Jesus, Gautama, Krishna, Mahavira, Lao-tze and the Platonic Socrates.[64]

This emergence, reunion, and enlightenment are the aims of the Master Game. But al-though it has been taught for centuries by sages of all traditions, it remains much misun-derstood and as DeRopp points out:

> It still remains the most demanding and difficult of games, and in our society there
> are few who play. Contemporary man, hypnotized by the glitter of his own gadgets,
> has little contact with his inner world, concerns himself with outer, not inner space.
> But the Master Game is played entirely in the inner world, a vast and complex terri-
> tory about which men know very little. The aim of the game is true awakening, full
> development of the powers latent in man. The game can be played only by people
> whose observations of themselves and others have led them to a certain conclusion;
> namely, that man's ordinary state of consciousness, his so-called waking state, is not
> the highest level of consciousness of which he is capable. In fact this state is so far

from real awakening that it could appropriately be called a form of somnambulism, a condition of "waking sleep."[68]

This then is the Master Game, perhaps the most profound and misunderstood of all games. How does this relate to shamanism? What I want to suggest is that, at their best, shamans were the earliest forerunners of the Master Game player. Alternately, one could say that shamans played the Master Game to the extent and depth they could in the ways allowed by their cultures and times. They were the first to systematically explore and cultivate their inner world and to use their insights and images for the benefit of their people.

To say that shamans were among our earliest Master Game players is not to claim, as some people do, that their techniques, experiences, and states of consciousness were identical to those of the saints and sages who followed them thousands of years later. No, the Master Game has evolved over millennia, sparking, molding, and reflecting the evolution of human consciousness.

Later we will examine how this game evolved. For now it is enough to suggest that some early shamans were, as Ken Wilber put it, "the true Heroes of the times, and their individual and daring explorations in transcendence could only have had a truly evolutionary impact on consciousness at large."[408]

Having decided that shamans at their best were, and are, Master Game players, we can now examine the common features of this game and the ways it plays out in the stages of the hero's journey. Campbell's book *The Hero with a Thousand Faces* traces the development of the composite hero: the warrior, ruler, and lover, as much as the Master Game-playing shaman, saint, or sage. Since we are concerned with the latter group, this account draws deeply and gratefully on Campbell's, but also differs from it in several ways.

The Master Game commonly progresses through five major stages. These are:

1) The hero's early conventional life

2) The call to adventure and awakening

3) Discipline and training

4) Culmination of the quest, and

5) The final phase of return and contribution to society.

CONVENTIONAL SLUMBER

The normal adjustment of the average, common-sense, well-adjusted man implies a continued successful rejection of much of the depths of human nature.

—Abraham Maslow [225]

At first the hero slumbers unreflectively within the conventions of society like the rest of us. To a large extent, the culture's conventional beliefs are accepted as reality, its morals deemed appropriate, its limits seen as natural. This is the developmental stage of conventionality, where most of us languish unquestioningly throughout our lives.

Conventionality is an essential stage on life's journey, but it can be a stopping point or a stepping-stone. Since our culture rarely recognizes further possibilities, most people settle here and die here. But if there is one point on which Master Game players agree, it is that though conventionality may be a necessary stage of life, it is definitely not the highest.

In fact, the conventional way of being and state of mind are considered as suboptimal, clouded, and inauthentic. In Asia, this clouded state is described as *maya*, illusion, or like a dream. In the West, existentialists describe it as automation conformity, everydayness, or inauthenticity, while psychologists label it as a shared hypnosis, a collective trance, or "the psychopathology of the average." Whatever its name, the painful implication is that most of us sleepwalk through life, ignorant of our potentials, and unaware of our trance because we are born into it, we all share it, and because we live in the biggest cult of all: *cult-ure*.

The hero's task is to go beyond these conventional limitations. This task involves more than simply reacting against social norms in blind countercultural defiance. Rather, it requires facing the inner fears and outer social sanctions that constrain and cripple our capacities, growing beyond conventional developmental stages, and realizing the fullness of our potential. This requires recognizing and awakening from the collective trance that is the source and sustainer of conventional beliefs and limits. Only in this way can the hero effectively help others to awaken.

One aspect of this awakening is "detribalization."[213] This is the process by which a person matures from a limited tribal perspective to a more universal one.[e] Such a person no longer wholly looks at life through his or her limiting and distorting biases, but rather begins to recognize, question, and correct them. In fact, this correction of cultural biases is one of the hero's great gifts. However, before this can succeed, many other tasks must be accomplished, and the first of these is to respond to "the call."

THE CALL TO ADVENTURE AND AWAKENING

At some point the hero's conventional slumber is challenged by a crisis, an existential confrontation that calls previous beliefs and ways of life into question. The call can come from within or without. Outer physical crises may take the form of sickness, as with some shamans; a confrontation with sickness in others, as with the Buddha; or suddenly staring death in the face.

An inner call may take the form of a powerful dream or vision, as with some shamans, or of a deep heartfelt response to a new teacher or teaching. It may also emerge more subtly as "divine discontent": a growing dissatisfaction with the pleasures of the world or a gnawing question about the meaning of life. No matter how this challenge arises, it reveals the limits of conventional thinking and living, and urges the hero beyond them. In our culture, this may appear as an existential or midlife crisis. Tragically, the deeper causes and questions of the crisis are rarely recognized, its potentials rarely fulfilled, and one of life's great opportunities is then missed.

As Jesus said, "Many are called, but few are chosen." Indeed, few choose to even recognize the call. And no wonder! For those who hear the call now face a terrible dilemma. They must choose whether to answer the call and venture into the unknown realms of life to which it beckons, or deny the call and retreat into their familiar cocoon. If the call is denied then there is little choice but to repress the message and its far-reaching implications. Only by such repression can non-heroes fall again into the seductive, anesthetic comforts of conventional unawareness, suppress the sublime, and sink into what the philosopher Kierkegaard so aptly called "tranquilization by the trivial." The result is a life of unconsciousness and conformity, which existentialists call inauthentic living and alienation.

But the call never really goes away. It lurks forever in the unconscious, alienated and repressed, but periodically sending into awareness bubbles of vague dissatisfaction and disease that demand still more defenses and distraction.[f] No wonder that a potential shaman who refuses the call is said to be at risk of sickness or insanity.

If the call is answered, then the hero's life must be reoriented and reordered. For if the purpose of the life has changed, then so too must one's priorities. What fosters growth is valued, what hinders it is discarded, and much that previously seemed valuable can now seem irrelevant. Renunciation may appear natural and appropriate. For if one is leaving family and home in order to find a teacher, possessions may seem more like hindrances than valuables. Indeed, the Latin term for baggage was *impedimenta*, from which we derive our word impediments. Many great spiritual heroes—Jesus, Buddha, Mahavira, Shankara—have been penniless wanderers who relinquished everything in their single-minded quest for awakening.

DISCIPLINE AND TRAINING

For the next phase a teacher is essential, and so the search for one begins. Then as DeRopp points out:

> The would-be player of the Master Game encounters at the outset one of the most difficult tests in his career. He must find a teacher who is neither a fool nor fraud and convince that teacher that he, the would-be pupil, is worth teaching. His future development depends largely on the skill with which he performs this task.[64]

Sometimes the teacher may be internal. The hero may find an inner guide, guru, or spirit, and this is particularly common among shamans. Even then, an external teacher is invaluable.

The teacher's job is to assess the would-be hero and then tailor a training program to fit his or her personality and development stage. This program will inevitably include at least some of the seven central practices and may involve physical, spiritual, and social disciplines, some of them of extraordinary severity. Physical disciplines develop will and disrupt the ordinary physiology and state of mind, thereby opening the mind to new possibilities. These disciplines include fasting, sleep deprivation, physical exertion, or exposure to extremes of heat or cold. Spiritual practices may involve meditation, yoga, ritual, or prayer, often combined with periods of quiet and solitude. Social disciplines may include compassionate service to cultivate generosity or menial tasks to instill humility.

The intensity with which some students have practiced these disciplines is remarkable. Prolonged starvation, exposure to arctic conditions, and days without sleep have been common fare for the more ascetic Master Game players. Indeed, extreme but unsuccessful players have sometimes starved and frozen themselves to death.

Whatever the method, the aim is the same. It is to work with body, heart, and mind so as to reduce the compulsions of greed and fear, to strengthen capacities such as will and wisdom, and to cultivate emotions such as love and compassion. In short, it is to develop the seven essential qualities of heart and mind.

THE CULMINATION OF THE QUEST

The study of virtue and vice must be accompanied by an inquiry into what is false and true
of existence in general and must be carried by constant practice throughout a long period…
at last in a flash, understanding of each blazes up, and the mind, as it exerts all its power to
the limit of human capacity, is flooded with light.

—*Plato*[288]

For successful players, years of discipline culminate in life-changing breakthroughs. These
may take the form of visions, insights, or experiences of death and rebirth. There may be
a sense of dissolving into the Absolute, a union with Spirit, God, or the Tao. The potential
experiences are numerous and the names many: salvation and *satori*, enlightenment and liberation, *moksha* and *wu*, *fana* and *Ruach Hakodesh*, death and rebirth, to name but a few. But
whatever the name, the result is similar: a realization of one's deeper nature and a resultant
self-transformation. For Master Game players, such breakthroughs represent their life goal.

RETURN AND CONTRIBUTION

The holy man goes to the lone tipi and fasts and prays. Or he goes into the hills in solitude.
When he returns to men, he teaches them what the Great Mystery has bidden him to tell.

—*Sioux Indian*[61]

With the great quest complete, the seeker has become a knower, the student a sage, the
pupil a potential teacher. But there is one more phase before the journey is complete: return and contribution. With one's own questions answered, the world's confusion begs for
clarification; with one's own suffering relieved, the pain and sorrow of the world cry for
healing. The desire to contribute becomes compelling, and the direction of the journey
now reverses. Whereas one had formerly turned away from society and into one's self, now
the hero turns back to society and out into the world.

There are numerous metaphors for this return. In Plato's parable, after escaping from
the cave, the hero reenters it to help others make their escape. In the famous "Ten Oxherd-
ing Pictures" of Zen, which portray in exquisite images the stages of spiritual life, in the
tenth and final picture, the enlightened one "enters the marketplace with help bestowing
hands." In shamanism, novices first tame their spirits and then use them for the benefit of
their tribe. For Christian mystics, this return is the final stage of the "spiritual marriage"
with God—the stage of "fruitfulness of the soul." After the mystic has united with God,

this spiritual marriage bears fruit for humankind as the mystic reenters the world to heal and help. In doing so, the mystic

> accepts the pains and duties in the place of the raptures of love; and becomes a source, a "parent" of fresh spiritual life….This forms that rare and final stage in the evolution of the great mystics, in which they return to the world which they forsook; and live, as it were, as centers of transcendental energy….Hence something equivalent to the solitude of the wilderness is an essential part of mystical education. But, having established that communion, re-ordered their inner lives upon transcendent levels—being united with their Source not merely in temporary ecstasies, but in virtue of a permanent condition of the soul, they were impelled to abandon their solitude; and resumed, in some way, their contact with the world in order to become the medium whereby that Life flowed out to other men. To go up alone into the mountain and come back as an ambassador to the world has ever been the method of humanity's best friends.[375]

This fruitfulness of the soul is the final stage of the Master Game player's life cycle, a cycle that the historian Arnold Toynbee called "withdrawal and return."[371] These heroes withdraw from society to wrestle with the fundamental questions of life, find insights and inspiration within their own depths, and then return to help, heal, and teach.

This is one form of the hero's journey. It is a journey that has been played out over countless years in countless cultures. Its greatest players, the saints and sages, have been said to represent the fullest flowering of humanity and to have given the greatest gifts to society. So at least said the historian Toynbee, the philosophers Bergson, Schopenhauer, and Nietzche, as well as the psychologists James, Maslow, and Wilber.

Of course the spiritual hero's journey can be, and usually is, played out less fully and dramatically. Many set out on the path but few attain the greatest heights. Nor do the "stages of the soul"[246] always constitute a single great circle of withdrawal and return. Rather, the journey may consist of a series of circles like a spiral in which one returns again and again, but each time to a higher vantage point.

Fortunately, the hero's journey is not limited to saints and sages. It is available to us all to greater or lesser degrees, depending on the sincerity and intensity with which we undertake it.

Let us return to the earliest heroes—the shamans—and see to what extent their lives correspond to this universal template.

PART III

THE LIFE OF THE SHAMAN

The words "many are called, but few are chosen" are singularly appropriate here, for the development of personality from the germ-state to full consciousness is at once a charisma and a curse, because its first fruit is the conscious and unavoidable segregation of the single individual from the undifferentiated and unconscious herd.

—*Carl Jung*[185]

CHAPTER 7

Times of Trial:
The Initial Call and the Initiation Crisis

If you bring forth what is within you
What you bring forth will save you
If you do not bring forth what is within you,
What you do not bring forth will destroy you.
—*Jesus,* The Gospel of Thomas

For shamans, the hero's journey usually begins in early adulthood with unusual experiences interpreted as signs from the spirits. In other cases, a shaman's child is selected at birth to continue the family tradition, or occasionally individuals themselves choose the career.

When selection occurs at birth, it can place enormous responsibilities on the future shaman, the family, and even the whole community. Appropriate rituals and taboos must be maintained in minute detail and can be painfully restrictive.

RITUAL, TABOO, AND SUPERSTITION

Knud Rasmussen, whose description of both American and Iglulik Eskimo shamans is a classic, wrote in 1929: "So seriously are all preparations considered, that some parents, even before the birth of the shaman-to-be, set all things in order for him beforehand by laying upon themselves a specially strict and onerous taboo. Such a child was Aua, and here is his own story..."

Mother was put on a very strict diet, and had to observe difficult rules of taboo. If she had eaten part of a walrus, for instance, then that walrus was taboo to all others; the same with seal and caribou. She had to have special pots, from which no one else was allowed to eat. No woman was allowed to visit her, but men might do so. My clothes were made of a particular fashion; the hair of the skins must never lie pointing upwards or down, but fall athwart the body. Thus I lived in the birth-hut, unconscious of all the care that was being taken with me.

At last I was big enough to go out with the grown up men to the blowholes after seal. The day I harpooned my first seal, my father had to lie down on the ice with the upper part of his body naked, and the seal I had caught was dragged across his back while it was still alive. Only men were allowed to eat of my first catch, and nothing must be left. The skin and the head were set out on the ice, in order that I might be able later on to catch the same seal again. For three days and nights, none of the men who had eaten of it might go out hunting or do any kind of work….Even after I had been married a long time, my catch was still subject to strict taboo.[299]

Such a life, hemmed in by countless taboos, is hard to imagine. Yet for tribal peoples these rules are as essential to life as eating. To flout them means offending the spirits and thereby risking death and disaster. Thus the taboos may rule generation after generation even though, as Rasmussen found, "Everyone knew precisely what had to be done in any given situation, but whenever I put in my query: why? They could give no answer."[299]

For Western science, these are examples, plain and simple, of superstitious behavior based on false beliefs. Since shamanic traditions seem to comprise a mixture of both effective techniques and superstitious rituals, it is worth examining how superstitions are learned and maintained.

Psychological explanations center around faulty learning, and many stem from experiments originally conducted by the psychologist B. F. Skinner. Skinner was famous—or infamous, depending on your perspective—for arguing that all behavior could be understood simply in terms of reinforcement by the environment. Free will, he argued, was an archaic concept left over from a prescientific era, and in his book *Beyond Freedom and Dignity*,[340] he proposed a utopian society based on rational principles of reinforcement. Among other things, this would overcome superstition, which he saw as merely a matter of misunderstood, random reinforcement.

Figure 2. Aua and his wife.

Skinner based this claim on a classic experiment in which he gave a pigeon food every fifteen seconds, no matter what it was doing. The bird didn't have to lift a feather for these free meals. Nevertheless it soon started turning in circles. Other birds behaved even more bizarrely—bobbing their head up and down, stretching their neck toward a corner, or making brushing movements over the floor—apparently believing that their behavior caused the arrival of the food.

Whatever the bird was doing when it was initially fed was reinforced, and the animal, understandably but falsely, assumed that its behavior caused the food's arrival. Naturally enough, it repeated the behavior, and, sure enough, food arrived again. Though there was actually no causal relationship between behavior and food—the food invariably arrived every fifteen seconds—the bird assumed there was. Coincidental reward maintained both the behavior and the belief.[17]

Skinner was not shy about implying that people can be birdbrains and suggested that similar reinforcement mechanisms underlie much superstitious behavior in all cultures. Coincidental rewards or punishments can lead people to assume causal relationships where none exist. They then engage in unnecessary behavior, which, because it is randomly reinforced, can seem effective and over time can harden into socially enforced rituals and taboos.[g] Anyone who violates these taboos may then be ostracized or even executed.

Coincidental learning can be enhanced by further factors. The desire for understanding and control makes people uncomfortable with ambiguous situations. They therefore tend to postulate causal relationships, even where none exist. This may reduce feelings of helplessness, since a belief about how something is caused gives a sense of how to control it.

In addition, superstitions are easily learned from other people via "social contagion." Thus Aua told Rasmussen that "our fathers have inherited from their fathers all the old rules of life which are based on the experience and wisdom of generations. We do not know how, we cannot say why, but we keep those rules in order that we may live untroubled."[299]

The net effect of all these factors—coincidental reward and punishment, the desire to understand and control, learning from others—may partly account for the extent and severity of tribal superstitions and taboos, as well as the willingness to endure the severe life restrictions they demand.[h] For in the face of a mysterious, dangerous world, there is enormous pressure to adopt any behavior that promises some degree of control. Not surprisingly, rituals and taboos are widespread among tribal peoples and their shamans. A major task in examining shamanism is therefore to distinguish between effective techniques and ineffective superstitions.

One further point about superstitions is crucial: They do not necessarily imply an immature logic or irrationality. The old, all-too-neat division between "primitive" and "civilized" modes of thought is moribund, although "evidence does exist that some cultures and environments encourage advanced cognitive development and others do not."[208] Superstitions may be inaccurate beliefs, but the beliefs may be quite logical within a particular cultural worldview. After all, if one believes in malevolent spirits, then rituals designed to appease them make perfect sense. Equally logically, an adolescent who seems bothered by the spirits may have special connections with them and could therefore make an effective healer. And, of course, some shamanic beliefs and behaviors may reflect a sensitivity to forces and factors that escape untrained perception.

THE INITIAL CALL

Those called were most often men, though the American anthropologist Barbara Tedlock has proffered a strong argument that scholars have underestimated the number and importance of women.[362] Aua, whose life and taboos we examined above, was selected on the basis of heredity; others may be chosen because of some striking feature or experience. These can include unusual physical appearance, a disorder such as epilepsy, unexpected recovery from severe illness, or a variety of omens.

They may also have striking inner experiences. For example, the call may come in a dream or vision quest. A vision quest is a period spent in solitude and fasting devoted to receiving a guiding vision for one's life. Dreams about spirits may constitute a shamanic call in the Inuit Eskimo tribes, while in Californian Indian tribes it may be dreams about deceased relatives.[201] The significance of these dreams may require confirmation by mature shamans, who were among the world's first professional dream interpreters. A Nepalese shaman described his call at age sixteen as follows:

> I had a wonderful dream in which Bajra (the thunder god) stood before me....Bajra said, "It is time for you to learn to become a shaman. I will be your teacher...." Later that evening, I suddenly went into trance—I began to shake and I could not utter a word. My brother-in-law, who is a shaman, was summoned. He tried to find out which spirit had possessed me, but it would not reveal itself. I remained

in trance, without speaking, for a week....Then, one night, Bajra came to me in a dream and taught me a mantra.[13]

Election by dreams occurs in many religious traditions. Recall, for example, the Jewish Torah: "Hear my words: If there is a prophet among you, I the Lord make myself known to him in a vision, I speak with him in a dream."

The call to shamanism may be met with considerable ambivalence, and those who receive it may be regarded as "doomed to inspiration."[29] Some of the elect attempt to decline the invitation at first, in what Joseph Campbell termed "refusal of the call." However, the spirits or symptoms can be distressingly persistent and eventually win out. Indeed, many shamanic traditions, like many hero traditions, hold that refusal of the call can result in sickness, insanity, or death. One of the earliest shamanic researchers, Bogoras, claimed:

> The rejection of the "spirits" is much more dangerous even than the acceptance of their call. A young man thwarted in his call to inspiration will either sicken and shortly die, or else the "spirits" will induce him to renounce his home and go far away, where he may follow his vocation without hindrance.[29]

In a few tribes, individuals may also select themselves. However, such people are often regarded as less potent masters than those whose selection is ordained by outside forces. One notable exception is the Jivaro Indian tribe of South America. Here would-be shamans select themselves, and established practitioners sell them their knowledge. The Jivaro payment may be neither cheap nor benign. It can consist of such spiritual necessities as one or two shotguns, a blowgun, and a machete.[147]

THE INITIATION CRISIS

While some calls to adventure can be ignored and suppressed, the shamanic initiation crisis cannot. It explodes through the shaman-elect, disintegrating the old identity and demanding birth of the new.

It usually announces itself in adolescence with an onslaught of unusual experiences. These may sometimes include talents such as heightened sensitivity and perception. More often the shaman-to-be starts to exhibit unusual behavior, which can even be bizarre, dangerous, and life threatening. The result may be weeks, months, or even years of unpredictable chaos that disrupts the lives of the shaman, the family, and the tribe. The onset may be abrupt or gradual. Eliade notes that there are

> "sicknesses," attacks, dreams, and hallucinations that determine a shaman's career in a very short time….Sometimes there is not exactly an illness but rather a progressive change in behavior. The candidate becomes meditative, seeks solitude, sleeps a great deal, seems absent-minded, has prophetic dreams and sometimes seizures. All these symptoms are only the prelude to the new life that awaits the unwitting candidate.[83]

Bogoras describes the crisis among Chukchee Indians:

> For men the preparatory stage of shamanistic inspiration is in most cases very painful, and extends over a long time. The call comes in an abrupt and obscure manner, leaving the young novice in much uncertainty regarding it….He feels "bashful" and frightened; he doubts his own disposition and strength, as has been the case with all seers, from Moses down. Half unconsciously and half against his own will, his whole soul undergoes a strange and painful transformation. This period may last months, and sometimes even years. The young novice, the "newly inspired" (*turene'nitvillin*), loses all interest in the ordinary affairs of life. He ceases to work, eats but little and without relishing the food, ceases to talk to people, and does not even answer their questions. The greater part of the time he spends in sleep.[29]

The contemporary anthropologist Larry Peters obtained a powerful firsthand account from a Nepalese shaman:

> When I was 13, I became possessed. I later learned that the spirit was my dead grandfather, but at the time I did not know what was happening. I began to shake violently and was unable to sit still even for a minute, even when I was not trembling.
>
> Finally, all the people in the village came looking for me. When they caught up with me, I stopped shivering and woke up. I was taken home and given food. My family was very concerned. I had no appetite and that night began shaking again.[281]

In the West, such behavior would usually be regarded as psychopathology. However, in shamanic cultures, this crisis is interpreted as selection by the spirits, the victim is destined to be a shaman, and the "newly inspired" is understood to be undergoing a difficult but potentially valuable developmental process. If handled appropriately, this process is expected to resolve in ways that heal the shaman and help the tribe, providing them with new access to spiritual realms and powers. Handling the process appropriately requires training and discipline.

CHAPTER 8

A Life of Learning:
Shamanic Training and Discipline

The greatest of all wonders is not the conqueror
of the world but the subduer of himself.
—William Durant[77]

The extent to which the human mind and body can be developed is extraordinary. Master Game players develop them exquisitely, but for this a discipline is essential.

This discipline includes toughening the body, cultivating the mind, conquering cravings, facing fears, and cultivating capacities such as concentration and endurance. Not surprisingly, this is a lengthy process, where success is measured in months and years, and patience is not only a virtue but a necessity. The goal is to hone body and mind so as to first awaken to spirit and then become an effective instrument of it. The process was pithily summarized by Chuang Tzu, one of the greatest Taoist sages.

> First gain control of the body and all its organs.
> Then control the mind.
> Attain one-pointedness.
> Then the harmony of heaven will come down and dwell in you.
> You will be radiant with Life.
> You will rest in Tao.[236]

This is obviously no simple task, and some 2,000 years ago the Stoic philosopher Epictetus warned, "If you aim to live by such principles, remember that it won't be easy."[87]

Instructions come from both inner and outer worlds. In the outer world, they come via apprenticeship to a master. The apprentice shaman must learn both theory and practice: the myths and cosmology, rituals and techniques of the culture. With their aid, the apprentice's experiences are evoked and made meaningful within the tribal traditions.

In the inner world, the apprentice learns to cultivate and work with dreams, visions, and spirits. Ideally, both inner and outer worlds align. Together, they mold the novice into a mature shaman who can mediate effectively between these worlds, between sacred and profane, spiritual and mundane.

The apprenticeship may take months or years. The novice's first task may be a ritual purification and confession of breaches of taboo.[299] After this, actual instruction by the teacher—aided, of course, by the teacher's spirits—begins.

Much must be learned. On the theoretical side, the apprentice must become a mythologist and cosmologist. To become an effective "cosmic traveler," he must learn the terrain of the multilayered, interconnected universe in which he will quest for power and knowledge.

This cosmology is no dry mapping of inanimate worlds, but a guide to a living, conscious, willful universe, and the would-be shaman must become familiar with its spiritual inhabitants. He must learn their names, habitats, powers, likes and dislikes, how they can be called, and how they can be controlled. For it is these spirits who will help or hinder, battle or befriend him as he does his work. It is they who embody the power at work in the cosmos, and it is his relationship with them that will determine his success.

Much of this cosmic terrain and advice for relating to it are contained in the culture's myths. Throughout human history, myths have provided guidelines for the conduct of life. Only in our own time have so many cultures lacked a coherent myth—a grand, unifying story of the cosmos. Indeed, this lack of meaningful myth may underlie much of the fragmentation and alienation that haunts our lives, and our future may well depend on our ability to create a new, life-affirming myth that gives coherence and common meaning to our modern world.

Joseph Campbell[45] suggested that myths serve four major functions: developmental, social, cosmological, and religious. Their developmental function is to guide individuals through life's stages. Their social function is to support the social structure and offer a shared understanding of life and relationships. Their cosmological and religious roles are to provide an image and understanding of the cosmos and of humankind's role and responsibility in it.

Myths serve the shaman in all four ways. This is not surprising since some myths may have originated in shamanic journeys and reflect the terrain discovered there.[83] They guide the shaman's development, suggest his place in society and the cosmos, and indicate how he is to relate to them. In addition, myths provide the belief system he and his patients will share. This may be crucial since research suggests that a shared belief system or "healing myth" is vital to effective therapeutic relationships.

But there is much more to learn than myths. The would-be shaman must also develop therapeutic skills, master altered states and journeys, and acquire his own helping spirits. We will explore these arts in subsequent chapters.

Helping spirits constitute the shaman's inner teachers. Consequently, considerable training involves learning how to cultivate the circumstances and states of consciousness—such as dreams, journeys, or visions—that will coax the spirits to reveal themselves and their messages. The most dramatic of these circumstances include ascetic disciplines.

ASCETIC DISCIPLINES

Ascetic practices are the atom bombs of religious discipline. These powerful tools can strengthen and purify by forcing practitioners to confront their limits, fears, and self-deceptions. But they are tools of high risk and high gain, for though they can be beneficial, they can also be misused.

Traditionally, ascetic practices are said to strengthen and purify.[187] They can strengthen warrior qualities such as courage and endurance, strip away physical and mental impurities, and foster clarity and concentration.[25] The sum total of these benefits is power; not power over others, but far more important, power over oneself. This is the power to control one's faculties, overcome obstacles, master spirits, and benefit others.

How do ascetic practices achieve these benefits? In several ways. First, those who face challenges successfully develop "self-efficacy": a sense of confidence and effectiveness.[19] Ascetics who master extreme challenges may therefore develop an exceptional sense of personal power and freedom from fear.

The secret to overcoming fear is to confront it—face your fear and it will disappear—and ascetic practices are superbly designed to force an unrelenting confrontation with fear and self-doubt. As Abraham Maslow put it, "The person who hasn't conquered, withstood and overcome continues to feel doubtful that he could. This is true not only for external dangers; it holds also for the ability to control and delay one's own impulses, and therefore to be unafraid of them."[225] This confrontation with fear, whether through cold, hunger, isolation, or psychedelics, has long been central to shamanic training The early initiates who crawled far underground through the pitch black labyrinths of caves, such as Les Trois Frères millennia ago,[316] left behind not only stunning Paleolithic art, but probably also their fear.

By holding fast to their spiritual goals, despite the pull of conflicting egocentric cravings—such as the classic temptations of money, sex, and status—ascetics undermine these cravings. Unreinforced motives diminish, and this weakening of conflicting drives, which is a goal of most religions, is a crucial part of "purification."

Only by winnowing away distracting drives can shamans and other Master Game players direct all their energies to spiritual pursuits. So important is this winnowing and the nonattachment it produces that Meister Eckhart, one of the greatest of all Christian contemplatives, wrote: "I have inquired, carefully and most industriously, to find which is the greatest and best virtue…" and concluded that "I find no other virtue better than a pure detachment from all things…"[79]

Asceticism can also assuage that tricky and painful emotion: guilt. If practitioners believe they are evil or contaminated and must pay for their sins, then asceticism can seem a logical way to do so. But though this can work to some extent, it can also be tricky. Self-punishment may assuage guilt temporarily, but can also strengthen belief in the appropriateness of both guilt and punishment.

Any spiritual practice has its traps. Asceticism is no exception. It can arouse feelings of righteousness or a puritanical denial of the beauty and joy of life. Asceticism can also be carried to dubious and dangerous extremes, even to the point of self-torture, mutilation, and death. Because of such dangers, the Buddha, who at one stage practiced asceticism so fiercely that he almost killed himself, finally advocated a "middle way" between sensuality and asceticism.

Japanese Ascetics

Ascetic practices occur around the world and reach extreme forms in parts of India and Japan. Many Japanese ascetics have been described as shamans.[25] If we look closely, however, relatively few of them seem to meet our definition of shamanism. No distinction is made between shamans and mediums; beyond that, contemporary shamanism in Japan seems to have degenerated significantly from former times. Few contemporary Japanese shamans enter altered states and actually journey. It appears that most simply act out the classic trance in symbolic rituals.

Today this trance occurs only rarely. The capacity for this kind of dissociation, and for the visionary journey which goes with it, seems to have diminished in recent centuries, and today the journey is most commonly accomplished by symbolic action in fully waking consciousness.[25]

This is an example of what we might call the "ritualization of religion": a process in which transcendence-inducing practices degenerate into ineffective rituals, direct experience gives way to mere symbols of experience, and understanding and mastery of effective altered states are lost.

Whatever its current limitations, Japanese shamanism has historically been highly ascetic. Some of these practices offer graphic examples of the extremes that asceticism can reach. Three major types include dietary restriction, cold, and solitude, often accompanied by sleep deprivation.

Mild dietary restriction involves avoiding certain foods, such as meat, or any foods believed to inhibit the acquisition of power. Extreme forms of dietary restriction involve fasting, even to the point of death, such as in the mind-boggling discipline of "tree eating." Though "tree eaters" were not really shamans, the discipline is instructive in demonstrating the ascetic extremes to which some seekers go in their quest for salvation. Practitioners would begin by vowing to follow the discipline for one, two, or even three thousand days.

> During the first part of the discipline their diet consisted of nuts, bark, fruit, berries, grass and sometimes soy in fair abundance. The quantity of these things was then reduced, until by the end of their allotted period they had undergone a total fast of many days. Ideally, if the discipline were properly calculated, the man should die from starvation, upright in the lotus posture, on the last day of his avowed fast. His body should have been reduced to skin and bone.[25]

Such a practice was obviously not for the faint of heart.

A second major austerity is exposure to cold. Common in arctic areas and Japan, this technique is considered highly effective in developing power. Once again the severity of the practices can reach almost incomprehensible extremes.

> To stand under a waterfall, preferably between the hours of two and three in the morning and preferably during the period of the great cold in midwinter, is believed to be an infallible method of gaining power. Indeed, one female ascetic reported that such a practice "no longer felt in the least cold to her. It rather promoted an unrivalled concentration of mind…which formed the very basis of her ascetic power."[25]

A third major ascetic practice is solitude. This common practice marked the lives of several religious founders, such as Jesus's forty days of fasting in the wilderness, Buddha's solitary meditation, and Mohammad's isolation in a cave. For centuries, prolonged solitude has been part of the training of shamans, Hindu and Taoist yogis, Buddhist monks, and Christian contemplatives. "So, sit in your cell, and your cell will teach you everything," urged the Christian Desert Fathers.[237]

Solitude frees attention from the distractions and seductions of the world and redirects it toward the spiritual. This spiritual realm is ultimately found to reside within the seeker— e.g., "The Kingdom of Heaven is within you" or "Look within, you are the Buddha"—but to find it usually requires intense contemplation and introspection. One must concentrate and still the mind, quiet the clamor of competing desires, and birth a new sensitivity to one's inner world.

"Know thyself" is the motto of these practices. However, the cacophonous demands and distractions of society usually hinder deep inner searching and self-knowledge. Consequently, periodic withdrawal and solitude may be essential, since as Wordsworth explained so poetically:

> The world is too much with us; late and soon,
> Getting and spending, we lay waste our powers;
> Little we see in nature that is ours;
> We have given our hearts away.

Shamans were the first spiritual seekers to appreciate that, to use their own words, "The power of solitude is great and beyond understanding."[299]

The many trials faced by those who confront themselves in isolation have inspired countless spiritual biographies. The Eskimo shaman Aua, whose parents' rituals and taboos were outlined earlier, described his time of solitude as follows:

> Then I sought solitude, and here I soon became very melancholy. I would some-times fall to weeping, and feel unhappy without knowing why. Then for no reason, all would suddenly be changed, and I felt a great, inexplicable joy, a joy so powerful that I could not restrain it, but had to break into song, a mighty song, with only room for one word: joy, joy! And I had to use the full strength of my voice. And then in the midst of such a fit of mysterious and overwhelming delight I became a shaman, not knowing myself how it came about. But I was a shaman. I could see and hear in a totally different way.[299]

These extreme mood swings and lack of control are common initial reactions to solitude. After my own first retreat, I wrote of experiencing "sudden apparently unprecipitated wide mood swings to completely polar emotions. Shorn of all my props and distractions there was just no way to pretend that I had more than the faintest inkling of self-control over either thoughts or feelings."[387]

Those who face themselves in solitude quickly appreciate just how restless and out of control the untrained mind is. They soon come to understand claims such as Sigmund Freud's that "man is not even master in his own house…in his own mind"[106] and why "all scriptures without any exception proclaim that for attaining salvation mind should be sub-dued."[296] Solitude is a time-honored method for subduing the mind.

Not content with the rigors of solitude alone, shamans sometimes combined it with fasting and cold, as in the following account by an Eskimo shaman, Igjugarjuk. While still young he received his call to adventure in the form of mysterious dreams.

> Strange unknown beings came and spoke to him, and when he awoke, he saw all the visions of his dream so distinctly that he could tell his fellows all about them. Soon it became evident to all that he was destined to become an *angakoq* [a shaman] and an old man named Perqanaoq was appointed his instructor. In the depth of winter, when the cold was most severe, Igjugarjuk was placed on a small sled just large enough for him to sit on, and carried far away from his home to the other side of Hikoligjuaq. On reaching the appointed spot, he remained seated on the sled while his instructor built a tiny snow hut, with barely room for him to sit cross-legged.

He was not allowed to set foot on the snow, but was lifted from the sled and carried into the hut where a piece of skin just large enough for him to sit on served as a carpet. No food or drink was given him; he was exhorted to think only of the Great Spirit and of the helping spirit that should presently appear—and so he was left to himself and his meditation.

After five days had elapsed, the instructor brought him a drink of lukewarm water, and with similar exhortations, left him as before. He fasted now for fifteen days, when he was given another drink of water and a very small piece of meat, which had to last him a further ten days. At the end of this period, his instructor came for him and fetched him home. Igjugarjuk declared that the strain of those thirty days of cold and fasting was so severe that he "sometimes died a little." During all that time he thought only of the Great Spirit, and endeavored to keep his mind free from all memory of human beings and everyday things. Toward the end of the thirty days there came to him a helping spirit in the shape of a woman. She came while he was asleep and seemed to hover in the air above him. After that he dreamed no more of her, but she became his helping spirit. For five months following this period of trial, he was kept on the strictest diet, and required to abstain from all intercourse with women. The fasting was then repeated; for such fasts at frequent intervals are the best means to attaining to knowledge of hidden things.[298]

This is a beautiful account of not only solitude and asceticism, but also of the practice of attempting to fix one's mind unwaveringly on the Divine.

Igjugarjuk's conclusion from all this was that "the only true wisdom lives far from mankind, out in the great loneliness, and it can be reached only through suffering. Privation and suffering alone can open the mind of a man to all that is hidden to others."[271] Igjugarjuk would therefore probably have agreed with the French existentialist Albert Camus that "when a man has learned—and not on paper—how to remain alone with his suffering, how to overcome his longing to flee, then he has little left to learn."[423]

Practices such as solitude and fasting enhance access to the inner world and its visions, dreams, and spirits. For successful candidates these climax in culmination experiences, which indicate that a degree of shamanic mastery has been attained. Two of the most frequent shamanic culminations are of being immersed in light and of death and rebirth.

Figure 3. Igjugarjuk.

CHAPTER 9

The Culmination of the Quest: Shamanic Enlightenment

In order that the mind should see light instead of darkness, so the entire soul must be turned away from this changing world, until its eye can learn to contemplate reality and that supreme splendor which we have called the good. Hence there may well be an art whose aim would be to effect this very thing.

—Plato[287]

Some experiences are specific to certain paths, while others are far flung across different traditions. The experiences of light and of death-rebirth are widespread milestones on the spiritual path, and for shamans they suggest that their quest is complete.

THE INNER LIGHT

For the rest of my life I want to reflect on what light is.

—Albert Einstein[315]

It is no accident that one of the terms most often used to describe the goal of the spiritual quest is "enlightenment." The word has both literal and metaphorical meanings. Metaphorically, it refers to a dramatic sense of insight and understanding; literally, it refers to an experience of being illuminated or suffused with light.

As Eliade stated: "Clearly, the 'inner light' that suddenly bursts forth after long efforts of concentration and meditation is well known in all religious traditions."[83] In the West the best-known examples are Christian. The apostle St. Paul was literally blinded by the brilliance of his vision. Similarly the great church father St. Augustine "beheld with the mysterious eye of my soul the light that never changes."[375] The famous mystic shoemaker Jacob Boehme, while wrestling with his "corrupted nature," discovered that "a wonderful light arose within my soul. It was a light entirely foreign to my unruly nature, but in it I recognized the true nature of God and man."[239]

Illuminative experiences can also occur spontaneously. Some 5 percent of Americans have had them, and these people scored exceptionally well on a test of psychological health.[124]

A particularly moving account of spontaneous light is that of a French World War II hero, Jacques Lusseryan. While still a student, Lusseryan led a large resistance movement in Paris, and then after his capture organized groups in the concentration camps to which he was condemned. Amazingly, he did all this though totally blind, guided and nourished by an inner light. He wrote of his discovery of this light:

> This was much more than a simple discovery, it was a revelation....I was aware of a radiance emanating from a place I knew nothing about....I felt indescribable relief, and happiness so great it almost made me laugh. Confidence and gratitude came as if a prayer had been answered. I found light and joy at the same moment, and I can say without hesitation that from that time on light and joy have never been separated in my experience....Still, there were times when the light faded, almost to the point of disappearing. It happened every time I was afraid....Anger and impatience had the same effect, throwing everything into confusion....But when I was happy and serene, approached people with confidence and thought well of them, I was rewarded with light....Armed with such a tool, why should I need a moral code?.... at every waking hour and even in my dreams I lived in a stream of light....Light is in us, even if we have no eyes.[220]

Lusseryan's discovery that light is within us and an inseparable part of our deepest nature is a familiar spiritual theme. In the evocative words of a Christian text:

> Those who seek the light are merely covering their eyes. The light is in them now. Enlightenment is but a recognition, not a change at all.[10]

Of course inner light experiences are not all the same. Nor do all religious traditions evaluate them similarly. Some traditions see them as signs of progress; others, such as Zen, view them as seductive sidetracks to be noted and transcended. Yet for still others, such as Iglulik Eskimo shamans, they are essential and ecstatic.

SHAMANIC ENLIGHTENMENT

Thus after an Iglulik shaman has put a student through preliminary training, then according to Rasmussen

> the next thing an old shaman has to do for his pupil is to procure him anak ua by which is meant his "angákoq," i.e., the altogether special and particular element which makes this man an angákoq (shaman). It is also called his quamenEq, his "lighting" or "enlightenment," for anak ua consists of a mysterious light which the shaman suddenly feels in his body, inside his head, within the brain, an inexplicable searchlight, a luminous fire, which enables him to see in the dark both literally and metaphorically speaking, for he can now, even with closed eyes, see through darkness and perceive things and coming events which are hidden from others; thus they look into the future and into the secrets of others.
>
> The first time a young shaman experiences this light…it is as if the house in which he is suddenly rises; he sees far ahead of him, through mountains, exactly as if the earth were on a great plane, and his eyes could reach to the end of the earth. Nothing is hidden from him any longer; not only can he see things far, far away, but he can also discover souls, stolen souls, which are either kept concealed in far, strange lands or have been taken up or down to the Land of the Dead.[299]

For example, the Iglulik Eskimo Aua, whose remarkable career we have been following, finally experienced his *quamenEq* (shamanic enlightenment) alone in the wilderness. He first trained in the company of his teachers, but his quest remained incomplete. He therefore set out into the Arctic wilds to seek in solitude what had eluded him in society. There he was seized by wild mood swings, experiencing fits of melancholy and joy.

> And then in the midst of such a fit of mysterious and overwhelming delight I became a shaman, not knowing myself how it came about. But I was a shaman. I could see and hear in a totally different way. I had gained my quamenEq, my enlightenment,

the shaman-light of brain and body, and this in such a manner that it was not only I who could see through the darkness of life, but the same light also shone out from me, imperceptible to human beings, but visible to all the spirits of earth and sky and sea, and these now came to me and became my helping spirits.[299]

Like his shamanic forefathers for thousands of years before him, Aua finally experienced the inner light and vision that signified the culmination of his quest. This is the spirit vision that would enable him to "see" the cause and cure of his people's ills. For these people believed, quite literally, that as Jewish proverbs put it, "Where there is no vision, the people perish…" and shamans took upon themselves the task of providing this vision.

CHAPTER 10

The Culmination of the Quest: Death and Rebirth

It is only in the face of death that man's self is born.
—St. Augustine[423]

Both ancient religions and modern psychologies recognize the extraordinary impact of confronting death. "Let me know how fleeting my life is" sing the Jewish Psalms, while Christian monks chant "Death is certain, the hour uncertain," knowing that as Mohammad said, "Death is a good advisor."[9] Irvin Yalom, one of today's best-known psychotherapists, concluded from his extensive work with the dying that "a confrontation with one's personal death…has the power to provide a massive shift in the way one lives in the world….Death acts as a catalyst that can move one from one stage of being to a higher one."[423]

Spiritual practitioners must be willing to confront not only physical death but also ego death. This is the demise of an old, outmoded identity so that from its ashes can arise a new identity appropriate to spiritual life.

This motif of death and rebirth echoes through the world's cultures and religions and, according to Ralph Metzner, indicates "the most radical and total transformation that consciousness and identity can undergo."[239] In aboriginal societies, rites of passage are enacted as death-rebirth rituals at important life transitions. In puberty rites, the childhood identities "die," and boys and girls are reborn as adults. The Christian who undergoes a deep conversion may have a sense of dying to the old bodily self and being "born again" in the spirit or in Christ. "Unless ye be born again…" is a common warning in religious traditions.

Shamans have heeded these warnings, and death-rebirth experiences are widely regarded as essential for mastery. Rasmussen pointed out that

> before a shaman attains the stage at which any helping spirit would think it worth while to come to him, he must, by struggle and toil and concentration of thought, acquire for himself yet another great and inexplicable power: he must be able to see himself as a skeleton. Though no shaman can explain to himself how and why, he can, by the power his brain derives from the supernatural, as it were by thought alone, divest his body of its flesh and blood, so that nothing remains but his bones….By thus seeing himself naked, altogether freed from the perishable and transient flesh and blood, he consecrates himself, in the sacred tongue of the sha-mans, to his great task, through that part of his body which will longest withstand the action of sun, wind and weather, after he is dead.[299]

Such experiences can occur either spontaneously or as a result of willed imagination or ritual enactment. They can be interpreted either metaphorically or literally. Shamans may view their death-rebirth experiences quite literally as actual physical events in which their bodies are first dismembered by the spirits and then reconstructed. Thus shamans may believe that

> they are cut up by demons or by their ancestral spirits; their bones are cleaned, the flesh scraped off, the body fluids thrown away, and their eyes torn from their sock-ets. His bones are then covered with new flesh and in some cases he is also given new blood.[89]

The belief is that the practitioner now has a new stronger body fit for the rigors of sha-manic work.

This dismemberment experience is similar to the Tibetan tantric practice of *chö* (*gcod*). Here practitioners cultivate detachment and compassion by deliberately visualizing their bodies being dismembered and offered to hungry demons to eat. But whereas for the tantric these experiences are voluntary visualizations, for the shaman they are involuntary trials.

Similar experiences of dismemberment and reconstruction, of death and rebirth also occur among contemporary Westerners. They may happen during intensive psychotherapy or spiritual practice and occur most dramatically in holotropic or psychedelic therapy sessions.

The term holotropic means moving toward wholeness or aiming for totality. Holotropic therapy is a technique devised by Stanislav and Christina Grof that combines hyperventilation, music, and bodywork. This powerful combination induces significant altered states of consciousness (ASCs) and deep psychological insights. In fact, holotropic therapy may be one of the most powerful, nondrug means of inducing therapeutic altered states.[131]

Holotropic and psychedelic sessions provide some of the most dramatic accounts of death-rebirth, and we can therefore use these accounts to fill out the information from shamanic traditions. Stanislav Grof, a research psychiatrist whose several thousand case studies are the world's most extensive, portrays psychedelically or holotropically intensified death-rebirth as an experience of awesome power that shakes those who undergo it to their psychological and spiritual core. The following is a psychedelic account:

Physical and emotional agony culminates in a feeling of utter and total annihilation on all imaginable levels. It involves an abysmal sense of physical destruction, emotional catastrophe, intellectual defeat, ultimate moral failure, and absolute damnation of transcendental proportions. This experience is usually described as "ego death"; it seems to entail instantaneous and merciless destruction of all the previous reference points in the life of the individual.

After the subject has experienced the limits of total annihilation and "hit the cosmic bottom," he or she is struck by visions of blinding white or golden light. The claustrophobic and compressed world…suddenly opens up and expands into infinity. The general atmosphere is one of liberation, salvation, redemption, love, and forgiveness. The subject feels unburdened, cleansed and purged, and talks about having disposed of an incredible amount of personal "garbage," guilt, aggression, and anxiety. This is typically associated with brotherly feelings for all fellowmen and appreciation and warm human relationships, friendship and love. Irrational and exaggerated ambitions, as well as cravings for money, status, fame, prestige and power, appear in this state as childish, irrelevant and absurd. There is often a strong tendency to share and engage in service and charitable activities. The universe is perceived as indescribably beautiful and radiant. All sensory pathways seem to be wide open and the sensitivity to the appreciation of external stimuli is greatly enhanced. The individual tuned into this experiential area usually discovers within himself or herself genuinely positive values, such as a sense of justice, appreciation of beauty, feelings of love, and self respect as well as respect for others.[129]

This emotional power has been wonderfully portrayed by the artist Sherana Harriette Frances who was a subject in an early LSD research study.[101] Her exquisite drawings, some of which are reproduced here, not only offer a graphic account of an LSD-induced death-rebirth, but also portray amazing similarities to perennial shamanic experiences.

INTERPRETING THE DEATH–REBIRTH EXPERIENCE

Death is a mirror in which the entire meaning of life is reflected.

—*Sogyal Rinpoche*[306]

The process of death and rebirth has occurred numberless times throughout history, but interpretations have varied dramatically. Contemplatives esteem it as a spiritual death and resurrection, while contemporary psychedelic researchers might diagnose it as a disintegration and reconstitution of the self-image. Shamans, however, have traditionally taken it to be a literal destruction and reconstitution of their physical bodies. For them, images of bodily dismemberment are interpreted quite literally, and this literal, concrete interpretation of mental imagery is a theme echoed throughout much of shamanism.

What can we make of this recurrent experience of agonizing death and dismemberment, followed by a healing process of rebirth and reconstitution? Clearly this is a powerful, perennial experience that has been sought by many and has burst unsought on many others. It appears to represent a deep, archetypal process of the psyche, a process with considerable healing potential. The following hypothesis attempts to understand this process in contemporary psychological terms.

The death-rebirth experience appears to be a transformative process most likely to occur at times of overwhelming emotional arousal. This arousal activates psychological tensions and conflicts to levels unsustainable by the old conditioning and uncontainable by the old identity and worldview. The result is a crisis in which old patterning forces can no longer maintain the former psychological balance. Old conditioning, psychodynamic forces, beliefs, and identity are overwhelmed, and the psyche's organization temporarily collapses.[i] The key result of this collapse, says Grof, is that "what is destroyed in this process is the old, limiting concept of oneself and the corresponding restricting view of existence and of the universe."[129]

This process is projected and witnessed as "autosymbolic images," images that picture one's psychological state. The initial phase of unbearable psychological tension and breakdown may be experienced symbolically as visions of physical torture, bodily dismemberment, death and decay or as war and destruction.

This destructured chaos opens the way to reconstruction. With conditioning and dynamics dissolved, reorganization can be guided by the mind's innate holotropic drive toward health and wholeness. For one of the most hopeful of all contemplative and clinical discoveries is that the psyche is inherently self-organizing and self-optimizing, and under supportive conditions it can be not only self-healing but also self-actualizing, self-transcending, self-awakening, and self-liberating.[j] The result can be a reconstructed psyche and identity that are unbound from the past, and therefore less conflicted and less symptomatic, and consequently more healthy, integrated, and whole. The death of the old self allows birth of the new.

This reconstruction and rebirth are reflected in the accompanying imagery. The shaman may see the spirits reconstructing her body, the therapy patient may witness images of birth, or the contemplative may experience being "reborn in the spirit."

This process may account for the dramatic breakthroughs and benefits that can follow death-rebirth experiences. These benefits may include resolution of the initiation illness in shamans, relief of chronic psychopathology in patients, and freedom from egotism in spiritual practitioners. Just how dramatic these benefits can be is evident from both ancient and contemporary accounts. Stanislav Grof concludes that "powerful experiential sequences of dying and being born can result in dramatic alleviation of a variety of emotional, psychosomatic, and interpersonal problems that have previously resisted all psychotherapeutic work."[131]

Two thousand years ago, Jesus offered a metaphor that has echoed across centuries: "A grain of wheat remains a solitary grain unless it falls into the ground and dies; but if it dies, it brings a rich harvest." The experience of death-rebirth can bring a rich harvest and, as with so many psychological and spiritual transformations, it was shamans who first recognized and harvested it.

Figure 4. The death-rebirth process is exquisitely portrayed by Harriette Frances, a subject in one of the early LSD research studies. Her drawings demonstrate many of the key features of the LSD death-rebirth experience as well as their remarkable similarities to shamanic experiences. In the first drawing, the artist portrays herself beginning to enter an altered state of consciousness as the LSD takes effect. Perception is altered, and the environment takes on an unfamiliar appearance.

Figure 5. As her altered state deepens, she experiences falling downward through a whirlpool-like tunnel, past skeletal symbols of death and destruction, to a lower world.

Figure 6. In the lower world, she experiences being pierced and tortured and is surrounded by images of death and decay.

Figure 7. She is torn apart and reduced to a skeleton, but sees a light above her that she struggles desperately to reach.

Figure 8. As she struggles to escape from this realm of all-consuming death and destruction, she feels herself being offered assistance.

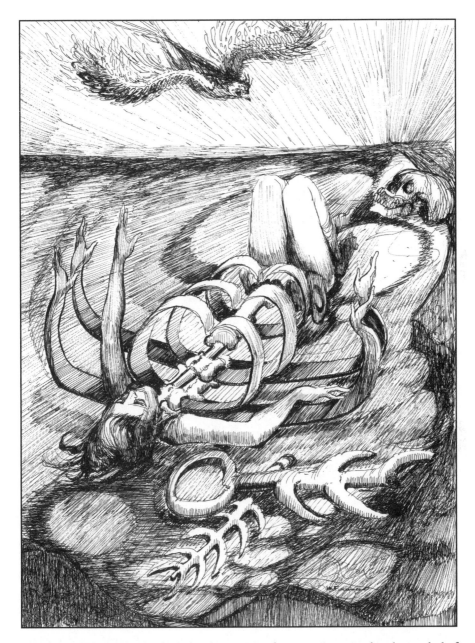

Figure 9. She sees a bird, which for shamans is often a power animal and a symbol of spirit, and appeals to it for help.

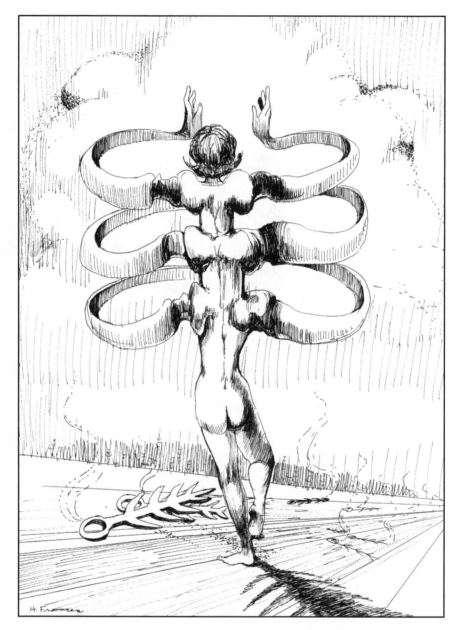

Figure 10. Her body begins to re-form. This is the shamanic experience of being provided with a new body. This new body is believed by the shaman to be stronger and better fitted for future shamanic work.

Figure 11. The repair of her body is completed.

Figure 12. She now experiences rebirth. Her body is completely constituted, and she is surrounded by birds. She is left with an ecstatic sense of having been cleansed, rejuvenated, and revitalized, and of having been through an experience of life-changing power and importance. Some forty years later the artist still regards this as one of the most significant experiences of her life.

PART IV

DIAGNOSING THE SHAMAN

Each investigator most readily sees that factor in the neurosis which corresponds to his peculiarity…each sees things from a different angle, and thus they evolve fundamentally different views and theories…

—*Carl Jung*[183]

CHAPTER 11

Devil, Madman, Saint, or Sage?
The Eye of the Beholder

Projection makes perception. The world you see is what you gave it, nothing more than that…it is a witness to your state of mind, the outside picture of an inward condition. As a man thinketh, so does he perceive.

—Anonymous[10]

What has been the most controversial topic in the study of shamans? Answer: their mental health.

Shamans have been demonized, pathologized, or sanctified with wondrous abandon. However, as Western culture has evolved, so too have the diagnoses given them. Roberte Hamayon suggests that this evolution has gone through three major stages. These she calls devilization, medicalization, and idealization, reflecting the ascendancy of religious, medical, and popularizing viewpoints.[141] While an oversimplification,[351] these three stages provide a useful framework.

DEVILIZATION

Early reports came from Christian clergy in the sixteenth and seventeenth centuries. French priests in South America found healers and spiritual consultants who may or may not fit our technical definition of shamanism. Nevertheless, the priests saw "people of evil custom who have given themselves over to serve the devil to deceive their neighbors"[365] and who "drink that rude potion of tobacco."[24] This disapproval of the "rude potion of tobacco" did not stop one of the priests, André Thévet, from introducing it to France, thereby leading to the addiction and death of millions.

But it was a seventeenth-century Russian priest who was exiled to Siberia, Avvakum Petrovich, who first published the word *shaman*. The expedition's leader consulted a Siberian "villain of a magician," and the villain assured the leader that a proposed war raid would be successful. Displaying less than full Christian charity, the enraged Reverend Petrovich prayed:

> May not one of them return! Dig a tomb for them there! Send them evil, Lord, send it to them! And lead them to their loss, so that the diabolical prophecy not be accomplished.[285]

Petrovich apparently got his wish, which did not exactly endear him to the survivors. However, such was the power of the church that Petrovich's view of shamans became the norm.

MEDICALIZATION: PSYCHIATRIC PERSPECTIVES

Shamans remained demons for centuries. However, with the rise of psychiatry, shamans became disturbed rather than evil. To start with some of the kinder diagnoses, the shaman has been described as a healed madman and a trickster. The labels hysteric, neurotic, epileptic, and schizophrenic have been applied liberally, while the shaman has also been called a charlatan, a "veritable idiot," or "an outright psychotic." The French psychoanalytically trained anthropologist George Devereux put it bluntly: "The shaman is mentally deranged….In brief, there is no excuse for not considering the shaman as a severe neurotic and even as a psychotic."[70] Such statements now seem painfully ethnocentric, but they held sway for many years.

In short, shamanism has often been dismissed as the unfortunate product of primitive minds, and seriously disturbed ones at that. The question of the shaman's psychological health is therefore no small matter; in fact, the status of this tradition hangs on it. It will therefore be crucial to carefully assess the medical evidence for the diagnoses given to shamans.

Of course there is no reason to assume that shamans are a homogenous group. In fact, psychological testing suggests they are not.[89] They may no more display a single personality type or neatly fit a single diagnosis than do all Western doctors. This may seem an obvious point, but it is amazing how often it is overlooked.

In making our assessment, we cannot examine the shaman's behavior alone. Rather, we need to consider the interaction between the shaman's behavior, our Western diagnostic assumptions, and the psychological skills and cultural perspectives of the researchers making the diagnoses. In addition, two shamanic behaviors need to be assessed carefully since they were frequently interpreted as pathological. The first of these is the initiation crisis, which we have already discussed.

The second is the shamanic journey. Here the shaman enters an altered state of consciousness (ASC), then experiences leaving the body and journeying to other worlds. The journey contains several experiences likely to arouse suspicion in Western researchers. The first is the ASC, the second is the rich imagery and visions that accompany it. Another suspicious experience (to Western minds) is the presence of spirits and the shaman's belief that these spirits are real. These, then, are the shamanic experiences and behaviors that have most often fostered pathologizing interpretations.

But what about the observers who make these interpretations? What about their possible biases and blind spots, such as biasing effects of Western cultural and psychological perspectives? Other concerns include early anthropologists' lack of psychological expertise and of personal experience of shamanic training and altered states.

DIAGNOSTIC BIASES

Today's anthropologists have developed considerable sensitivity to the ethnocentric dangers wrought by the distorting lens of cultural bias. When other people are judged by our own beliefs and standards, then all too often their behavior is interpreted as primitive or pathological. This was certainly true for shamanism.

The negative picture of the shaman, primarily (though not exclusively) found in the earlier anthropological literature, is the expression of a Zeitgeist, the spirit of the times.

That Zeitgeist assumed that the Western rationalistic-positivist ideology was the norm against which other cultures and institutions were judged. Non-Western systems of explanation, where they deviated from these Eurocentric positivistic norms, were considered an abnormal expression of "poor reality testing."[188]

For example, a Westerner who reported seeing and being persecuted by spirits might well be diagnosed as psychotic, since these experiences are not part of our usual cultural reality. However, in shamanic cultures they are the norm. Indeed, the person who did not believe in the possibility of spirit persecution would be considered strange. "What in shamanistic behavior may appear hysterical or psychotic to the Western psychiatrist is to the people concerned a time honored ritual."[210] Small wonder that some early researchers, blinded by their own cultural assumptions, labeled the shamanic initiation crisis and shamanic journey as psychotic episodes.

Lack of medical and psychological expertise also produced flawed interpretations. Because they did not know exactly what to look for, some anthropologists' reports lack crucial information that would allow us to determine the precise nature of shamanic experiences and whether they are pathological or not. For example, shamans' visionary experiences were commonly described as "hallucinations" or "neurotic dreams," without more precise description or explanation. Similarly, the supposed epilepsy that can occur during initiation crises was sometimes labeled as simply "fits," a description that makes accurate diagnoses impossible.

A recently recognized problem can arise when researchers have not themselves engaged in shamanic practices. This is a special problem with shamanism for two key reasons, both of which relate to the centrality of ASCs.

1) In shamanism, as well as other authentic[k] spiritual disciplines, altered states of consciousness play a crucial role.[l]

2) It can be extremely difficult to comprehend ASC experiences without direct experience of the state.

Without direct experience, talk of ASC experiences can remain at the level of what the philosopher Immanuel Kant famously called "empty concepts," concepts devoid of the richness, meaning, and significance that only direct experience can impart. This deficit can be dangerously distorting, as the psychologist Richard Noll pointed out:

> Devoid of the personal experience of ASCs (altered states of consciousness), yet quite familiar with the altered states of the diagnostic manual, the incredible sagas of shamans must indeed seem psychotic to an interpreter who only considers experiences in an ordinary state of consciousness to be valid, mentally healthy phenomena.[260]

This is an example of what Michael Harner calls "cognicentrism," the tendency to interpret (and denigrate) alternate states from the limited perspective of our own state.[146]

Unfortunately, this tendency has been particularly marked in psychoanalysis, the perspective initially most often used to interpret shamanic experiences. Psychoanalysis has made enormous contributions to our understanding of mind and behavior, but like any psychology it contains its limitations and blind spots. Its major focus has been on sickness and early development, and as the humanistic psychologist Abraham Maslow said, "It is as if Freud supplied to us the sick half of psychology and we must now fill it out with the healthy half."[225] Consequently, there has been a tendency for healthy behavior to be interpreted in terms of early or pathological development. Richard Noll concludes that the anthropological result has been a "virulent influence of Freudian psychoanalytic tradition in culture and personality studies in nurturing unnecessary psychopathological interpretations of cross-cultural behaviors."[261]

The risks of misunderstanding other cultures become particularly dangerous when altered states are involved. Until quite recently Western psychology and anthropology recognized only a limited range of normal states: primarily waking, dreaming, and non-dreaming sleep. States falling outside this narrow range were automatically considered pathological. Richard Noll points out that "states of consciousness that are altered in some fashion are traditionally viewed as pathological merely because they deviate from…the ordinary states against which all other states are contrasted."[260]

This view has now changed dramatically. The range of healthy states of consciousness is considerably broader than previously imagined, and studies of other cultures and contemplative traditions have revealed a startling plasticity of consciousness. States of remarkable concentration, calm, clarity, and sensitivity are among the many identified in recent years.[398]

However, these are recent recognitions. For many years even states of exceptional joy or compassion were often pathologized. Mystical experiences, for example, were interpreted as neurotic regressions, ecstatic states viewed as narcissism, and enlightenment dismissed as regression to intrauterine stages.[399] Witness the painful example of a classic psychiatry textbook, which stated that "the obvious similarities between schizophrenic regression and the practices of yoga and Zen merely indicate that the general trend in oriental cultures is to withdraw into the self from an overbearingly difficult physical and social reality."[7]

In short, Western psychiatry has a long history of viewing mystics as madmen, saints as psychotics, and sages as schizophrenics. And this in spite of the fact that saints and sages may represent the heights of human development and have had the greatest impact on human history. So, at least, said the philosophers Bergson and James, Schopenhauer and Nietzsche as well as the psychologists Maslow and Wilber.[407] The historian Arnold Toynbee posed the question, "Who are...the greatest benefactors of the living generation of mankind?" He answered, "I should say: Confucius and Lao Tzu, the Buddha, the Prophets of Israel and Judah, Zoroaster, Jesus, Mohammed and Socrates."[372]

This historical argument against equating mystical and pathological states now has considerable scientific support. Several hundred studies make it quite clear that the altered states induced by meditation and yoga, for example, are healthy and valuable.[398] As Ken Wilber stated emphatically, these states can be equated with pathology "only by those whose intellectual inquiry goes no further than superficial impressions."[410]

In summary, religious experiences and states of consciousness have all too often been viewed as pathological because of cultural bias, lack of psychological expertise, psychoanalytic emphasis on pathology, and ignorance of the potential range and value of certain altered states. Fortunately, this situation has begun to change.

IDEALIZATION

With the popularization of shamanism in the West has come idealization. Where some clergy saw demons, some popularizers see saints; where psychoanalysts found neurotics, enthusiasts find spiritual masters. Indeed, the depths of pathology formerly attributed to shamans are almost matched by the heights of sanctity now accorded them by extreme enthusiasts. Among other things they have been called yogis, psi masters, and "masters of death."[189] We will dissect such claims later. For now it is enough to point out that in idealizing shamanism, enthusiasts "brush aside its dark truths,"[36] and that there are dangers in any extreme view.

CHAPTER 12

Primitive Madmen: Assessing Traditional Views of Shamans as Psychologically Disturbed

It is the mind that maketh good or ill, that
maketh wretch or happy, rich or poor.
—Edmund Spencer

Times change and with them our views of shamans. No longer devils and no longer madmen, the psychological state of shamans can finally be reviewed objectively.

An objective assessment is long overdue. For there is something very curious about the shift away from seeing shamans as psychologically disturbed. Curiously, this shift is not based on careful medical assessments, but rather seems to largely reflect a shift in the Western Zeitgeist, the spirit of the times. Now that researchers recognize the dangers of ethnocentric assumptions that label other people as inferior or disturbed, they seem to simply assume that shamans are usually healthy, but without carefully examining the data. This we need to do.

What is required is some detective work. We need to examine field reports and psychological tests of shamans and then compare them with contemporary diagnostic criteria. Only in this way can we hope to get accurate assessments and, as much as the available data permits, definitively lay to rest old myths about shamanic psychopathology.

The most common diagnoses given to shamans have been—to use the imprecise language found in early anthropological literature—epilepsy, hysteria, schizophrenia, imposter, or con man. Let us first examine the evidence for and against each of these diagnoses and then consider more recent interpretations.

EPILEPSY

Shamans were diagnosed as epileptics because of their "fits" during initial crises. However, these fits have rarely been observed by anthropologists. Rather, any information usually comes from shamans' recollections many years afterward. This alone would make diagnosis difficult, since recollections of past illness can be notoriously inaccurate. Complicating things further, because they were not medically trained, anthropologists did not know the correct questions to ask in order to make accurate diagnoses. The results are descriptions so vague that it is impossible to determine whether the condition was in fact epilepsy, let alone what type of epilepsy might be involved.

One of the few researchers to actually see "fits" was the Russian ethnographer Shirokogoroff, who conducted important studies of Siberian shamanism. He observed a would-be shaman who was not accepted as one by her tribe. He concluded that

> the most typical picture of hysterical character, with strong sexual excitement was beyond any doubt: she was lying on the stove-bed in a condition varying between great rigidity ("arch") and relaxation; she was hiding herself from the light....there was temporary loss of sensitiveness to a needle....at times continuous movements with the legs and basin were indicative of a strong sexual excitement....Her cognition of reality was rather doubtful, for during her fit she did not recognize persons being around her. However, from time to time, or at least at the end of her fits, she was quite conscious of her surroundings and before a fit she looked for isolation and for certain comfort for herself during the fit.[335]

This description is one of the most detailed in the literature yet still insufficient to allow certain diagnosis. The description is consistent with "hysterical epilepsy," but a definitive diagnosis would require more precise information about the episode, the patient's experience, and laboratory data.[m] And in any event, this was a would-be shaman and not an accepted practitioner.

In summary, available descriptions are so vague that it is impossible to make any definitive statement about the occurrence of epilepsy in shamans. There is precious little evidence for organic epilepsy. Whatever fits do occur may well be psychological in origin and may simply be expressions of intense emotional agitation. In addition, only some shamans experience fits, and epilepsy could certainly not account for experiences such as the shamanic journey. Consequently, it is clearly incorrect to conclude that all shamans are epileptics or to imagine that shamanism can be either explained or dismissed on the basis of epilepsy.

"HYSTERIA"

The second condition that was often used to diagnose and dismiss shamanism is hysteria. "Hysteria" is actually an old term for a variety of fascinating disorders that are now called "conversion disorders" and "dissociative disorders."[8] Conversion disorders occur when a person unconsciously converts psychological conflicts into physical symptoms.

In dissociative disorders, the symptoms are psychological rather than physical. The key element is loss of conscious awareness and control of mental processes such as memory, perception, or identity. Dissociative disorders include dissociative amnesia, fugue, depersonalization, and dissociative identity disorder, which was formerly known as multiple personality disorder.

Dissociative amnesia involves memory loss of important personal information, usually stressful or traumatic information.

Dissociative fugue patients suddenly become confused about who they are and are unable to recall their past; they may leave home and be found wandering far away.

In *dissociative identity disorder,* there exist within the person two or more distinct personalities that alternate in their control of the person's identity and behavior.

Depersonalization involves a sense of detachment and alienation from one's experience. The shamanic experiences that might conceivably be related to dissociation include the initial crisis, mediumship, and the shamanic journey.

The Initiation Crisis

With its many bizarre experiences and behaviors, it is not surprising that the shamanic initiation crisis has been labeled "hysterical." The dramatic changes in consciousness and behavior that can accompany it might, perhaps, be classifiable as an unusual, culturally specific form of dissociation. However, once again, the descriptions we have of initiation crises are too imprecise to allow accurate diagnosis. Consequently, all we can conclude is that dissociation *might* play a role in *some* initiations.

Mediumship

The second aspect of shamanism that might reflect dissociation is mediumship, or "channeling" as it is now popularly known. During this process, one or more spirits seem to speak through the shaman, who may range from being alert to experiencing a complete absence of personal awareness. During this absence, the spirit(s) may seem to displace the shaman's personality, whose behavior, mannerisms, and voice may change dramatically.

This phenomenon has occurred throughout diverse cultures and times. In the West, one of the earliest and most famous examples was the Greek oracle at Delphi who was consulted by peasants and kings. Spirit messengers were much in vogue around the end of the nineteenth century when the process was known as mediumship, and interest has recently surged again under the name of channeling.

Western psychiatry tends to regard this as a form of dissociation. Witness the *Comprehensive Textbook of Psychiatry* that says: "A curious and not fully explored or understood form of dissociation is that of the trance states of spirit mediums who preside over spiritual séances."[255]

There is an interesting clash of worldviews here. For psychiatry, mediumship is a form of dissociation in which the "spirits" are assumed to be splintered fragments of the psyche. For the shaman, on the other hand, and also the Western medium or channeler, the "spirits" are experienced as distinct entities. To decide between these two views is far trickier than it first appears, as we will see in a later chapter.

Mediumship/channeling can be a complex phenomenon, which, though producing much nonsense, can sometimes produce meaningful, even profound, information.[158; 195] To simply dismiss it as "hysteria" or dissociation would be an unfortunate error that would prevent us from exploring an unusual capacity of mind. We will return to it later.

The Shamanic Journey

A third phenomenon that might be considered dissociative is the shamanic journey. Here the shaman enters an ASC and experiences traveling as a soul or spirit to other worlds, having complex visions and meeting spirit beings.

The journey *might* be considered a dissociative disorder for several reasons:

1) The ASC has traditionally been described imprecisely as a "trance"; trances are listed as a culturally specific form of dissociative disorder.[8]

2) Some of the shaman's experiences and behavior may be involuntary, and

3) The experiences may seem bizarre, at least to Westerners.

However, there are several arguments against diagnosing shamanic journeys as dissociative disorders. First, the journey is culturally valued, and so to label it as a disorder may be to "fail to distinguish clinic and culture."[424, n]

Moreover, the shaman has control over her trance; she enters and leaves it at will. This is very different from classic dissociative disorders that appear to overtake and control their victims. For example, "The Siberian shaman may fall into a state of partial hysterical dissociation like the hysteric in, say Britain, but this state he voluntarily seeks and in doing so he obtains authority and respect from the tribe."[424]

Nor does the shamanic journey seem to function as a psychological defense mechanism. In clinical disorders, dissociation functions as a defense mechanism by reducing and distorting consciousness in order to protect the self by avoiding psychological pain. The shamanic journey seems to do just the opposite. Here the shaman deliberately opens herself to either her own pain and suffering, that of her people, or even that of spirits in other worlds, in order to resolve the pain.

This is not to deny that the journey can *sometimes* be used as a psychological defense, since almost anything can be used defensively. However, this is very different from saying that the journey serves primarily as a defense. Therefore, it seems that there are several arguments against interpreting the shamanic journey as a dissociative disorder.[o]

LIVING IN A WORLD APART:
PSYCHOSIS AND SCHIZOPHRENIA

Epileptics and neurotics have trouble with the world, but psychotics live in their own world. Lost in private fantasies and beliefs, yet unable to recognize them as the hallucinations and delusions that they are, psychotics suffer in their own virtual realities, unwitting victims of their mind-created nightmares. Small wonder that psychotics can seem bizarre and incomprehensible to the rest of us.

Even though shamans' experiences make perfect sense to them, they can seem completely bizarre to someone from another culture. Not surprisingly, some Westerners therefore decided that shamans are psychotic. Gross examples include the French anthropologist George Devereux, who described the Mohave shaman as "an outright psychotic,"[69] and a contemporary psychiatrist who concluded that schizophrenia and shamanism share "grossly non-reality-oriented ideation, abnormal perceptual experience, profound emotional upheavals, and bizarre mannerisms."[338]

The experiences that have most concerned observers have been the initial crisis and the visionary experiences during the shamanic journey. Consequently, we need to examine both of these.

The shamanic journey can be assessed accurately since we possess many detailed accounts of it from native shamans and also from Westerners who have undertaken authentic shamanic training and their own journeys. When the shamanic journey is carefully compared to a schizophrenic episode, as is done in a later chapter, it becomes clear that they are very, very different.

Initiation Crisis

For initiation crises, the situation is less clear since we have so little firsthand data on them. Two questions need to be addressed. These are whether the crises are consistent with psychosis and, if so, whether they are consistent with schizophrenia.

The diagnosis of psychosis during the initial crisis has been based on both the shaman's experience and behavior. At this time the shaman-to-be may experience herself as tormented and controlled by spirits. She may also exhibit confusion and emotional turmoil, may withdraw from society, and exhibit bizarre behavior such as going naked, refusing food, and biting herself.

However, this belief in spirit possession and persecution is fully consistent with the cultural worldview. In fact, at one time or another many people in the tribe may feel persecuted. What is unique about the shaman is *not* that she complains of persecution by spirits; it is that she eventually learns how to master and use them.

Given the limited data and the cultural setting, all we can conclude is that the bizarre behavior associated with *some* initiation crises *could* be consistent with a psychotic episode. However, it is important to note that initiation crisis disturbances are usually temporary, and only a small percentage of shamans undergo them. This means that only a very small percentage of all shamans, if any, would suffer a psychosis. For a more technical discussion of the possible kinds of psychosis that might occur during an initiation crisis, see endnote p.

This is not to say that all shamans are models of health or model citizens. However, it is to say that contrary to centuries of pathologizing, the vast majority of shamans cannot be diagnosed as mentally ill. In short, shamanism certainly cannot be neatly dismissed as the confused productions of primitive or pathological minds. Something much more remarkable, rewarding, and profound is going on.

CHAPTER 13

Putting Shamans to the Test: Measuring Personality and Spiritual Mastery

...the question of whether the shaman is a disturbed individual (neurotic, psychotic or schizophrenic) or is, on the contrary a gifted, balanced and perfectly well adjusted person, constitutes one of the oldest of anthropological debates.[244]

If the health of shamans is one of the perennial puzzles of anthropology, then how best to assess health is one of the perennial puzzles of psychology. Debate has raged for half a century over the relative merits of clinicians using their intuitive judgment as compared to objective measurement. Both have their place, but carefully designed psychological tests can sometimes best even experienced clinicians.[405] It is therefore unfortunate that we have so few objective studies of shamans. Still, these few offer interesting clues.

PROJECTIVE TESTS

The assessment measures used most often with shamans have been projective tests in which ambiguous images are shown to subjects. The pictures they see, the meanings they give, and the stories they tell in response to these images are then interpreted and mined for information about personality and perception. Projective tests have a mixed reputation, and it is not clear that all the subjects tested were in fact shamans as we are defining them. Therefore we will need to be cautious in drawing conclusions from the following studies.

When the Holtzman ink blot technique was given to Mexican Zinacanteco shamans, it revealed no significant differences between shamans and control subjects. However, the shamans did show a greater variability of psychological characteristics than the controls.[89]

This is an important finding since it is often assumed that shamans share a common psychological profile. However, this study suggests otherwise. And when you think about it, why should we expect shamans to exhibit a common personality or level of health any more than we expect this of physicians or psychologists?

The Rorschach Test

The most famous of all psychological tests may well be the Rorschach. It may also be the most controversial. An American Psychological Association group lauded it as "perhaps the most powerful psychometric instrument ever envisioned," while the *New York Review of Books* damned it as "a ludicrous but still dangerous relic."[58] Certainly, as it is usually used, the Rorschach is neither particularly valid nor reliable,[58, 422] and claims made from using it therefore need to be accepted cautiously.

This is particularly true of one of the most famous of all studies of shamans. This investigated Mescalero Indian reservation Apaches and compared shamans, pseudoshamans, and controls. *Shamans* were defined as native medicine men who claimed supernatural powers and were accorded shamanistic status by their people. *Pseudoshamans* were either regarded as shamans by the tribe but denied possessing any power, or else were claimants to shamanic status who were not regarded as such by others.

Overall, the shamans received a positive report. While they displayed more responses suggestive of hysteria, overall they seemed healthier than their peers. Some of their positive features included a high degree of reality testing, keen awareness of peculiarities, and a capacity to regress in the service of the ego. The experimenters concluded of the shamans that "In general, based on their greater capacity to test reality and their ability to use regression in the service of the ego, they are healthier than their society co-members."[31] By contrast, the pseudoshamans were said to display "impoverished personalities."[31] However, the poor design of the study renders these conclusions tentative.[89, q]

Further support for the health of shamans comes from a survey of Bhutanese refugees in Nepal that included forty-two people (most of them male) who claimed to be shamans. Interviews revealed no significant differences between them and non-shamans, although shamans tended to display fewer anxiety disorders.[377]

SPIRITUAL MASTERY

Spiritual masters have supposedly realized potentials of heart and mind that only lie dormant in the rest of us. How remarkable it would be to test these masters and find out precisely who and what they are. It would be even more remarkable to compare masters from different traditions. Recently the first such study appeared and revealed striking similarities between an outstanding Apache shaman, a Hindu swami, and an advanced female Buddhist meditation teacher.[181] The study compared Rorschach responses, and we have already discussed the problems with this test. However, in this case it may be useful for two reasons:

- Though the Rorschach is not particularly reliable, it can still be valuable in exploratory studies looking for patterns that deserve further investigation.

- The findings are striking. In fact, they suggest something quite remarkable has occurred in these subjects.

While there were major differences between their responses, there were also striking similarities among the masters. What did they show?

Transpersonal Concerns

Unlike the rest of us, their responses had very little to do with their individual concerns. Rather, their perceptions were centered around their religious traditions. For example, the Apache shaman who was named Black Eyes gave responses involving the powers of nature and the seasons of the earth; Swami Sivananda described the forces of Shiva and Shakti and the unity underlying diversity; the Buddhist master saw human and animal forms representing the causes of suffering. In each case their responses mirrored the worldview and teachings of their tradition.

The researcher, Diane Jonte-Pace, interpreted these responses as being culturally embedded or impersonal. However, a better term would likely be "transpersonal," since individual perspective and personality seemed to be replaced by a transpersonal perspective grounded in the teachings and experiences offered by the tradition. Jonte-Pace concluded that "the masters were enmeshed in their spiritual tradition to such a degree that inner life became indistinguishable from the spiritual teachings."[181]

These findings offer support for several perennial spiritual claims. Diverse traditions hold that their practices include transpersonal shifts in identity and perception. Spiritual practices are said to gradually winnow away egocentricity and to replace our usual separate or egoic self-sense with a transpersonal identity that grows to encompass humankind, life, and the cosmos.

Along with this goes a transformation of understanding and perception. The conventional view gradually yields to a post-conventional, transpersonal understanding, and perceptual transformation awakens sacred vision.[392]

Integrative Style

When given the ten Rorschach images one after the other, people usually give unrelated responses to each. Not so the masters. Each one of them organized their responses into a single coherent account that laid out the basic teachings of their tradition. The masters transformed the test into a teaching for the testers. An amazed Jonte-Pace wrote:

> One would almost believe that the masters had been given the Rorschach cards in advance with the request that each prepare a lecture on his or her spiritual tradition based on the sequence and the imagery of the cards....The shaman communicated his ecstatic flights through space; the swami taught the central elements of Vedantic doctrine; and the enlightened Buddhist master related her knowledge and experience of the means to end suffering. The integrative and unitive styles reveal the masters' remarkable intellectual capacities, the presentations of cultural/spiritual truths support the earlier suggestion that individual perceptions seem to disappear as individual identity is subsumed by spiritual identity, while the didactic style demonstrates a deep embeddedness in the therapeutic and salvific role of master.[181]

Toleration of Ambiguity

A third unusual characteristic was the large number of responses related to shading, amorphous forms, and inanimate movement. Curiously, such responses are usually viewed as pathological. However, Jonte-Pace interprets these suggestions of change and lack of boundaries more positively in the case of these masters. She suggests they developed tolerance of ambiguity as well as a familiarity and comfort with flux and change. Recognizing and becoming comfortable with constant change is certainly one of the benefits of Buddhist meditation[121] and this study suggests that it may also be a benefit of other practices.

Conclusions

Even given the limitations of the Rorschach, this is an exciting study with several important implications. First, intensive spiritual practices of diverse kinds can produce overlapping effects. Second, spiritual masters of different traditions may share several kinds of remarkable capacities, perspectives, and identities. Several findings support centuries-old claims about the effects of spiritual practice and the qualities of spiritual masters. Finally, the study opens a new era of testing and comparing spiritual masters.

CHAPTER 14

Spiritual Emergency and Spiritual Emergence? New Views of Shamans' Health

...of external facts we have had enough and to spare, more than the squirrel like scholars will ever be able to piece together into a single whole, enough to keep the busy popularizers sprouting in bright-eyed knowledgeability the rest of their days; but of the inner facts—of what goes on at the center where the forces of our fate first announce themselves—we are still pretty much in ignorance...

—*William Barrett*[22]

Despite decades of attempts to pigeonhole them, shamans simply do not slip neatly into traditional psychiatric categories. Much has been made of the initiation crisis, and yet what is most important is not the crisis itself but what comes out of it. For the shaman "is not only a sick man" said Eliade, "he is a sick man who has been cured, who has succeeded in curing himself."[83] From this perspective, "shamanism is not a disease but being healed from disease."[4]

In fact, shamans are often the most functional members of their community, and according to Eliade, "show proof of a more than normal nervous constitution."[83] They can display remarkable energy and stamina, unusual levels of concentration, high intelligence, leadership skills, and a grasp of complex myths and rituals.[83, 302, 311] What can we make of this curious combination of initial disturbance and subsequent health? Are there any data and diagnoses that can encompass *both* the initial disturbance *and* the subsequent recovery?

DISTURBANCE AS DEVELOPMENT

The answer is clearly yes. Shamans are not alone in becoming better after a psychological disturbance. Over 2,000 years ago, Socrates declared that "our greatest blessings come to us by way of madness, provided the madness is given us by divine gift."[219] More recently the eminent psychiatrist Karl Menninger observed that "some patients have a mental illness and then they get weller! I mean they get better than they ever were....This is an extraordinary and little realized truth."[219]

Fortunately, it is becoming better recognized. Responses to stress can span a spectrum from regression to growth. This spectrum extends from pathological regression (at the negative extreme) to resilience (continued normal functioning) and even to post-traumatic growth (also known as stress-related growth, positive adaptation, and thriving).[214]

Likewise, some psychological disturbances can function as growth experiences that somehow result in greater psychological or spiritual well-being. These disturbances shed new light on shamanic initiation crises.

The general process is one of temporary psychological disturbance followed by resolution and repair to a new and higher level of functioning. What seemed at the time to be purely a crisis of disturbance and disease can now be seen as a stage of development and growth. Each of the many names given to such crises illuminates a different facet of the process. These names include "positive disintegration," "regenerative processes," "renewal," "creative illness," and "resilience."[62, 86, 96, 275, 278]

Some psychological crises include mystical or transpersonal experiences. These have been described as "mystical experiences with psychotic features," "divine illnesses," "metanoiac voyages," "visionary states," "spiritual emergencies," and "transpersonal crises."[127, 128, 135, 206, 219] What these names make clear is that psychological disturbances may sometimes be followed by significant growth. Consequently, we can now recognize some psychological disturbances as developmental crises.

Developmental Crises

Developmental crises are periods of psychological stress that accompany turning points in our lives. They may be marked by considerable psychological turmoil, sometimes even of life-threatening proportions. These transitions can occur spontaneously, as in adolescent and midlife crises, or can be induced by growth-accelerating techniques such as psychotherapy and meditation.

These crises occur because psychological growth rarely proceeds smoothly. Rather, growth is usually marked by periods of confusion and questioning or, in extreme cases, disorganization and despair. The twin lions that guard the gates of Eastern temples are said to represent confusion and paradox, and anyone who seeks wisdom must be willing to pass through both.

Even clarity can become a trap. We cling to an old familiar understanding of ourselves and the world because it saves us from having to face the ever-changing novelty and uncertainty of life. We cling to the familiar, not knowing that mystery is a necessary prelude to the dawning of wisdom. As Castaneda succinctly put it, clarity "dispels fear, but also blinds," and the person who holds fast to it no longer learns.[46]

If these crises are successfully negotiated, then the turmoil may turn out to be the means by which constricting, outdated life patterns are cast off. Old beliefs and goals may be released and new, more life-affirming modes adopted. In short, psychological pain and confusion can be symptoms of either disease or development.

Developmental crises can occur spontaneously as a result of inner forces that compel growth, whether the individual wants it or not. The mind is designed to grow, and the drive powering that growth has been variously described as an *actualizing tendency* (Carl Rogers), *individuation urge* (Carl Jung), *holotropism* (Stan Grof), *equilibration* (Jean Piaget), or *eros* (Ken Wilber). The result is a dynamic tension between these forces of growth and the seductiveness of stagnation, between the pull of transcendence and the inertia of the familiar. The Jungian psychiatrist John Perry observed that

spirit [is] constantly striving for release from its entrapment in routine or conventional mental structures. Spiritual work is the attempt to liberate this dynamic energy, which must break free of its suffocation in old forms....[I]f this work of releasing spirit becomes imperative but is not undertaken voluntarily with knowledge of the goal and with considerable effort, then the psyche is apt to take over and overwhelm the conscious personality....The individuating psyche abhors stasis as nature abhors a vacuum.[278]

In other words, the psyche may be unwilling to risk the unhappiness that Abraham Maslow warned against when he said, "If you deliberately plan to be less than you are capable of being, then I warn you that you will be deeply unhappy for the rest of your life."[227] Rather than tolerate stagnation, the psyche may willfully create crises that force development.[278]

Such is the case with shamans. Many are not at all pleased by the prospect of their new profession and resist the initial signs with all their might. According to Devereux, "Among the Sedang Moi, a person who receives the 'call' may even drink his own urine, in the hope that this act will so depreciate him in the sight of his divine sponsors that they will take back the power they had given him."[70] However, resistance is no easy matter, and many tribal myths hold that the person who resists the call will sicken, go mad, or die.

When the forces of growth overwhelm the forces of inertia, a developmental transition or crisis occurs. The symptoms of this crisis vary depending upon the individual's personality and maturity and can range from regressive pathology at one extreme to transpersonal or spiritual concerns at the other.[413] These transpersonal crises, which are also called *spiritual emergencies* or *spiritual emergences*,[127, 128, 135] seem close to, and helpful in understanding, some shamanic initiation crises.

THE VARIETIES OF SPIRITUAL EMERGENCIES

Although they have been described for centuries as complications of spiritual practices, the careful study of spiritual emergencies has only just begun. Varieties particularly relevant to shamanism and its initiation crises include "mystical experiences with psychotic features," "shamanic journeys," "possession," "renewal," "kundalini," and "psychic opening."

Mystical experience with psychotic features and "psychotic disorder with mystical features" are terms used to describe psychoses in which significant mystical experiences occur.[219] The episodes are usually short-lived and have a better prognosis than other psychoses. This curious combination of mystical and psychotic is consistent with the bizarre behavior and mystical experiences of some shamanic crises.

Shamanic journey emergencies echo themes commonly encountered in both shamanic initiations and journeys. As Christina and Stan Grof observe:

Transpersonal crises of this type bear a deep resemblance to what the anthropologists have described as the shamanic or initiatory illness....In the experiences of individuals whose transpersonal crises have strong shamanic features, there is great emphasis on physical suffering and encounter with death followed by rebirth and elements of ascent or magical flight. They also typically sense a special connection with the elements of nature and experience communication with animals or animal spirits. It is also not unusual to feel an upsurge of extraordinary powers and impulses to heal.... Like the initiatory crisis, the transpersonal episodes of a shamanic type, if properly supported, can lead to good adjustment and superior functioning.[127]

The striking similarity of these contemporary crises to classic shamanic experiences suggests that initiatory crises reflect a deep psychological process, not limited to particular cultures or times. This process seems capable of exploding from the depths of the psyche in contemporary Westerners surrounded by cars and computers as well as in ancient shamans in tepees and igloos. Clearly some deep, perhaps archetypal, pattern is being played out here, and the Grofs' therefore conclude that "Individuals whose spiritual crises follow this pattern are thus involved in an ancient process that touches the deepest foundations of the psyche."[127] We may therefore have much to learn from ancient shamanic wisdom about the appropriate handling of these crises.

Experiences of *possession* have been described throughout history and can constitute a major feature of shamanic crises. Individuals experience being taken over by inner forces or beings beyond their control. Sometimes these forces feel so alien and malevolent as to seem literally demonic, and victims may fear that they are engaged in a desperate battle for their life and sanity. So dramatic are these experiences that even some contemporary psychiatrists, most notably Scot Peck, have concluded that demonic forces are to blame.[274] However, most health professionals assume that possession is an expression of powerful psychological dynamics that can be treated therapeutically. Indeed, Christina and Stan Grof claim that "with good support, experiences of this kind can be extremely liberating and therapeutic."[127]

John Perry described the *renewal process* as an experience of destruction followed by regeneration. Individuals undergoing it are overwhelmed by images in which they see both themselves and the world being destroyed. Yet this destruction is not the end but a prelude to rebirth and regeneration. Out of the images of ruin comes a sense of personal renewal and world regeneration. Images of death and rebirth are of course common in the shamanic crisis.

This renewal process may entail considerable stress and even reach psychotic proportions. Psychiatrists rarely distinguish this particular process from other psychoses and usually suppress them all with drugs. However, John Perry claims:

> If a person undergoing this turmoil is given love, understanding and encouragement, the spiritual crisis soon resolves itself without the need for interruption by suppressive medication. The most fragmented "thought disorder" can become quite coherent and orderly within a short time if someone is present to respond to it with compassion. Such a relationship is far better than a tranquilizer in most instances.[278]

The fundamental change in this "renewal process" is thought to be a dissolution of the old self-image and its replacement with a new, more appropriate one.

Kundalini awakening has been most fully described in the yogic tradition of India, where kundalini is the creative energy of the universe. Humans partake of this energy, but it usually lies dormant and unrecognized. Under the prodding of spiritual practice, or occasionally spontaneously, the kundalini can be aroused and unleash enormous, even overwhelming, physical and psychological energy.

The result is a complex array of intense physical, psychological, and spiritual experiences that can be ecstatic or terrifying. These can manifest physically as tremors and spasms or psychologically as intense emotions, agitation, energy, lights, and vivid imagery. Kundalini could account for the unusual symptoms and intense agitation of some shamanic crises. Kundalini crises are now occurring more frequently in the West as more people begin intensive meditative and yogic practices.

The last type of spiritual emergency is that of *psychic opening*. Here individuals feel they have suddenly become capable, sometimes quite against their will, of one or more psychic abilities. These can include out-of-body experiences, visions, and mediumship or channeling—all common experiences among shamans. Such people may encounter significant difficulties, feel overwhelmed, and fear for their sanity. We will explore the question of the validity of psychic phenomena in a later chapter.

These are the forms of spiritual emergency most relevant to shamanic initiation crises. An important implication is that there may be several kinds of shamanic crises, and future descriptions and diagnoses will need to be more nuanced.

DIAGNOSIS AND TREATMENT

Clearly spiritual practices and awakenings (to use religious terms) can revive and exacerbate unresolved conflicts. This is not necessarily bad since the process can bring to the surface issues and difficulties requiring attention, and it can result in considerable healing and personality integration.[128]

Two major diagnostic errors can be made. One is reductionistic: to fail to recognize a spiritual emergency and reduce it to pure pathology. The other is "elevationistic": to overlook a pathological process such as schizophrenia and elevate it to a spiritual emergency. The task is complicated by the existence of hybrid forms in which both mystical and pathological experiences coexist.[219]

If correctly diagnosed and appropriately supported, then spiritual emergencies can be valuable growth experiences; hence their other name of "spiritual emergences." Several factors are helpful. The first is a trusting relationship where the patient feels cared for and safe. The second is a positive attitude in which the patient expects that the process will prove valuable and healing.[233] Third, opening to and talking about the experience can be helpful and can be facilitated by psychotherapy.[135]

Shamans discovered these principles long ago. Their crises involve symptoms and behaviors that appear bizarre, even pathological. However, the outcome may be positive when the shaman-to-be is recognized as such by the tribe and then receives culturally appropriate support, guidance, and "therapy." This support includes a relationship with an experienced shaman, a positive reinterpretation of the disturbance as part of a shamanic awakening, and practices that enable the novice to work with the emerging experiences. With this assistance, the initiate may not only recover but may emerge stronger and able to help others. In short, shamanic crises and contemporary spiritual emergencies seem to be related, difficult, but potentially valuable maturation crises. Shamanic cultures have long provided the types of support that contemporary therapists are now rediscovering.

CHAPTER 15

Shamanic Trickery: The Tricks of the Trade

Truth is so very precious, man is naturally economical in its use.
—Mark Twain

To add insult to injury, shamans have not only been diagnosed as disturbed, but have also been dismissed as charlatans. However, whereas the evidence for disturbance is debatable, the evidence for trickery is clear. Yet as we will see, there can be much of value in these tricks and more to them than simple deceit.

THE VARIETIES OF SHAMANIC TRICKERY

Since shamans' reputations rest largely on their ability to display supernatural powers, it is not surprising that they may be tempted to lend the supernatural a helping hand. This they do in several ways.

One approach is to employ spies who can assess a potential patient's health and help the shaman determine whether to take the case. This is no small decision, since if the patient should die, the shaman loses his reputation and, in some tribes, his life.[311] Spies can also provide personal information about patients that can later be revealed by the spirits.

Shamans also use tricks to add dramatic flair to their treatments. When sucking out spirit intrusions, the healer may hide an object such as a worm or a bloody tuft of hair in his mouth and then spit it out as proof of therapeutic success. Eskimo shamans of St. Lawrence Island in Alaska may pretend to first crush a stone to sand and then reform it back into a stone.[400] Long observation of Eskimo shamans led the anthropologist Bogoras to conclude that

> there can be no doubt, of course, that shamans, during their performances, employ deceit in various forms, and that they themselves are fully cognizant of the fact. "There are many liars in our calling," Scratching Woman said to me....Of course, he was ready to swear that he never made use of any of these wrong practices. "Look at my face," he continued, "he who tells lies his tongue stutters. He whose speech, however, flows offhand from his lips, certainly must speak the truth." This was a rather doubtful argument, but I refrained from making any suggestions.[29]

Shamans may also pretend to do physical battle to vanquish evil spirits. Rasmussen witnessed this:

> During our stay at South Hampton Island I was witness to such a case, where a Shaman named Saraq went out to fight against evil spirits, but I discovered that he had taken some Caribou blood with him beforehand and rubbed himself with this without being discovered by anyone else. When he came in, he stated that the shaman who had been out with him had been unable to hold the evil spirit, but he, Saraq, had grasped it and stabbed it, inflicting a deep wound. It had then made its escape, but the wound was so deep that he could not conceive of the possibility of it surviving. All believed his report, all believed that he had driven the evil spirit which had been troubling the village, and no one was afraid any longer.[299]

Acquiring such tricks may be part of an apprentice's training. For example, a Kwakiutl apprentice from the Vancouver area of Canada learns:

> A curious mixture of pantomime, prestidigitation, and empirical knowledge including the art of simulating fainting and nervous fits, the learning of sacred songs, the technique for inducing vomiting, rather precise notions of auscultation and obstetrics, and the use of "dreamers," that is, spies who listen to private conversations and secretly convey to the shaman bits of information concerning origins and symptoms of the ills suffered by different people. Above all, he learned the *ars magna* of one of the shamanistic schools of the Northwest Coast: the shaman hides a tuft of down in a little corner of his mouth, and he throws it up, covered with blood, at the ap-

propriate moment—after having bitten his tongue or made his gums bleed—and solemnly presents it to his patients and the onlookers as the pathological foreign body extracted as a result of his sucking and manipulations.[212]

Dangerous Trickery

These are harmless tricks that might even be helpful inasmuch as they bolster faith and inspire a placebo response. However, not all trickery is benign. Some shamans have been reported to give toxins or psychedelics to their patients in order to make the disease and its cure more dramatic.[311] A Jivaro shaman may bewitch disliked neighbors and then refer them to his shaman partner for treatment.[147] Shamans may even attempt to kill and Rasmussen reported:

> If now a shaman desires to injure a person by magic, someone who he does not like and of whom he has grown envious, he will first endeavor to obtain some object belonging to the person concerned; this he takes and speaks ill over it and keeps on speaking ill over it hoping thus to pass on the evil to the person he desires to hurt and should he discover a powerful destructive force, which may lie concealed in a grave, then he must rub the object he is speaking ill over into the grave. This may give rise to sickness, madness or enmity ending in homicide.[299]

Small wonder that shamans have been such ambivalent figures, revered and sought for healing, while feared and hated for their malevolence.

QUESTIONS RAISED BY SHAMANIC TRICKERY

Clearly, *some* shamans may engage in all manner of trickery, and this raises the following questions:

1) Do all shamans engage in trickery and deceit?

2) Is part of the trickery done for the benefit of the patient and tribe? In other words, is some of the trickery a kind of pious fraud?

3) Are shamanism and all shamanic practices ineffective and fraudulent, as some people have claimed, or are there also practices that are therapeutic and valuable?

4) Do shamans use more trickery than other healers and professionals?

5) Do shamans deceive themselves as well as their patients?

Let's begin with the question of whether all shamans engage in trickery and deceit. Though trickery is widespread, many anthropologists have been impressed by the sincerity of shamans and their desire to help. There is also the question of whether trickery should be regarded as fraudulent when a healer believes that using it helps the patient. In short, there is no reason to assume that all shamans are tricksters.

EXPECTATIONS OF HEALING

Can shamanic trickery benefit patients? Research shows that the expectations of both patient and therapist tend to become self-fulfilling prophecies and that faith in a physician can exert a powerful placebo effect. Indeed, the environment, the physician's status, and the rituals involved in giving and taking medicine can sometimes be as important as the drug itself. Psychiatrists treating depression or anxiety are well aware that they had better exude confidence to ensure that their drugs work optimally.

Sharp observers that they are, shamans may have reached similar conclusions. They may radiate confidence to remove their patients' doubts and perhaps also their own. Rasmussen, for example, described a shaman who stated that "I believe I am a better shaman than others among my countrymen. I will venture to say that I hardly ever make a mistake in the things I investigate and what I predict. And I therefore consider myself a more perfect, a more fully-trained shaman than those of my countrymen who often make mistakes."[299]

Shamanic tricks and abundant self-confidence may increase patients' expectations and therefore their likelihood of being cured since:

> Plainly, the shaman's tricks serve as a symbol of his healing power. They impress the audience with his magical skill and knowledge, and provide a concrete visible representation in the form of a worm, or bloody down of the patients' illness. In that the tricks reinforce the belief of the patient and the community in the shaman's power, they add tremendously to the force of his suggestion and the patient's expectant faith in the healing process.
>
> We need have no doubt that the healing rituals, relying heavily as they may do on the power of suggestion, are effective. Their value in aiding the recovery of emotional and physical illnesses has been repeatedly observed and amply recorded.[400]

A special case occurs when shamans operate in ASCs. For example, a shaman may pull out a worm he has hidden in his mouth and announce that it is the patient's illness. An outsider, understandably enough, might dismiss the shaman as an outright charlatan.

However, the shaman in an altered state has a very different view. In his visionary state, he may see the illness sucked into the object in his mouth so that this object now has both ordinary and supernatural aspects. As Michael Harner explains:

> He then "vomits" out this object and displays it to the patient and his family saying "now I have sucked it out. Here it is." The non-shamans think that the material object itself is what has been sucked out and the shaman does not disillusion them. At the same time, he is not lying because he knows that the only important thing about the *tsentsak* (spiritual force or helper) is its supernatural aspect, or essence, which he sincerely believes he has removed from the patient's body. To explain to the layman that he already had these objects in his mouth would serve no fruitful purpose and would prevent him from displaying such an object as proof that he had affected the cure.[145]

So from the shamans' perspective, at least some of their "tricks" are essential parts of the healing process, done primarily for the patient's benefit.

BEYOND TRICKERY

Are trickery and deceit all there is to shamanism? While some critics have thought so, several lines of evidence argue otherwise.

First, there is the enormous durability of the tradition. Shamanism has thrived for millennia, and it is hard to imagine a tradition surviving for so long in so many cultures unless there were effective components to it. Certainly, anthropologists have been impressed by the sincerity of many shamans.

Many shamanic techniques make good psychological and scientific sense. As we will explore in later chapters, shamans draw on an array of individual and group techniques also employed by psychotherapists, while pharmaceutical companies are investigating traditional healing potions.

Importantly, shamanism presents a coherent worldview that offers an explanation of the cause and cure of illness. Within this worldview, shamanic practices seem logical and appropriate to both shaman and patient. This is crucial since a shared understanding of the cause and cure of illness provides what is called a "healing myth": a curative context that fosters the placebo effect and healing. What is essential is that this healing myth is plausible to both patient and therapist.[104]

DECEPTION AND THE HEALING PROFESSIONS

Do shamans deceive more than other healers? Few of us could claim that we never use dubious means to bolster our personal or professional image. Indeed, "there is hardly a legitimate everyday vocation or relationship whose performers do not engage in concealed practices which are incompatible with fostered impressions."[119]

Certainly the shaman is not unique in using placebo effects both consciously and unconsciously. It has been said that "the history of (Western) medical treatment for the most part until relatively recently is the history of the placebo effect."[331] Indeed, a considerable amount of the effectiveness of current psychotherapy may be due not to the cherished theories and techniques of the therapist, but to her empathy and the warmth of the relationship. In this regard shamanism and psychotherapy have much in common.[400]

Shamans and psychotherapists may both deceive themselves. Both may mistakenly believe that their cures are due to specific techniques, such as unearthing and interpreting childhood traumas in psychotherapy or extracting and battling spirits in shamanism. Yet much of their effectiveness may stem simply from the warmth and support of a caring relationship.[423]

Moreover, both shamans and therapists must face the fact that their techniques are not always effective. Both are repeatedly confronted by a distressingly large number of patients and illnesses that they cannot help, and both may sometimes lose faith in their craft.

Yet shamans, like healers of all kinds, confront powerful social and psychological forces pushing them to maintain faith in their trade. After all, they have invested significant amounts of time and resources in their training, and their income and status depend on it. Faced with this painful conflict, both shamans and psychotherapists may resort to self-deception to bolster their faith in their own effectiveness.[400] These self-deceptions may include a variety of psychological defense mechanisms such as rationalization, repression, and selective memory. With the help of rationalization, a failure to cure may be explained away by attributing it to outside forces such as patient resistance or spirit malevolence. Repression and selective memory enable shamans and therapists to forget failures, while recalling their cures with vivid clarity.

These defenses are supported by the needs of the patients and society. People eager for help project healing ability onto the healer in a desperate attempt to believe that they can be cured. "It is difficult for a healer to doubt his own worth if he is constantly assured of it by his patients, their relatives and the whole community. If the social consensus is that someone has the power to heal, then he is a healer."[400]

SUMMARY

Some shamans may use trickery and deceit but they are hardly unique in this. Conscious and unconscious bolstering of one's professional image occurs in most professions. In fact, trickery is so much a part of human nature that it is portrayed across cultures as the *trickster*: a mythological figure who continuously deceives and upsets the traditional order and appearances.[352]

Shamans may believe in some of the techniques that seem like deceit to outsiders. In addition, shamanic trickery may not be entirely self-serving. Patients who believe they can be healed are more likely to recover. As Henry Ford supposedly said, "Those who believe they can do something and those who believe they can't are both right." Finally, some "tricks" may be ritually enacted symbols of deeper healing processes.

PART V

THE SHAMAN'S UNIVERSE

Many of the transpersonal experiences that are potentially of great therapeutic value involve such a basic challenge to the individual's world view that he or she will have serious difficulty in letting them happen unless properly intellectually prepared.

—*Stanislav Grof*[130]

CHAPTER 16

Many Worlds

A sensible man prefers the inner to the outer eye.
—*Lao Tzu*[39]

What is the nature of the shamans' cosmos? There are numerous cultural variations, but also cross-cultural similarities.

One similarity is that the shaman's universe is often three-tiered. It comprises an upper, middle, and lower world, and the upper and lower worlds may be multilayered. What makes shamans "cosmic travelers" is their experience of being able to traverse these multiple worlds at will. Eliade claimed that

> the pre-eminently shamanic technique is the passage from one cosmic region to an-
> other—from earth to the sky or from earth to the underworld. The shaman knows
> the mystery of the break-through in plane. This communication among the cosmic
> zones is made possible by the very structure of the universe.[83]

"The very structure of the universe" to which Eliade refers is its interconnectedness. The three worlds are often linked by the *axis mundi* or world axis. Eliade pointed out that in diverse myths:

> The essential schema is always to be seen, even after the numerous influences to
> which it has been subjected; there are three great cosmic regions, which can be suc-
> cessively traversed because they are linked together by a central axis. This axis, of

course, passes through an "opening," a "hole"; it is through this hole that the gods descend to earth and the dead to the subterranean regions; it is through the same hole that the soul of the shaman in ecstasy can fly up or down in the course of his celestial or infernal journeys.[83]

Three forms of the central axis are common to diverse cultures and myths. The first is the "cosmic mountain" at the center of the earth, such as the seven-story mountain that the Yakut shaman climbs.[83] The second is the "world pillar" that often holds up the sky. Third is the "world tree"—symbol of life, fertility, and sacred regeneration—that the shaman climbs to other worlds. But whatever its form, the world axis symbolizes the connection between worlds, a connection that the shaman alone is able to traverse.

But the shaman's worlds and levels are more than interconnected; they also interact with one another. Shamans believe that these interactions can be perceived and affected by one who knows how to do so and that the shaman, like a spider at the center of a cosmic web, can feel and influence distant realms.

All parts of this interconnected universe are seen as alive and conscious to some degree. In contemporary philosophical language, these would be the doctrines of hylozoism and animism. *Hylozoism* is the belief that all objects are imbued with life. *Animism* is the belief of tribal people that every object is invested with a mind or soul. When this same belief is held by Western intellectuals, it is renamed *panpsychism*. Needless to say, panpsychism is most unfashionable in these materialistic times, even though historically it has been supported by such first-rank philosophers as Leibniz, Schopenhauer, and Whitehead.

As metaphysicians, shamans tend to be ontological realists. Where Westerners might regard the upper and lower worlds as mental constructions, shamans regard them as independently existing realms. Michael Harner points out that for the shaman, "the mind is being used to gain access, to pass through a door into another reality which exists independently of that mind."[149] This is another example of the literal and realist interpretation of experience that often characterizes the shamanic worldview.

For the shamans' tribespeople, this multilayered cosmos is a myth and article of faith. For shamans it is a direct experience. They alone traverse these layers and turn a cosmology into a road map, which they then use to acquire information and power. They alone, said Eliade, transform a cosmotheological concept into a "concrete mystical experience." This point is important. It explains the difference between, for example, the religious life of a North Asian people and the religious experience of its shamans; the latter is a *personal and ecstatic experience*.[83]

CULTURE, COSMOLOGY, AND INDIVIDUAL EXPERIENCE

Since shamans directly experience the realms described in tribal myth and cosmology, an obvious question is whether their journeys also shaped these myths and cosmology. Put more generally, this question becomes an extremely important one: To what extent do spiritual practitioners *create* their tradition's cosmology from their experience, and to what extent is their experience *created by*, or at least molded by, their cosmology? Do religious practice and experience create beliefs, or do beliefs create religious experience? Which is chicken and which egg, or are they mutually co-creative?

Eliade argued that cosmology determines shamanic experience. But while he acknowledged that some epic stories may derive from shamanic journeys, he denied the impact of these journeys on cosmology.

> The shamans did not create the cosmology, the mythology, and the theology of their respective tribes; they only interiorized it, experienced it, and used it as the itinerary for their ecstatic journeys.[83]

On the other hand, Michael Harner claims that what defines shamanism are its techniques and that the experiences they elicit allow practitioners to reach their own conclusions and cosmology.

> Shamanism ultimately is only a method, not a religion with a fixed set of dogmas. Therefore people arrive at their own experience-derived conclusions about what is going on in the universe, and about what term, if any, is most useful to describe ultimate reality.[149]

So here we have two experts disagreeing. Eliade believed that preexisting cultural cosmologies determine shamans' experiences. However, Harner claims that shamans simply do their practices, observe their experiences, and deduce their own cosmology largely independent of cultural conditioning. Who is correct, and how can we decide?

We have no research data so we will need to fall back on general principles concerning the relationship between individual experience and collective culture. The relationship turns out to be at the heart of postmodern thinking.

It used to be assumed that individual experience arose freely and autonomously and that all a person had to do to see unvarnished truth was to "look within." Meditative disciplines and modern phenomenology are based on this assumption. Certainly much can be learned, and much insight, healing, and transcendence can be gained from careful introspection.

However, one of the absolutely crucial contributions of postmodernism—and one of the great intellectual advances in the twentieth century—is the recognition that individual experience is deeply, pervasively, and unconsciously molded by culture. Before experiences arise to awareness, they are constructed, filtered, and interpreted by the "cognitive unconscious" according to often unrecognized background cultural frameworks such as language, values, beliefs, and biases.[411] In fact, a central thrust of the whole field of Critical Studies is to unveil unconscious collective biases such as those of, for example, culture, gender, and class, which create respectively ethnocentrism, sexism, and classism. (For a popular introduction, see *Introducing Critical Theory*.[339])

In religious studies, a similar "constructivist" movement argues that religious experiences are also constructed and interpreted by prior cultural concepts categories.[r] In short, experiences in general, and shamanic ones in particular, are molded and interpreted by the individual's culture and cosmology. Expectation evokes experience as, for example, with the technique of dream incubation where one attempts to dream about a particular topic.

Certainly shamans bring some beliefs and cosmology to their practice. After all, why would a shaman want to journey to the upper world without believing there was one? Furthermore, there are wide cultural variations in myths, and shamans tend to have experiences consistent with their culture.

However, pioneering explorers can have novel experiences that transcend the conventions of their culture and eventually transform it. These transconventional experiences remain grounded in some cultural contexts and presuppositions—such as linguistic categories and parts of the prevailing worldview—while breaking free of others. This is the process of "detribalization" by which an individual disidentifies from certain cultural assumptions. He or she is thus able to look *at* them rather than look *through* them and can then work *on* them to transform them and the culture. One goal of spiritual practices is precisely to foster this kind of liberation from conventional illusions. But one of the great traps unveiled by the postmodern critique was to assume that spiritual practices alone could reveal and liberate all cultural conditioning.[411]

Individuals such as shamans who break through into transconventional experiences can exert a transforming effect on culture. Their impact is a function of their social status and resultant "idiosyncrasy credit" and the openness of the social structure. In general, the greater an individual's status, the more leeway he or she has to be idiosyncratic and challenge old ideas. Likewise, the less structured the social and religious institutions, the less they are likely to be threatened by individual religious revelations. Shamans generally have high status and reside in relatively simple societies, so their potential for modifying their culture and cosmology would presumably be high. Thus in the short term, shamanic experiences are clearly shaped by cultural cosmology, but in the long run, shamanic experiences may reshape and enrich this cosmology.

CHAPTER 17

Many Spirits

Glendower: I can call spirits from the vasty deep.
Hotspur: Why, so can I, or so can any man;
But will they come when you do call for them?
—*William Shakespeare,* Henry IV

For shamans, the answer to Hotspur's question is "yes, the spirits will come." For shamans reside in a living, conscious universe teeming with spirits that exert an enormous influence on individuals and the tribe.

Ordinary people are largely helpless victims who have little control over the spirits. Their only recourse is to pray, to sacrifice, to obey the tribal taboos, or to have the shaman intercede on their behalf. For the shaman alone can control spirits. Indeed, for many anthropologists, this control is a defining characteristic of shamans. But in order to control the spirits, shamans must first learn to see them.

SPIRIT VISION

Since the spirits are usually invisible to the untutored eye, a major part of shamanic training involves acquiring the power of "spirit vision" by which they can be recognized. This accounts, said Eliade, for "the extreme importance of 'spirit visions' in all varieties of shamanic initiations."[83]

Given the value of this spirit vision, it is not surprising that considerable effort is invested in acquiring it. The spirits are usually sought under specific conditions that enhance awareness of visual images, conditions such as ASCs and reduced lighting. For example, the Jivaro Indian initiate of South America may spend days fasting and ingesting drugs until finally a spirit is seen. In another tribe, the instructor rubs herbs on the eyes of the apprentice and then:

> For three days and nights the two men sit opposite each other, singing and ringing their bells. Until the eyes of the boy are clear, neither of the two men obtains any sleep. At the end of the three days the two again go to the woods and obtain more herbs....if at the end of seven days the boy sees the wood-spirits, the ceremony is at an end. Otherwise the entire seven day ceremony must be repeated.[215]

How does spirit vision develop? One psychological explanation is that shamans learn to recognize and interpret the flux of visual images seen during altered states. If you close your eyes right now, especially in a darkened room, and gaze into the inner space of awareness, you will gradually become aware of a kaleidoscopic flux of visual images. In altered states these images can become more distinct, meaningful, and archetypal.

Shamans may organize this flux into spirits and other images consistent with their expectations. A study of Zinacanteco natives of Mexico revealed significant perceptual differences between shamans and non-shamans.[336] When shown a series of blurred, out-of-focus photographs and asked what they saw, shamans were much less likely than non-shamans to say "I don't know," even when the photographs were blurred to the point of being completely unrecognizable. Furthermore, when the experimenter offered suggestions as to what the image might be, shamans were more likely to ignore the suggestions and to give their own personal interpretations.

These findings indicate that shamans can create meaningful patterns from unclear data, organizing ambiguous experiences into coherent, meaningful images. Moreover, for shamans these images are likely to reflect their own personal categories and worldview. This suggests that shamans are adept at finding what they expect to see. Consequently, they may be particularly able to find spirits amid the many images they encounter during their séances. Of course, it remains for future research to see whether these findings hold for shamans in other parts of the world.

The psychologist Richard Noll has suggested that shamans may also be intense fantasizers.[260] Studies of excellent hypnotic subjects suggest that some 4 percent of the population are so-called "fantasy-prone" personalities. These are people who "fantasize a large part of the time, who typically 'see,' 'hear,' 'smell,' 'touch,' and fully experience what they fantasize."[414] Perhaps some shamans are "fantasy-prone" personalities who are able to organize and learn from their intense images in personally and socially beneficial ways.

The term "fantasy" is sometimes used derogatorily, as in idle daydreaming. However, at its deepest, imagery may open into profound, revelatory visions. This is not to say that psychological processes fully account for experiences of spirits or that spirits are only visual images. But whatever the nature of spirits, shamans clearly exemplify the words of the great sixteenth-century physician Paracelsus who claimed that "everyone may educate and regulate his imagination so as to come thereby into contact with spirits, and be taught by them."[263]

Stabilizing Spirit Vision

The novice's task of learning to see the spirits involves two stages. The first is simply to catch an initial glimpse of them. The second is to develop a permanent visionary capacity in which the spirits can be summoned and seen or felt at will. In Eliade's words:

> All this long and tiring ceremony has as its object transforming the apprentice magician's initial and momentary and ecstatic experience…into a permanent condition—that in which it is possible to see the spirits.[83]

This is the "challenge of stabilization," a challenge that faces spiritual practitioners of all traditions.[396] The task—for shamans, yogis, and contemplatives alike—is to stabilize temporary gifts into permanent abilities, altered states into altered traits, and epiphanies into personality, or as Huston Smith so eloquently put it, to transform "flashes of illumination into abiding light."[346]

THE VARIETIES OF SPIRITS

While there are many kinds of spirits, the shaman can control only some of them. For as Eliade pointed out, the shaman is "a man who has immediate concrete experiences with gods and spirits; he sees them face to face, he talks to them, prays to them, implores them—but he does not 'control' more than a limited number of them."[83]

Those he controls are his helping spirits. Many of these are animals, sometimes called power animals, and "they can appear in the form of bears, wolves, stags, hares, all kinds of birds,"[83] and in numerous other forms as well.

Similar encounters also occur outside shamanism. Growing numbers of psychotherapists use guided visualization techniques to evoke images of "power animals" or "spirit guides" and then encourage clients to interact with and learn from them.[110]

Encounters with "spirit guides" occur spontaneously in psychedelic therapy and, according to Stanislav Grof, can be "most valuable and rewarding phenomena."[131] It is remarkable how often ancient shamanic experiences are echoed in contemporary psychedelic ones, suggesting that shamans have long mined deep, archetypal realms of the psyche that remain hidden to most people.

FUNCTIONS OF SPIRITS

Whatever their form, spirits assist the shaman in four ways. They may teach, assist with journeys, provide strengths and abilities, or possess the shaman as in mediumship.

The spirits may travel with the shaman on ecstatic journeys, accompanying or even carrying her to the sky. They may defend her from threats and battle on her behalf. Their strength may become hers if she voluntarily merges with them and thereby partakes of their powers and capacities. She may see herself turned into an eagle and soar into the sky, or become a wolf and feel infused with its power. After returning from the journey she may perform her "power animal dance," moving and sounding like the animal, as a way of experiencing and maintaining its presence. The following example of finding a power animal is drawn from my own experience as a participant in one of Michael Harner's core shamanism workshops. It demonstrates the experiential power of these encounters.

This was a journey to the lower world to meet and request assistance from power animals. I began my journey by entering a cave in Hawaii and went down a tunnel until I reached the lower world that first appeared as a small green globe. On landing I found myself in a lush green jungle filled with animals.

I was immediately drawn to a lion. I appealed to him to be with me during the workshop and to let me share his power, strength, suppleness, keen sensitivity, and agility.

I then asked him what I needed to know or do. Immediately the lion leaped into me and merged with me, so that my shamanic body was human/lion, and I felt its power. This sense of power was very helpful since it seemed to counteract feelings of fear, guilt, and contraction that I had been experiencing.

At the end of the journey, I returned up the tunnel into the cave and then back into the workshop room. Yet there was a clear sense that the "lion" returned with me, and I felt healed, empowered, and strengthened.

What are we to make of these reports of merging with power animals? Several psychological mechanisms may be at work. These include role playing, identification, permission giving (being given permission to feel powerful, effective, etc.), and "acting as if" (acting as if one had a particular desired quality). But whatever the mechanism, it is clear that visualizing oneself merging with a powerful figure is widespread across religious traditions, is dramatically empowering, and is increasingly used in psychotherapy.[92] Even contemplating an animal can bring benefits, as the great yogi Patanjali described some 2,000 years ago: "From *sanyama* [meditation] on the strength of an elephant, or other creatures, we gain that strength."[333]

Some of the most dramatic examples are the "deity yogas" of Hindu yoga and Tibetan Buddhism. Here the yogi visualizes herself as first creating and then merging with a sacred figure—the *ishtadeva* of Hinduism or the *yidam* of Buddhism—who symbolizes spiritual qualities such as unconditional love, boundless compassion, or profound wisdom. Afterward the yogi attempts to speak and act as the deity. In other words, after merging with their allies, both shamans and yogis attempt to experience and express their allies' qualities.

However, there is a crucial difference. For the shaman, the power animal ally is real. However, for the yogi, the deity is considered a mental creation, a projection of one's own as yet unrecognized transpersonal potentials, which the visualization will allow the yogi to recognize and claim.

The impact of these visualizations is suggested by the fact that Tibetans regard Deity yoga as one of their most powerful practices. In one of the world's most dramatic claims for effectiveness, they claim that Deity yoga allows practitioners to become a Buddha in a single lifetime, rather than in the "three countless eons" it would otherwise take.[166] However, despite the claim, Buddhas seem to be in short supply.

The spirits also instruct and teach. In fact, "During the period of initial contact the spirits function above all as teachers."[337] The spirits are most likely to instruct during altered states, such as dreams or journeys, or during the curious process of mediumship.

CHAPTER 18

Mediums: Channels for the Spirits?

CHANNELING

Shamans have many roles, one of which can be as a medium, and in more than half of twenty-one cultures where shamans journey, they also act as mediums.[284] Korean shamans describe their first experience of mediumship as the "opening of the gate of words."[385]

The process of mediumship, or channeling as it is now popularly known, involves a supposedly spiritual entity speaking through a person. The medium's state of consciousness may vary from full awareness (conscious channeling) to complete unawareness and amnesia (trance channeling).[35] The medium's voice, accent, and behavior may change dramatically, suggesting that the original personality has been replaced by one quite different. The effect can be dramatic.

MEDIUMSHIP THROUGH THE AGES

Mediumship is a worldwide phenomenon, and in a survey of 188 cultures it was found in over half of them.[30] It has been called by many names: prophecy, revelation, oracle, spirit communication, possession, inspiration of the muses, or channeling. But whatever its name, its impact has been remarkable. It sculpted many religions and, on several occasions, changed the course of history.

Of the many famous examples, the best known is probably the Greek oracle at Delphi. For over 1,000 years the Delphi temple priestesses regularly became possessed, supposedly by Apollo, the god of prophecy, purification, and healing, and dispensed advice to princes and paupers alike. It was the oracle who famously dubbed Socrates the wisest man in Athens, much to Socrates' surprise.

The king Croesus, whose fabulous wealth inspired the saying "rich as Croesus," was one of the oracle's more famous customers. Craving yet more wealth, he wanted to know whether to attack his neighbors. The oracle's sage advice was: "After crossing the Halys [a river], Croesus will destroy a great empire."[158] Greatly inspired, Croesus crossed the river and, in fact, did destroy a great empire: his own.

The oracle was also approached for military strategy to defend against the marauding Etruscans. The oracle's advice was to "use as few ships as possible." Displaying admirable faith in the oracle, the people sent out a mere five ships against the entire Etruscan fleet. Not wishing to be embarrassed by seeming to need a larger force, the Etruscans also fielded only five ships. These were promptly sunk. The Etruscans then sent out another five. These were also sunk. The scenario was then repeated yet a third and fourth time. Finally the Etruscans retired from the scene.[158] Of course, not all advice was so dramatic or accurate. Yet the oracle had a track record respectable enough to impact Greek history and to stay in business for over a thousand years.

Mediumship has also figured centrally in many religions. Among the great religions, there are references to it in Christianity's Old and New Testaments, and it played significant roles in Jewish and Taoist mysticism.[162, 421] Some influential religious texts that are widely regarded as profound were apparently produced in this way, including parts of the Islamic Koran, Jewish Kabbalah, and Tibetan Buddhist scriptures.[158]

MODERN MEDIUMS

Mediumship has become popular in the West where it is now known as channeling, and its influence continues to be surprising: Witness the remarkable popularity of the book *Conversations with God*.[386, s] Like historical mediumship, today's channeled productions include literary, musical, metaphysical, and spiritual works.

However, there are also novel features. An emphasis on psychology is new as are some supposed sources. In ancient times, gods and angels kept themselves busy being channeled, while in the nineteenth century Orientals, American Indians, and deceased spirits were much in vogue. Today, however, spiritual masters, extraterrestrials, and more evolved beings on other planes are all the rage.

The range of quality of channeled materials is enormous. They include the abysmal and trite, the ego serving and self-aggrandizing, as well as the clearly erroneous and ridiculous. Some of the more amusing examples include "Leah, a sixth density entity from the planet Venus six hundred years in the future."[325] Since the surface temperature of Venus is some 500°C, hot enough to melt lead, Leah and her friends must be impressively heat resistant. Likewise, the nineteenth-century astronaut Mademoiselle Helene Smith journeyed to Mars with her spirit guide Leopold, "whence she returned with colorful descriptions of the Martian countryside and samples of the inhabitants writing and language."[255] This is considerably more than the dry dust and rocks that recent space probes have found. Productions such as these led the philosopher Ken Wilber to sigh, "Higher intelligences have got to be smarter than the drivel most of these channels bring through."[406]

If this were all there were to channeling we could happily dismiss it with a laugh. But channeled works also include, though much more rarely, remarkable artistic and intellectual creations. Artistic works include favorably reviewed poetry, novels, paintings, and music.[158] On the intellectual side are sophisticated mathematics, complex and coherent (though not necessarily verifiable or correct) metaphysics, and helpful—even profound—spiritual works.

Famous literary productions include those of William Blake, William Butler Yates, and Pearl Curran. In fact the most renowned of all such literary productions were those of either (depending on your belief system) Pearl Curran, a little-educated St. Louis housewife, or of Patience Worth, the spirit of a seventeenth-century Englishwoman.

Beginning in 1913, Pearl/Patience performed many remarkable feats. She could dictate a poem on a specified topic faster than a scribe could write it in shorthand. She could even alternate lines from two different poems as she did so; the first line from poem one, the second from poem two, the third line from poem one, and so on. The author Edgar Lee Masters witnessed one such writing session and shook his head in disbelief, saying, "It simply can't be done."[158] Altogether, Pearl/Patience channeled over twenty volumes of poetry, novels, and advice, which were widely published and favorably reviewed.

Among the many contemporary spiritual works, one of the most interesting is a three-volume set with the unlikely name of *A Course in Miracles*.[10] The *Course* is a Christian teaching channeled by an astounded Jewish psychology professor at Columbia Medical

School. "Having no belief in God," she said, "I resented the material I was taking down, and was strongly impelled to attack it and prove it wrong."[342]

But no matter how negative the reluctant scribe felt about it, others have felt just as strongly positive. The first review stated that "the three books comprise one of the most remarkable systems of spiritual truth available today."[342] A Stanford University professor called it "perhaps the most important writing in the English language since the translation of the Bible."[342] Ken Wilber's comments about channeled "drivel" suggest that he is no big fan of channeling. Yet he concludes: "The *Course* is clearly inspired. Its insights are genuinely transcendental....I know of no other channeled material that even comes close to it."[409] Needless to say, not everyone is a fan, and some theologians and Christian fundamentalists have assailed it.

The *Course* displays several remarkable features. It is psychologically sound, philosophically penetrating, and eminently practical. Practically, it offers a series of 365 lessons—one for each day of the year. Psychologically, these comprise a kind of cognitive therapy that aims to eliminate painful, false beliefs and to substitute healthy, accurate ones. Philosophically, it embodies a Christian form of the perennial philosophy (the common wisdom at the contemplative core of the great religions).[t] In his well-researched study of channeling, *With the Tongues of Men and Angels*, author Hastings concludes that "the *Course* is the most systematic spiritual system that has come through a channeling mode."[158] Its practical and psychological appeal is suggested by readers of a psychotherapy journal, *Common Boundary*, who rated it as the most influential book they had read.

Features such as these help explain its astounding publishing record that includes over one million copies sold, all without advertising. When one also considers classic texts, such as some of the prophets of Israel, parts of the Koran, as well as certain Taoist and Tibetan Buddhist writings, it becomes clear that a few channeled spiritual works may be profound and have a great impact.

Of course, skeptics deny that channeled productions are ever profound. For the determined skeptic, all such productions "consist solely of strings of loosely associated gobbets of naive ideas" produced by people "of hysterical personality, displaying dissociative features" and in some cases "all the hallmarks of schizophrenia."[301] Now there is no argument whatsoever that most channeled productions are trite or nonsensical. However, this does not prove that all of them are, and shallow skeptics tend to carefully ignore challenging cases such as classic channeled religious texts or the writings of Pearl Curran.[u]

Clearly, mediumship is no simple matter. Meaningful and profound productions occasionally occur so that the phenomenon cannot be simply dismissed as pure nonsense or pathology.

Unfortunately, most people take extreme positions. On one side are true believers who doubt not a single word of their favorite spirit guide. On the other side are skeptics for whom every word is necessarily false, and channeling is summarily dismissed as self-deceit at best. Either approach serves as a pleasant anesthetic that saves having to investigate the issue in any depth. Yet channeling is clearly a complex and curious phenomenon from which we can learn much about little known mental capacities.

EXPLANATIONS OF CHANNELING

Many theories, none entirely satisfactory, have been offered. These range from fraud to dissociation to possession by spiritual entities. Needless to say, it is easier to explain trivial works than profound ones.

Fraud may account for some cases, but certainly not for all. Dissociation is perhaps the most common explanation. In this process, aspects of the psyche are split off from conscious awareness and control. These aspects can then function independently as subpersonalities or as more or less full-fledged separate personalities in multiple personalities. Thoughts from such personalities are then perceived by the conscious personality as coming from outside itself.

Multiple personalities provide dramatic examples of dissociation and divided consciousness. However, the implications of research on dissociation extend much further and suggest that *all* of us live in some degree of dissociation. A book with the suggestive title *Divided Consciousness* opens with the claim, "The unity of consciousness is illusory. Man does more than one thing at a time—all the time—and the conscious representation of these actions is never complete."[160]

One crucial implication is that anyone—ancient shamans, modern channelers, and all the rest of us—may be able to receive information from aspects of our own psyches that lie outside conscious awareness. This information may seem to come not from our mind but from another entity, as hypnotists can easily demonstrate. Moreover, some of the information may consist of long-forgotten facts and memories, a process called *cryptomnesia* that is sometimes mistaken for evidence that the message is from a separate entity.[325]

So purely psychological mechanisms may account for most, if not all, superficial chan-neled productions, and there seems little need to invoke spirits. In addition, the long-stand-ing philosophical "principle of parsimony" argues for keeping explanations as simple as possible.

Unfortunately, very little experimental research has been done on channeling. Sarah Thomason, a professor of linguistics at the University of Pittsburgh, made an interesting beginning. She analyzed the voices of eleven different channelers and found curious contra-dictions and peculiarities.

Several findings were highly suspicious. Two entities sported British accents yet claimed to be thousands of years old. However, British accents as we know them have probably not existed for more than 1,000 years at most. Likewise, another entity's pronunciation became increasingly inconsistent and American the more excited he became. According to Thoma-son, this is a real giveaway and "just the opposite of what one would expect, if he were a non-native speaker of American English."[368]

Yet other findings were puzzling. The well-known "entity" Lazaris, who does telephone interviews and has a waiting list over two years long, was a case in point. "Lazaris's accent sounds fake to me," said Thomason, "but there are no obvious inconsistencies in his sound pattern." Channeling is nothing if not puzzling, and it clearly needs more research.

This still leaves the problem of accounting for the occasional profound channeled work. For while it is easy to conceive of a sub-personality producing trivial nonsense, it is more difficult to imagine it creating major literary or spiritual works far beyond the channel's level of knowledge and skill. However, it is possible to imagine such creations coming from the psyche if we grant that there may be transpersonal aspects of the psyche that are "transcendent" to the ego or conscious personality. Indeed, some channelers find that over time they eventually come to experience their "spirits" as aspects of their own mind and unacknowledged wisdom.[223] Sadly, we understand remarkably little of ordinary creativ-ity—which is one of the great mysteries and miracles of human existence—let alone of channeled creativity.

However, if we are honest, we need to admit that none of these ideas actually rule out the possibility that "spirits," whatever they may be, are the actual source of some channeled materials. Therefore, we need to examine a tricky question: "What is a spirit?"

CHAPTER 19

What Is a "Spirit"?

Several volumes would be needed for an adequate study of all the problems that arise in connection with the mere idea of "spirits" and of their possible relations with human beings...
—*Mircea Eliade*[83]

What then is a spirit? The Oxford dictionary defines it as "a supernatural, incorporeal, rational being or personality, usually regarded as imperceptible at ordinary times to the human senses, but capable of becoming visible at pleasure, and frequently conceived as troublesome, terrifying or hostile to mankind." This has been a widespread view of spirits throughout history. However, if we set aside historical notions such as these, we need to ask questions such as the following: Are "spirits" mental or nonmental? Part of, or separate from, the medium? Expressions of health or pathology? In short, what is the psychological and ontological status of spirits? We can best explore these questions by examining both shamanism and other traditions.

To do this, we need to first look carefully at how exactly a "spirit" is experienced. Essentially, it is an interaction with what is felt to be an intelligent, nonmaterial entity separate from the ego or self. In the shaman's case, the entity may provide information or power that the shaman believes she cannot access alone.

ENCOUNTERING SPIRITS AND GUIDES

Spirits may be seen outside or sensed inside. Outer spirits may appear as spirit intrusions in a patient's body and require exorcism. Shamans can recognize intrusions with their trained, and sometimes psychedelically enhanced, spirit vision. However, an occasional anthropologist has been shocked, and had their Western belief system rattled, by seeing spirits themselves. An astounded Edith Turner reported that during a Zambian ritual, "I saw with my own eyes a large gray blob of plasma emerge from the sick woman's back. Then I knew the Africans were right, there is spirit affliction, it isn't a matter of metaphor and symbol, or even psychology."[373] This is a powerful example of the potential impact of open-minded, participatory anthropological research.

If spirits can be seen, could they be photographed? At the height of nineteenth-century spiritualism, a veritable industry of spirit photography flowered briefly. However, it quickly sputtered out under the weight of pictures which were "for the most part, grossly and transparently fake."[320]

Encounters with spirits can be either troublesome or beneficial. In a religious context, troublesome examples include being tormented or possessed by unfriendly entities such as spirit intrusions, ghosts, or demons. In fact, dealing with troublesome spirits is one of the shaman's most frequent tasks. In a psychological context, these same "spirits" might be interpreted as hallucinations.

Interactions with spirits can also be beneficial. Here the spirits may be valuable sources of information, guidance, and wisdom. In a religious context, such sources might be viewed as transcendent beings. Examples include the shaman's "helping spirits," the Hindu's "inner guru," the Quaker's "still small voice within," the Naskapi Indian's "great man," and for Christians, the "Holy Spirit." However, mainstream Western psychology would regard all such inner sources as aspects of the psyche, such as sub-personalities.

A transpersonal psychological interpretation straddles these two views. Since transpersonal psychologists acknowledge capacities of mind transcendent to our usual egoic awareness, they might interpret these inner sources of wisdom in several ways. The first would be, like the traditional psychologist, as mundane sub-personalities. However, transpersonal psychologists might also view these sources of wisdom as transcendent aspects of the psyche "above and beyond" the ego. Examples include the "higher self"; the "transpersonal witness"; the Jungian "self," which is the center of the psyche; and the "inner self-helper," which is a helpful and apparently transcendent personality that can occur in multiple personalities.

Many religions and some psychologies recognize the possibility of accessing wisdom from inner sources that seem wiser than the ego. Indeed, considerable effort has gone into refining methods for facilitating this access.

Religious methods include diverse rituals, prayers, and altered states of consciousness. These altered states include possession, soul travel, or quieting the mind so as to be able to hear the "still small voice within."

In psychology, major techniques include hypnosis and guided imagery. In fact, it is relatively easy to create an experience akin to channeling with hypnosis, as Charles Tart describes:

> From my studies with hypnosis I know I can set up an apparently independent exis-
> tent entity whose characteristics are constructed to my specifications and the person
> hypnotized will experience it as if it's something outside of his own consciousness
> talking. So there is no doubt that some cases of channeling can be explained in a
> conventional kind of way. There is nothing psychic involved.[195]

Schools of psychology, such as Jungian, post-Jungian, and Gestalt, use guided imagery to access inner wisdom. In a technique called "dialogue with the sage or inner teacher," the therapist asks the patient to imagine himself in a pleasant environment where he meets a person of great wisdom. The patient is then encouraged to allow a dialogue to emerge spontaneously and to ask whatever questions seem most helpful. Such dialogues can elicit novel, valuable information, and a growing number of authors, artists, and businesspeople now employ these methods for inspiration.[378] Such techniques have obvious similarities to shamanic journeys to find a spirit teacher.

Inner teachers can also arise spontaneously and have life-changing effects. Some major historical figures have been directed by such inner teachers. The philosopher Socrates, the political leader Gandhi, and the psychologist Carl Jung all reported that they were advised by inner guides who arose unbidden from the depths of the psyche.

Carl Jung provided dramatic examples. One inner teacher, whom he called Philemon, provided Jung with a wealth of information about the psyche. Philemon first appeared dur-ing a fantasy of Jung's in which suddenly there appeared from the right a winged being sailing across the sky. I saw that it was an old man with the horns of a bull. He held a bunch of four keys, one of which he clutched as if he were about to open a lock. He had the wings of the kingfisher with its characteristic colors....Philemon and other figures of my fantasies brought home to me the crucial insight that there are things in the psyche which I do not produce, but which produce themselves and have their own life. Philemon represented a force which was not myself. In my fantasies I held conversations with him, and he said things which I had not consciously thought. For I observed clearly that it was he who spoke, not I....I understood that there is something in me which can say things that I do not know and do not intend, things which may even be directed against me.

Psychologically, Philemon represented superior insight. He was a mysterious figure to me. At times he seemed to me quite real as if he were a living personality. I went walking up and down the garden with him, and to me he was what the Indians call a guru.[184]

Even a single experience of an inner guide can have life-changing effects. A dramatic example is given by a woman called Lillian who suffered chronic pelvic pain for which no medical cause could be found. Lillian began practicing visual imagery and obtained some benefits. She started by imagining

a stream of cool water circulating through her pelvis, and knotted ropes being untied. What felt like a cement block in her lower back was imaged as dissolving. She said she felt better; the burning was still there, but covered a smaller area.

Then one night when Lillian was practicing her imagery at home, a coyote named Wildwood flashed into her mind. He advised her to stay by his side, and watch what was about to happen, and told her that what she saw would be related to the fire in her body. She then sensed herself sitting by a campfire, in the midst of a hostile tribe of Indians who held her captive. She experienced the horror of being brutally gang-raped and murdered. "At the instant of my death....I woke up and was back in my body in the room, only my pain was completely gone, and hasn't returned since.[3]

What is one to make of such an experience and its dramatic outcome? Lillian attributed it to a past life. A shamanic interpretation would be that her helping spirit guide or power animal, the coyote Wildwood, had taken her on a journey in which she had undergone rape, death, and a healing rebirth. A psychological explanation would be that her own mind had, by a wisdom and means far beyond our present understanding, provided her an experience of profound psychosomatic healing power. Whatever the explanation, one can only feel awe for the healing power of the psyche, its images, and its inner guides.

Of course, not all inner guidance is beneficial. Consider the case of a young World War I soldier who sat down in a trench to eat a meal when he heard an inner voice tell him to get up immediately and move to the far end of the trench. He did so, and a minute later a shell exploded, killing everyone in the group where he had been sitting. The soldier's name? Adolf Hitler.[158]

THE ONTOLOGY OF SPIRITS

How are we to understand these sources of inner guidance? What exactly is their nature, or, in philosophical terms, what is their ontological status? Asking the sources themselves is not particularly helpful, because the answers may range all the way from "I am part of you" to "I am God." Clearly we're not going to get much help here, although some people swallow channeled claims totally. However, those of us who are more cautious need to think our way through the issue very carefully, and to make our own decisions about the sources of information and the processes involved.

From a psychological perspective we can account for inner guides and channeling if we recognize transpersonal aspects of the psyche. In this view, inspired channeled works would be creations of transpersonal facets of mind "above and beyond" the ego, such as psychosynthesis's "higher unconscious," Aurobindo's "intuitive mind," Tibetan Buddhist "yidams," or certain Jungian archetypes.

However, psychological explanations do not disprove the existence of spirits (intelligent, nonmaterial entities independent of the channel's mind) or their role in some channeling. Indeed, it is not at all clear that it is possible to either prove or disprove them.

In fact, the nature of "spirits" may be one of the great puzzles at the heart of shamanism, a puzzle at the intersection of three major philosophical conundrums: incommensurability, underdetermination of theory, and ontological indeterminacy.

In brief, *incommensurability* argues that there can be major difficulties in comparing or deciding between competing theories or worldviews. The shamanic worldview and theories, on one hand, and conventional psychological worldview and theories, on the other, hold such different assumptions, beliefs, and values that adjudicating between their different interpretations—of spirits, for example—is inherently problematic.

Underdetermination of theory by data suggests that it is always possible to come up with more than one theory to explain observations. Put another way, there may never be sufficient information available to decide definitively between two competing theories.[v]

Ontological indeterminacy implies that we may be unable to determine the precise nature or the ontological status of something. In this case, the ontological status of "spirits" cannot be decided definitively (i.e., is indeterminate) because the available information can be interpreted in many ways (underdetermination of theory by data), and we have no absolute method by which to decide which interpretation(s) are best (incommensurability).

Practically speaking, what this means is that people's interpretations of phenomena in general, and of spirits in particular, are determined by their "world hypothesis": their fundamental assumptions about the nature of the world and reality. Since fundamental beliefs are rarely questioned, most people's decisions about the nature of spirits and channeling will be decided by these beliefs. Thus a philosophical materialist who assumes that everything is composed of matter will obviously view "spirits" very differently from the contemplative who believes in a transcendent realm of pure consciousness or spirit. For the philosophical materialist, shamanic spirits and worlds are merely mental projections that shamans mistake for independent entities and realities. All sources of inner wisdom, all perceived entities, all voices and visions are simply the expressions of neuronal fireworks, and probably deranged fireworks at that.[w] Michael Winkelman attempted to relate spirit possession to temporal lobe dysfunction, but cites no actual neurophysiological studies of mediums to support this.[418]

Things are very different for the believer in panpsychism. This is the view that everything in the universe, even including plants and inanimate objects, has some kind of psychological being or awareness. For panpsychists, some of the shaman's helpers, voices, and visions could indeed be spirits. For psychologists, such as post-Jungians, spirits are best interpreted in terms of images and imaginal realities.[259]

Of course we have no proof whatsoever that all sources of inner wisdom have the same nature. For all we know, some might be merely aspects of mind, and not terribly impressive aspects at that, while others might be transcendent sources within or beyond us. We may simply be unable to decide definitively between such interpretations. Consequently, an agnostic view of spirits and channels, in which we confess their indeterminacy and our epistemological limitations, may be the most intellectually honest conclusion. It also avoids the danger of what Edith Turner calls "intellectual imperialism" in which we force native experiments into our own conceptual categories.

This conclusion may be honest but not terribly satisfying. Indeed, it can be downright annoying. But annoyance reflects attachment to our opinions as well as discomfort with ambiguity.

Yet psychology, philosophy, and religion all agree that life is fundamentally and inescapably mysterious, and that being willing to tolerate ambiguity and to open to the ultimate mystery of existence are essential for maturity. For Hinduism, *maya* is forever unknowable; for Buddhism, reality is *shunyata* (beyond all concepts), and for Taoism, "Tao is beyond words."[236] "Things keep their secrets," observed Heraclitus,[159] so much so that the great religious scholar Huston Smith concluded: "Reality is steeped in mystery; we are born in mystery, we live in mystery, and we die in mystery."[347]

Yet this sense of bottomless mystery can bless as much as stress. It can release us from rigidity and dogma, open us to awe and humility, and, according to Albert Einstein, "stands at the cradle of true art and true science."[224] "Keep don't know mind" urges Zen.

So the fact that we cannot decide about the existence of spirits is actually not surprising. Rather, it reflects both the mystery of existence and the limitations of our knowing. This may not be wholly satisfying, but it is usefully humbling."ˣ

Mediumship can be interpreted in many ways. However, it certainly points to capacities of mind that remain as yet little understood and reminds us that we have underestimated the wisdom and creative powers latent within us. Long ago shamans became the first pioneers to explore and cultivate these powers.

CHAPTER 20

Cosmic Traveling: The Shamanic Journey

We must close our eyes and invoke a new manner of seeing…
a wakefulness that is the birthright of us all, though few put it to use.
—Plotinus[269]

At the heart of shamanism lies the journey. It is this that helps to distinguish shamans from other ecstatics, healers, and mystics. "Any ecstatic cannot be considered a shaman," wrote Eliade, because "the shaman specializes in a trance during which his soul is believed to leave his body and ascend to the sky or descend to the underworld."[83] Eliade's focus on the journey as the defining feature of shamanism has been much debated, but it is certainly a distinctive feature of the tradition. Others may enter altered states, minister, or heal, but it is shamans who primarily engage in soul flight.

During this flight the shaman's soul seems to leave the body and roam at will through the upper, middle, and lower worlds. The shaman is a cosmic traveler because, according to Eliade:

> he commands the techniques of ecstasy—that is, because his soul can safely abandon his body and roam at vast distances, can penetrate the underworld and rise to the sky. Through his own ecstatic experience he knows the roads of the extraterrestrial regions. He can go below and above because he has already been there. The danger of losing his way in these forbidden regions is still great; but sanctified by his initiation and

furnished with his guardian spirit, a shaman is the only human being able to challenge the danger and venture into a mystical geography.[83]

The precise experiences—the worlds visited, the spirits met, the dangers faced—depend on the journey's purpose. However, the general principles are similar.

THE NATURE OF THE JOURNEY

The shamanic journey involves three phases: preparation, induction of an ASC, and the actual journey.

The initial phase is one of preparation and purification. It may involve a period of isolation, fasting, and celibacy, perhaps alone in the wilderness or in a solitary hut. The journey is usually begun at night when visions are clearer. The shaman begins the appropriate rituals and then uses a variety of techniques—such as singing, dancing, drumming, or drugs—to induce an altered state.

The journey may traverse numerous worlds and can be dramatic and dangerous, ecstatic or horrendous. Emotions may range from terror to bliss, yet, in Michael Harner's words, often there is "an ineffable joy in what he sees, an awe of the beautiful and mysterious worlds that open before him. His experiences are like dreams, but waking ones that feel real and in which he can control his actions and direct his adventures."[146]

Lower World Journeys

For these journeys the shaman usually visualizes an entrance into the earth. Common entrances include caves, a hollow tree stump, or a water hole. The shaman sees himself entering this hole and diving deep into the earth until he eventually emerges into another world. Michael Harner describes the experience as follows:

> Entrances into the Lowerworld commonly lead down into a tunnel or tube that conveys the shaman to an exit, which opens out upon bright and marvelous landscapes. From there the shaman travels wherever he desires for minutes or even hours, finally returning back up through the tube...to emerge at the surface, where he entered.[146]

Once in the lower world the shaman begins the next phase of his mission. This may range from acquiring knowledge and power to recovering lost souls or placating angry spirits. Rasmussen gave a classic example of placation, namely the Eskimo shaman's journey to the depths of the sea to placate the spirit *Takánakapsâluk*. It is this stern goddess of fate who controls the sea animals on which Eskimos depend for food. When she becomes angry—most often because of breeches of taboo—she withholds these animals. Then the Eskimos hunt in vain, and hunger haunts the tribe.

At this time their fate rests on the shaman. It is he alone who can journey to the bottom of the sea, the dwelling place of *Takánakapsâluk,* brave the barriers and beasts with which she protects herself, and beg her forgiveness. Rasmussen[299] described the sea spirit and the shaman's journey to her as follows:

A shaman about to make this journey is said to be *nak'a'*: one who drops down to the bottom of the sea. This remarkable expression is due perhaps in some degree to the fact that no one can rightly explain how the journey is made. Some assert that it is only his soul or his spirit which makes the journey; others declare that it is the shaman himself who actually, in the flesh, drops down into the underworld....

The shaman sits for a while in silence, breathing deeply, and then, after some time has elapsed, he begins to call upon his helping spirits, repeating over and over again:..."the way is made ready for me; the way opens before me!"

Where at all present must answer in chorus:..."let it be so!"

And when the helping spirits have arrived, the earth opens under the shaman, but often only to close up again; he has to struggle for a longtime with hidden forces, ere he can cry at last: "Now the way is open." And then all present must answer: "Let the way be open before him; let there be way for him."

And now one hears, at first under the sleeping place: "*Halala—he—he— he, halala—he—he—he!*" and afterwards under the passage, below the ground, the same cry: "*Halele—he!*" And the sound can be distinctly heard to recede farther and farther until it is lost altogether. Then all know that he is on his way to the ruler of the sea beasts....

An ordinary shaman will, even though skillful, encounter many dangers in his flight down to the bottom of the sea; the most dreaded are three large rolling stones which he meets as soon as he has reached the seafloor. There is no way round; he has to pass between them, and take great care not to be crushed by these stones, which churn about, hardly leaving room for a human being to pass. Once he has passed beyond them, he comes to a broad, trodden path, the shamans' path; he follows a coastline resembling that which he knows from on earth, and entering a bay, finds himself on a great plain, and here lies the house of *Takánakapsâluk*, built of stone, with a short passage way, just like the houses of the Tunit. Outside the house one can hear the animals puffing and blowing, but he does not see them; in the passage leading to the house lies *Takánakapsâluk's* dog stretched across the passage taking up all the room; it lies there gnawing at a bone and snarling. It is dangerous to all who fear it, and only the courageous shaman can pass by it, stepping straight over it as it lies; the dog then knows that the bold visitor is a great shaman, and does him no harm.

These difficulties and dangers attend the journey of an ordinary shaman. But for the very greatest, a way opens right from the house whence they invoke their helping spirits; a road down through the earth, if they are in a tent on shore, or down through the sea, if it is in a snow hut on the sea ice, and by this route the shaman is led down without encountering any obstacle. He almost glides as if falling through a tube so fitted to his body that he can check his progress by pressing against the sides, and need not actually fall down with a rush. This tube is kept open for him by all the souls of his namesakes, until he returns on his way back to earth.

Should a great shelter wall be built outside the house of *Takánakapsâluk*, it means that she is very angry and implacable in her feelings towards mankind, but the shaman must fling himself upon the wall, kick it down and level it to the ground. There are some who declare that her house has no roof, and is open at the top, so that she can better watch, from her place by the lamp, the doings of mankind. All the different kinds of game: seal, bearded seal, walrus and whale, are collected in a great pool on the right of her lamp, and there they lie puffing and blowing. When the shaman enters the house, he at once sees *Takánakapsâluk*, who, as a sign of anger, is sitting with her back to the lamp and with her back to all the animals in the pool. Her hair hangs down loose all over one side of her face, a tangled, untidy mass hiding her eyes, so that she cannot see. It is the misdeeds and offenses committed by men which gather in dirt and impurity over her body. All the foul emanations from the sins of mankind nearly suffocate her. As the shaman moves towards her, Isarrataitsoq, her father, tries to grasp hold of him. He thinks it is a dead person come to expiate offenses before passing on to the Land of the Dead, but the shaman must then at once cry out: "I am flesh and blood" and then he will not be hurt. And he must now grasp *Takánakapsâluk* by one shoulder and turn her face towards the lamp and towards the animals, and stroke her hair, the hair she has been unable to comb out herself, because she has no fingers; and he must smooth it and comb it, and as soon as she is calmer, he must say:

"pik'ua qilusinEq ajulErmata": "those up above can no longer help the seals up by grasping their foreflippers."

Then *Takánakapsâluk* answers in the spirit language: "The secret miscarriages of the women and breaches of taboo in eating boiled meat bar the way for the animals."

The shaman must now use all his efforts to appease her anger, and at last, when she is in a kindlier mood, she takes the animals one by one and drops them on the floor, and then it is as if a whirlpool arises in the passage, the water pours out from the pool and the animals disappear in the sea. This means rich hunting and abundance for mankind.

It is then time for the shaman to return to his fellows up above, who are waiting for him. They can hear him coming a long way off; the rush of his passage through the tube kept open for him by the spirits comes nearer and nearer, and with a mighty *"Plu—a—he—he,"* he shoots up into his place behind the curtain: *"Plu-plu,"* like some creature of the sea, shooting up from the deep to take breath under the pressure of mighty lungs.

Then there is silence for a moment. No one may break this silence until the shaman says: "I have something to say."

Then all present answer: "Let us hear, let us hear."

But the shaman does not answer immediately. Rather, he uses this dramatic moment to force the audience to confess their breaches of taboo. All must acknowledge their sins, a process which produces a powerful group confession and cohesion. Only when this is complete does the shaman sigh with relief. Then at last "the cause of *Takánakapsâluk*'s anger is explained, and all are filled with joy at having escaped disaster....This then was what happened when shamans went down and propitiated the great Spirit of the Sea."[299]

Middle and Upper World Journeys

Middle or upper world journeys have the same general features as those of the lower world. However, there are some differences in purpose and in the types of entities likely to be encountered. The lower world is often a place of tests and challenges. However, it is also a place where power animals are acquired and the shaman is guided and empowered to victory. The upper world is more likely to be where teachers and guides can be found, and journeys here may be particularly ecstatic.[12]

The middle world is this world. In their visions, shamans journey over it at will, unimpeded by barriers or distance, and returning with information about hunting, weather, or warfare. Middle world journeys are particularly common in the near artic areas of North America and Siberia where food supplies are precarious and migrating animal herds must be located.[151]

The journey to the upper world usually begins from a raised area such as a mountain, tree top or cliff, from which the shaman ascends into the sky. At some stage a membrane may temporarily impede the ascent. When this is pierced the shaman finds himself in a different realm: the upper world, populated with strange animals, plants, and people. Like the lower one, the upper world may have several levels that the shaman can usually move between at will, perhaps assisted by a helping spirit.

The ascent may also occur in other ways. In some variations the shaman may be transformed into a bird soaring to the upper world. At other times the ascent may involve climbing the world axis, which runs between upper, middle, and lower worlds. Sometimes this axis takes the form of a tree, the "world tree." Alternately, the shaman may ascend a mountain, rainbow, or ladder. But whatever the specifics, the common theme is an ascent into a world above where spirits abide.

Only the shamans can master this journey to other worlds, and there placate or even overpower the spirits, win knowledge and power, retrieve the souls of the sick, or act as a "psychopomp": one who guides the souls of the dead to their resting place. The ability to journey therefore gives the shaman a measure of power over the mysterious forces and spirits that rule the lives of ordinary mortals.

CHAPTER 21

A World of Ecstatics:
Journeys in Other Religious Traditions

Divine reality is infinite,
and infinite are the ways to realize it.
—*Ramakrishna*[161]

That shamanic journeys have endured for millennia around the world is remarkable. Just as remarkable is that similar journeys have shaped so many great religions and so much of history.[55] Each of the great Western monotheisms—Judaism, Christianity, and Islam—was impacted, as was Chinese Taoism. In contrast, soul flights had less effect on Confucianism, with its greater social and political emphasis, or on the Indian traditions of Hinduism and Buddhism, where yogic practices dominated.

THE WESTERN MONOTHEISMS

In the West, three of the most influential religious leaders, Mohammad and the Christian saints Paul and John, were spontaneously born upward through the heavens.

Mohammad's Night Journey

Mohammad's *Mi'r j* (night journey or ascent) was originally described very briefly, but has been elaborated over the centuries and is apparently alluded to in the Koran in the verse "glory be to Him, who carried his servant by night….that we might show him some of our signs."

Asleep in Mecca, the Prophet was awakened by Gabriel, the archangel who had previously revealed the Koran to him and, centuries earlier, had announced Jesus's birth to Mary. Gabriel escorted Mohammad first to Jerusalem, where he prayed with the great prophets of history. Then he ascended up through the seven heavens to the throne of Allah. Even the great archangel could not ascend this far and sighed, "If I would go one step further, my wings would get burned."[323]

The Koran tells us that Mohammad's "eyes swayed not, nor swept astray. Indeed, he saw one of the greatest signs of his Lord." Of course we are told almost nothing about the nature of this ultimate theophany (vision of God), which is assumed to be far beyond anything words could convey.

However, we are told that the Muslims were instructed to pray fifty times a day. Moses, however, had other ideas. When the Prophet descended to the sixth heaven where Moses presided, he was ordered to go back and request a smaller number better suited to the limited capacities of humans. This was repeated several times until, at five prayers a day, Mohammad felt ashamed to beg yet again for another reduction.

During his descent to Mecca he saw camel caravans trekking across the desert. The next morning, his report of the journey was met with mocking hostility by skeptics. Then the caravans arrived.[118]

The nature of the journey—whether a dream, a purely spiritual vision, or a literal transport of the body—has been debated for centuries. But whatever its nature, its impact has been extraordinary. For fourteen hundred years, devout Muslims have prayed five times a day, while the great mystics of Islam, the Sufis, use the language of ascension to describe their own spiritual experiences. In the West, the medieval poet Danté apparently fashioned part of his famous allegorical journey in the *Divine Comedy* on Mohammad's experience, though as a conventional Christian he consigned Mohammad to one of the lowest hells. Note that Mohammad's journey, like those of the saints Paul and John, was spontaneous, unlike those of shamans or Jewish and Taoist practitioners.

Early Christian Ascents

Saint Paul was also "caught up into Paradise." Paul was no stranger to visions, having been transformed from a merciless persecutor of Christians to one of their foremost leaders by a vision of Jesus so overwhelming that "he fell to the ground." Afterwards "he could see nothing," and "for three days he was without sight, and neither ate nor drank." Later Paul underwent a spontaneous journey, which he reluctantly revealed to maintain his authority in the face of competition from other Christian visionaries.

> I will go on to visions and revelations of the Lord. I know a person in Christ who fourteen years ago was caught up to the third heaven—whether in the body or out of the body I do not know; God knows, [and] was caught up into Paradise and heard things that are not to be told, that no mortal is permitted to repeat.

Paul's visions braced him with an unwavering faith that endured persecution and torture, fortified the precarious early church, and shaped Christian doctrine for 2,000 years. But the impact of even Saint Paul's journeys are dwarfed by those of John, author of the Book of Revelation. John reported a voice:

> Which I had heard speaking to me like a trumpet, said,
> "Come up here, and I will show you what must
> Take place after this." At once I was in the spirit…

John's detailed, highly symbolic visions portray perennial Christian themes such as future trials and tribulations, the millennium, and Armageddon, the final cosmic battle between the forces of good and evil. The nature of John's visions—symbolic or literal—has been hotly debated and even today is having an enormous religious and political impact. Literalists have long expected their fulfillment at any time and are now agitating politically to bring about the political conditions for their fruition.

In addition, the best-selling novels in the United States today are the *Left Behind* series, which have sold more than sixty million copies. Based on John's visions, the books portray the head of the United Nations as the Antichrist, and jubilantly celebrate the massacre of millions of non-Christians by a militant and curiously unforgiving Jesus. If a Muslim wrote an Islamic version delighting in Christian genocide, Christians would have a fit.[202] In short, literalist interpretations of visions are potentially dangerous.

The Chariot Mysticism of Judaism

Judaism and Taoism provide examples of religions in which spiritual journeys mushroomed into major traditions. In fact, Judaism's earliest mystical tradition, the *Merkabah* or

"Chariot Mysticism" centered on journeying. It was sparked by the spontaneous journey of the prophet Ezekiel, who in 592 BCE had an overwhelming vision of a chariot and of the throne of God.

For over a thousand years, Jewish seekers strove to emulate Ezekiel's vision. To do this, they elaborated a complex and demanding discipline that required "moral purity, rabbinic learnedness, ritual purity, and thorough mastery of the special knowledge necessary to negotiate the supernal realm."[28] Thus prepared, the seeker readied himself for the journey through the heavens and the halls of the divine palace by fasting, solitude, and prayer. An eleventh-century account tells us:

> …when a man is worthy and blessed with certain qualities and he wishes to gaze at the heavenly chariot and the halls of the angels on high he must follow certain exercises. He must *fast* for a specified number of days, he must place his head between his knees *whispering softly* to himself the while certain praises of God with his face towards the ground. As a result he will gaze in the innermost recesses of his heart and it will seem as if he saw the seven halls with his own eyes, moving from hall to hall to observe that which is therein to be found.[11]

It was not an easy journey. Standing watch at every level were guardians who were "harsh, fearful, terrifying.…Bolts of lightening flow and issue forth from the balls of their eyes… and torches of fiery coals from their mouths."[28] Fires scorch the seekers, complex prayers were demanded at every level, and the unworthy suffered insanity or death. For the successful, the reward was an ecstatic vision of the throne of God.

Powerful as this vision is, contemporary Jewish scholars point out that it is also curiously lacking.[28, 324] There is little devotional love, no penetrating insight into the fundamental nature of humankind or the world, no new moral ideal, no practices for ordinary people, and certainly no sense of union with God. Gershom Scholem concluded that "the mystic who in his ecstasy has passed through all the gates, braved all the dangers, now stands before the throne; he sees and hears—but that is all."[324] Perhaps these factors help explain why the chariot tradition eventually died out.

Of course, spontaneous journeys continued. For the Baal Shem Tov, the remarkable eighteenth-century founder of Hasidism, journeys were a vital source of inspiration. He wrote:

For on the day of the New Year of the year 5507 (= September, 1746)

> I engaged in an ascent of the soul, as you know I do, and I saw wondrous things....
> That which I saw in my ascent is impossible to describe or to relate...[374]

So impactful was the Baal Shem Tov that he inspired a new movement of ecstatic Judaism in which joyous prayer, singing, and dancing assumed a central place.

TAOISM

Chinese shamans traveled the cosmos for centuries before the birth of organized religions. The most famous of all Chinese soul flights is described in the classic poem "The Far-off Journey," dating to the third century BCE. The author described how he toured the universe:

> Up to the Cracks of Heaven,
> Down to the Great Abyss....
> Going beyond-nonaction, I reach the Clarity,
> Become a neighbor of the Great Beginning.[198]

Like Judaism, ecstatic journeys became a central practice of Taoism. Beginning in the fourth century CE, the Highest Clarity (*Shang Qing*) Tradition transformed "the ancient shamanistic practice...into a formal meditation procedure."[198] To do so, it developed the art of visualization to a degree never found before or since in Chinese religion. The body now became a micro-cosmos, and the practitioner journeyed within it and in the heavens.

The Highest Clarity school also created an enormous pantheon of gods and goddesses residing in the body and in the stars. These deities the practitioner visited, drew power from, and even took as a lover.[310]

Journeys aimed for knowledge, power, ecstasy, union with a divine lover, and ultimately immortality. These Taoists obtained knowledge and power "by sinking deep in rapture within the confines of the sacred space of his meditation chamber and traveling through the world searching for virtue and instruction....The practitioner absorbs the essences of the stars and guides them to remain in certain parts of the body."[310]

It is not all hard work. While the practitioner draws nourishment from the stars, he also "frolics in the paradise protected by them, where the divinities originate and reside."[310] Ecstatic union with a divine lover is also possible:

Adepts visualize the pure energy of the sun or the moon, then imagine a goddess in its midst. The goddess grows stronger and more vivid with prolonged practice until she is felt present in the flesh. Pressing her mouth to his, she dispenses celestial vapors to increase the adept's vitality. After a long courtship and regular visualizations, she will even lie with him.[198]

But ecstasy demands preparation, and the Taoist training could be long and arduous. Years of discipline, purification, and meditation were necessary, and a classic text urged: "In all cases, first undertake purifications and fasts, make an effort to control your thoughts, and focus your mind firmly on the mystery."[198]

As in mystical traditions the world over, purification was regarded as essential, and "to attain the Tao through ecstatic excursions, the soul and spirit of the Taoist must be freed completely from the concerns of this world."[198] A classic text, "Three Ways to Go Beyond the Heavenly Paths," gives the following instructions for a journey to a favored celestial destination, the Big Dipper and its attendant deities.

> To practice the Tao excursion to the seven stars [of the Dipper] first summon the Jade Emperor and his nine lords and let their mysterious essence radiate within your body. Block off the root of death, calm your mind, and darken the room.... Concentrate your mind and make a strong effort to control your thoughts. Visualize the gods in creative imagination, but do not fall asleep. Practice this for seven years; then a jasper carriage with a flying canopy and cinnabar shafts will come to receive you and take you to ascend through the Heavenly Pass.[198]

Having arrived at the Big Dipper, the adept either rested on it, imbibed nourishment from its stars and divinities, or traveled the cosmos in it. "Once the tour of the whole universe is completed, the kings of the Thirty-six heavens will enter his or her name into the registers of immortality."[310] At this point the long discipline is complete, and the practitioner has become an immortal.

SUMMARY

One can only marvel at the far-flung distribution and world-changing impact of journey experiences. They occur across religions, cultures, and centuries, both spontaneously and after arduous preparation. In their wake, they have transformed individuals, religions, societies, and history. Their impact continues to this day.

Journeys are strikingly culture-specific. Mohammad traversed seven heavens, Saint Paul only three; the Jewish seeker arrived at the throne of God, while the Taoist retraced a familiar route through the stars.

Where journeys are deliberately sought, their goals are also culture-specific. The most common goal is *kratophany* (a revelation of power), in whatever form power is conceived. The Taoist also journeyed for pure pleasure, for ecstatic union with a divine lover, or ultimately for immortality and union with the Tao. On the other hand, Tibetan Buddhists—whose journey practices were not described since they form a relatively minor part of the vast array of Tibetan practices—seek enlightenment and liberation from suffering and delusion.

Techniques

Though physical disciplines of fasting and posture remained, the methods used for inducing journeys in Judaism and Taoism differed from the methods of shamanism. Intensely energetic methods such as dancing and drumming gave way to greater reliance on meditation, calm, and mind control. This demonstrates a general principle of the evolution of both the technology of transcendence and the religious states of consciousness it induces. Over the centuries, techniques become increasingly subtle, internal, and focused on mental training and control. The original reliance on entrainment by powerful external stimulation is replaced by a more subtle inner control of mental processes. According to Ramakrishna, one of the greatest of Hindu sages, the defining characteristic of such a yogi is that "the mind is under his control; he is not under the control of his mind."[294] So widely is this kind of self-control praised by sages, psychologists, and philosophers that the great historian William Durant concluded: "The greatest of all wonders is not the conqueror of the world but the subduer of himself."[77]

Interpretations and Metaphysics of Journeys

Interpretations of the metaphysical nature of journeys in the great religions span the spectrum of possibilities. Saint Paul humbly acknowledged that he did not know whether his journey was "in the body or out of the body," and there has long been debate about whether Mohammad's ascent was bodily or visionary. Taoists embraced both views and saw themselves able to travel within the body and the heavens simultaneously. For Tibetan Buddhists, spiritual travels are explicitly mind creations, as is the entire physical universe.

Clearly, cosmic travelers in diverse religions learned to create inner worlds consistent with the maps of their tradition, worlds that the religious scholars Mircea Eliade and Henri Corbin called, respectively, "creative imagination" and "active imagination." Adepts learned to tame and train their own minds and thereby to traverse their inner world. Through these journeys, they were able to break the bonds of ordinary physical life and attain the transcendent goals of their traditions.

At the other extreme are literal interpreters of the Book of Revelation, some of whom are trying to direct world politics so as to fulfill its predictions. The implications of how journeys are interpreted are not minor.

CHAPTER 22

The Varieties of Journey Experiences: Dream, Out-of-Body, Near-Death, and Abduction Experiences

> Maybe you and I are still in a dream and have not yet awakened....
> As we speak now, we do not know whether we are awake or dreaming.
> —*Chuang Tzu*[90]

Shamans learn to induce and direct the journeys that are their hallmark. Yet people who have never even heard of shamanism may have journey-like experiences. Spontaneous journeys include out-of-body experiences (OOBEs), lucid dreams, near-death experiences, and abduction experiences, while deliberately induced journeys are now employed in psychotherapy.

SPONTANEOUS JOURNEYS

Out-of-Body Experiences

Spontaneous OOBEs have occurred throughout history and were traditionally called "astral traveling." Among the best-known travels were those of the eighteenth-century Swedish genius, Emmanuel Swedenborg. Around his fifty-fifth year, this brilliant scientist underwent a religious crisis and then began to describe spontaneous journeys to heaven and hell and meetings with their inhabitants. So powerful were his reports that today, over two hundred years later, the Swedenborgian movement is still thriving.

Perhaps the best-known contemporary examples of spontaneous out-of-body experiences are those of Robert Monroe. Monroe was a conventional businessman who feared he was going crazy, and he actually sought medical treatment when he found himself having OOBEs. He had never even heard of such a thing and didn't believe it possible. Yet eventually shock turned to pleasure as he found himself able to control and explore the experiences. Like Swedenborg, Monroe assumed that the worlds he visited and the creatures he met were real, and he produced elaborate maps and guidebooks of them. He chronicled his explorations in the widely selling book *Journeys Out of the Body*.[245] The similarity of such travels to those of shamans is obvious, and since they occur spontaneously and then later become controlled, this may be one way shamanic journeying was originally learned.

Near-Death Experiences

"May I ask about death?" inquired a disciple of Confucius, to which the master replied, "You do not understand even life. How can you understand death?"[207]

Death is a great mystery, but also a great teacher. "Visit the graves," urged Mohammed,[322] for "death is a good adviser."[9]

It has long been known that those who have a brush with death may describe remarkable experiences. Near-death experiences, or NDEs as they are now called, occur most often in people who come close to death—for example, after a heart attack—but are resuscitated at the last moment.

The experience typically progresses through several stages. The first is a sudden switch from the agony of desperately fighting for survival to profound peace and well-being. Then comes the bewildering shock of finding one's "self" outside the body, able to hear and see everything in the environment, including one's own body lying inert and comatose. Some revived patients have dumbfounded their doctors with detailed descriptions of the resuscitation procedure and of what the doctors said while they were "dead."[247]

Next comes a sense of moving through a vast, dark tunnel. At the end of the tunnel is a spiritual figure or light of incomprehensible brilliance, with which the dying person merges in ecstatic love. The experience ends with a sense that death would be premature and that the person must return to the world.[247] NDEers commonly report that this was the most profound, important, and life-changing moment of their life, and almost 90 percent say they would be willing to repeat it.[303]

NDEs can cause dramatic, long-lasting personality changes similar to those produced by other mystical experiences. Not surprisingly, there is a reduced fear of death, greater belief in an afterlife, and a deeper sense of the preciousness of life, love, and relationships. This is accompanied by increased interest in learning, self-knowledge, and helping others, together with less concern with materialistic goals and worldly possessions. These dramatic changes are as much as would be expected from years of psychotherapy. As the famous astronomer Carl Sagan said after a severe illness, "I recommend almost dying to everyone, it's character building. You get a much clearer perception of what's important and what isn't, the preciousness and beauty of life."[200]

As yet, no single explanation—either biological, psychological, or spiritual—has proved adequate to account for the near-death phenomenon.[304] But whatever their nature, because of improved resuscitation techniques, the number of people having such experiences is multiplying. Consequently, near-death experiences are increasingly impacting our culture in far-reaching ways.[304, 399]

There are obvious similarities—detachment from the body, journey to other realms, meeting spirits—between NDEs and shamanic journeys. One writer even went to the extreme of suggesting that "The shaman, then, is a master of death, he actually dies and is actually reborn....The shaman is the classic investigator of the realm of death; he explores the routes of travel to and in the beyond and thereby produces a map of the postmortem terrain."[189]

However, it is safer to say that, while there are similarities between shamanic journeys and NDEs, there are also significant differences. For example, the shaman deliberately induces the journey, has a wider range of potential experiences, and, unlike the person approaching death, has considerable control over the process. Perhaps NDEs inspired some shamans, since one of the traditional calls to practice is unexpected recovery from illness. If some shamans-to-be survived near-death experiences, they may have sought ways to recreate their profound transformative and healing effects.

Dream Journeys

We are such stuff
As dreams are made on, and our little life
Is rounded with a sleep
—*Shakespeare*, The Tempest

We are all familiar with the flights and journeys of dreams. Within minutes of closing our eyes, we may journey to unknown worlds and interact with their inhabitants. Most amazing of all, we assume that these worlds, creatures, and our dream body are all utterly solid, material, and "real."

Dream journeys can be rich sources of insight. In many religions, dreams are regarded not only, to quote Freud, as "the royal road to the unconscious," but also as a way to wisdom and awakening. Small wonder that some shamans and tribal cultures regard dream experiences and journeys as no less real or valuable than waking ones.

A valuable variation is "lucid dreaming" in which the dreamer knows she is dreaming. Lucid dreamers can direct their dreams much as shamans do their journeys. The dreamer can travel consciously through diverse worlds, meet other beings, explore, question, and learn.

Until recently, psychologists dismissed lucid dreaming as impossible. Yet it has long been valued in many religions, which regard it as a capacity to be cultivated. Almost a thousand years ago, the great Sufi mystic Ibn El-Arabi—who was a towering religious and philosophical genius known to Muslims as "the greatest master"—said, "A person must control his thoughts in a dream….Everyone should apply himself to the attainment of this ability of such great value."[330] The technique has been developed most exquisitely in Tibetan dream yoga. Tibetan yogis continue spiritual practice throughout their dreams, during which they explore the nature of mind, seek inspiration, or receive teachings from the Buddha.[265]

Advanced yogis practice "witnessing the process of dreaming or dreamless sleep."[333] That is, the most advanced practitioners attain what Hindu yoga calls *turiya*, a unique fourth state of consciousness in which they never lose awareness. Rather, they remain continuously and imperturbably lucid and aware during dreams, dreamless sleep, and waking life.[399] At this point, practice continues unbroken through day and night, and, according to the Christian Saint Isaac the Syrian, "Then prayer never stops in a man's soul."[157] Electroencephalographic (EEG or brain wave) studies of advanced TM (Transcendental

Meditation) practitioners have validated some of these remarkable claims for continuous, unbroken awareness twenty-four hours a day.[228] There is no evidence that shamans developed these advanced skills, but they were surely inspired by spontaneous lucid dreams, and a few probably went on to develop some yogic capacities.

Instructions for cultivating lucid dreams are now widely available. A good introduction is the book *Lucid Dreaming*,[165; 205] which is summarized in *Paths Beyond Ego*.[399]

Alien Abductions

Many cultures have myths of alien beings who appear from the stars to help or abduct humans.[179] Of late, the aliens have been very busy, abducting some 2 percent of Americans.[317] This would amount to more than 100 million people worldwide and an abduction every few seconds. As Carl Sagan quipped, "It's surprising that more of the neighbors haven't noticed."[317]

Typical abductees might report awaking at night paralyzed and being transported by small humanoid creatures to spacecraft. There they are medically examined and sometimes healed, perhaps sexually probed or even fertilized, and educated about spiritual matters or the ecological devastation wrought by human destructiveness. They are left with a mélange of emotions and a sense of bewilderment, numinosity, and sacred mission.

What are we to make of such reports? Many abductees take them literally. A handful of researchers agree, of whom the most famous was John Mack, a Pulitzer Prize-winning Harvard psychiatrist.[221] But the evidence Mack adduced seems painfully weak, not least because there was no physical proof, and many stories were garnered via hypnotic recall—a notoriously unreliable method that can strengthen or even implant false memories.[53]

The many similarities to shamanic journeys are obvious[179] and viewing the abduction as a spontaneous upper-world journey makes good sense. After all, asked Carl Sagan, "Which is more likely—that we're undergoing a massive but generally overlooked invasion by alien sexual abusers, or that people are experiencing an unfamiliar mental state?"[317]

This in no way denies the power, or even value, of these experiences for some abductees. Rather, it demonstrates the remarkable prevalence of journeys and "alien" or "spirit" encounters, shows that even spontaneous encounters can sometimes be healing and educational, and reminds us how much we still have to learn about the roots of shamanism, our minds, and ourselves.

Conclusions

Out-of-body, dream journey, near-death, and abduction experiences all center on apparent "soul travel" and encounters that are often powerful, healing, and informative. The capacity for them may be partly hardwired into the brain.[209] They doubtless occurred throughout history and, as such, may have inspired belief in a soul and soul travel. Since these experiences can be healing and helpful, the techniques and circumstances that favor them would likely have been carefully cultivated. Whenever these skills were collected into a coherent body of techniques, wedded to an explanatory mythology, and transmitted across generations, the shamanic tradition would be reborn.

This suggests a partial answer to the puzzle of shamanism's far-flung distribution. If journey-like experiences recurred spontaneously, they could have inspired related practices and beliefs in widely separated cultures. This would favor the idea that our ancestors developed shamanism in many parts of the world. It would also help explain why the tradition shows striking similarities across cultures and why it has survived for so long. But of course there is no way to test this theory, and the origins of shamanism and religion will probably forever remain a mystery of history.

DELIBERATE JOURNEYS

Psychotherapy

Given the healing potential of journeys, it is not surprising that psychotherapists use visualization to evoke similar experiences. A wide range of imagery techniques is used, with names such as active imagination, visualization, guided imagery, guided meditation, or waking dreams.[250] Commonly patients are asked to visualize themselves going to meet people or entities that will provide understanding and healing.[3]

Such experiences have much in common with shamanic journeys but also differ in several ways. Unlike guided imagery, journeys usually occur in significantly altered states of consciousness, often involve travel to other realms, and are viewed as real rather than imaginary by the shaman.

Hypnotic experiences can be closer to the shamanic journey. While in the ASC of deep hypnosis, other worlds and entities can seem unquestionably solid, material, and independent of our own minds. Both hypnotic and shamanic travels can be therapeutic, but only the shaman enters and leaves the state at will.

These two worlds are now converging as more therapists study shamanism and employ its journeys and other techniques in their consulting rooms.[109, 172] The effects on both disciplines will be intriguing.

Neoshamanism

Journey-like experiences are surprisingly common, but can ordinary contemporary Westerners learn to journey shamanically? The popularity of neoshamanism demonstrates that for many people the answer is yes and that, with the aid of drumming, most people find journeying surprisingly easy and helpful. Of course, this is not to say that all people have equal talents. Michael Harner, who has taught many thousands of people, reports that "approximately nine out of ten persons have the capacity for the visualization necessary to the shamanic journey."[148]

Notice the marked contrast between the large number of people capable of at least some journeying and the small number who traditionally did. While most people may have been capable, it was shamans alone who engaged in cosmic travel, while their compatriots remained firmly earthbound.

CHAPTER 23

Interpreting and Researching Journeys

What is this awesome mystery that is taking place within me?....
My intellect sees what has happened, but it cannot explain it.
It can see, and wishes to explain,
But can find no word that will suffice...
—*Symeon, The New Theologian*[235]

INTERPRETATIONS

How are we to understand the nature of journey experiences? For shamans this question is not even an issue: the realms, worlds, and spirits are all real, as real as this world, and perhaps even more so.[146] However, this position is unlikely to satisfy contemporary Westerners who are more likely to regard the experiences as examples—dramatic examples, granted—of vivid imagery or imagination.

Philosophically speaking, we have here two different ontological perspectives. The shamanic view is a realist one since it regards the phenomena found in the journey as real, objective, and independent of the shaman's mind. The shaman views the journey as truly "exosomatic" (outside the body) rather than as "imaginal" (mind-created imagery).[173]

This perspective is consistent with the shamanic worldview, which holds that other worlds and spirits exist independent of the human mind and can be accessed directly through cosmic traveling. Since this worldview may have been derived from shamanic journeys, the consistency is hardly surprising. Some people who have out-of-body and near-death experiences interpret them similarly. They believe that the soul separates from the body, journeys through realms, and meets beings that are quite separate from themselves.

Certainly the idea that there is a soul and that it can leave the body to travel to other realms is an ancient one. Plato described the soul as imprisoned in the body like an oyster in his shell. Likewise Socrates claimed that the mind only perceives absolute truths "when she takes leave of the body and has as little as possible to do with it, then she has no bodily sense or desire, but is aspiring after true being."[182]

More common today is the imaginal perspective that interprets shamanic journey experiences as mind-created images. These images may be interpreted as either pathological or beneficial. Pathological interpretations of such images label them as hallucinations, whereas positive interpretations see them as helpful, healing products of the imagination.

A more radical perspective is that of Tibetan Buddhism. Here the realms to which yogis travel in dreams or meditation are regarded as mind creations, but so too is everything in ordinary waking experience. This world and all worlds are ultimately regarded as creations of consciousness or mind. As Ramana Maharshi summarized: "There is no difference between the dream and waking states except that the former is short and the latter long. Both are the product of the mind."[270] Waking from all dreams, both sleeping and waking, is said to occur only with enlightenment. When asked for proof for this position, the yogi might give either a philosophical argument or the centuries-old advice: "To see if this be true, look within your own mind." Of course, none of these perspectives deny that the journey may yield significant benefits.

Shamanism in a Post-Metaphysical Age

Metaphysical claims for the existence of independent ontological realms—whether heavens and hells or the worlds and spirits of shamanic journeys—cannot hope to withstand the onslaught of contemporary philosophical criticism. Over two centuries ago, Immanuel Kant—widely regarded as the most important European philosopher of the modern era—launched a devastating critique against metaphysical claims of any kind. Kant demonstrated that experience and perception are largely constructed by the perceiver's mind and that there are inescapable limits on our knowledge of "things-in-themselves." The claim that there are mind-independent ontological realms, such as shamanic worlds just waiting for us to journey to and objectively perceive, cannot withstand Kant's famous *Critique of*

Pure Reason. So devastating is Kant's critique that contemporary philosophy is described as post-Kantian and post-metaphysical, and any spiritual tradition that simply assumes the presence of realms that can be objectively perceived and described is doomed to theoretical oblivion.[411]

Of course, there is an obvious escape clause. Kant's critique is of metaphysical or ontological claims, not of experiential descriptions. One can legitimately talk of spiritual *experiences* in general, or of shamanic *experiences* in particular, and there is no problem. Specific spiritual practices evoke specific experiences, and these experiences can be insightful, valuable, healing, and even liberating. We only run into problems when we leap from making statements about experiences to making assumptions about some reality that they supposedly reveal. The so-called "principle of parsimony," otherwise known as "Ockham's razor," wisely argues for using as few assumptions, metaphysical or otherwise, as possible.

RESEARCH STUDIES

We know very little about the effects of journeying on the shaman's psychology and physiology. However, we do know more about other kinds of journeys. Since the publication of Stephen LaBerge's book *Lucid Dreaming*[205] in 1985, thousands of people have flocked to workshops, and many laboratory studies have appeared. This ancient yogic skill, which psychologists once dismissed as impossible, is now proving psychologically and spiritually beneficial and is yielding insights into sleep, dreams, and the brain.

Numerous studies of near-death experiences confirm their many far-reaching effects on personality and priorities.[304] Likewise, a few studies have been done on abductees. Intriguingly, these people show some of the same value shifts as NDEers, specifically a greater concern with ecology and spirituality.[305] Of course, these investigations of aftereffects tell us little about the actual nature of the experiences.

Out-of-body experiences offer an intriguing opportunity to test whether people can actually see, and accurately report on, the places they supposedly visit. The psychologist Charles Tart, whose valuable analyses of ASCs we will draw on later, reported occasional evidence of extrasensory perception (ESP) and some unusual EEG patterns during his subjects' OOBEs.[360]

However, a more intensive study was decidedly negative. Stephen LaBerge tested approximately one hundred subjects, all of whom believed they could readily induce OOBEs and employ ESP while having them. The subjects were asked to visit a specific room while in the OOBE and subsequently to describe what they saw. The result? There was virtually no correspondence whatsoever between the room and the descriptions.[205]

LaBerge interpreted these findings as supporting his hypothesis that OOBEs are actually misinterpreted, partly lucid dreams. This hypothesis would explain some of the curious features of OOBEs and why they usually occur at night. There is no firm evidence that out-of-body experiences actually involve consciousness separating from the body. How one could even test such a question is unclear.

However, whatever interpretations one adopts and whatever future research reveals, it is clear that experiences of leaving the body and traveling to other realms are perennial, worldwide phenomena. Many of these experiences are so intriguing and helpful that most cultures value them, develop techniques to induce them, and create traditions to support them.

PART VI

SHAMANIC TECHNIQUES

This is why it is so difficult to explain the path to one who has not tried; he will see only his point of view of today or rather the loss of his point of view. And yet, if we only knew how each loss of one's viewpoint is a progress, and how life changes when one passes from the stage of closed truth to the stage of the open truth—a truth like life itself, too great to be trapped by points of view, because it embraces every point of view...a truth great enough to deny itself and pass endlessly into a higher truth.

—*Satprem*[321]

CHAPTER 24

The Politics of Consciousness

We are all prisoners of our minds.
This realization is the first step on the journey to freedom.
—*Ram Dass*[293]

CULTURE AND CONSCIOUSNESS

Anthropologists divide cultures into *monophasic* and *polyphasic*.[208] Most of the world's cultures, including shamanic ones, are *polyphasic*, meaning that they recognize and utilize multiple states of consciousness, such as dreams and meditative and contemplative states. Polyphasic societies value and cultivate these states, honor those who master them, and derive much of their understanding from them of the mind, humankind, and the cosmos.

By contrast, *monophasic* cultures—of which the modern Western world is the prime example—recognize very few healthy ASCs and derive their view of reality almost exclusively from the usual waking condition. These societies give little credence to alternate states and may denigrate those who explore them, especially if they involve drug use. People reared within monophasic blinders can have great difficulty recognizing unfamiliar states, let alone their healing or spiritual potentials.

For example, hypnosis was long dismissed as a sham. During the nineteenth century, the British physician James Esdaile went to India, learned hypnosis, and used it for surgery. At a time when there was no anesthesia and even the most devastating operations were performed without pain relief, this was obviously a momentous discovery. Yet Esdaile's reports were dismissed as impossible, and medical journals refused to publish them. After returning to England, he arranged a demonstration for the British College of Physicians and Surgeons. As Charles Tart describes:

> After hypnotizing a man with a gangrenous leg, he amputated it in front of them while the man lay there calmly smiling. The conclusion of his skeptical colleagues? Esdaile was fooling them. He had hired a hardened rogue for a gold piece to lie there and pretend that he was feeling no pain. They must have had very hard rogues in those days.[355]

The Western world's belief that altered states such as hypnosis, lucid dreaming, and *satori* are impossible or pathological has cost us dearly. But times are changing. Much of the social turmoil beginning in the 1960s reflects the West's initial, tumultuous transition from a monophasic to a polyphasic culture.[y] The popularization of the powerful psychedelic LSD, together with its chemical cousins, such as mescaline and psilocybin, unleashed experiences of such intensity that in the 1960s they shook the very foundations of our culture. A Pandora's box of altered states, heavens and hells, highs and lows, trivia and transcendence cascaded into a society utterly unprepared for any of them. [396]

The West also began to discover contemplative and spiritual practices and their states of consciousness. Meditation and yoga flooded in from the East; Jewish Kabbalah, Christian contemplation, and Islamic *Zikr* reemerged in the West; and shamanic practices immigrated from tribal cultures.

Their impact reverberates to this day, and the Western world will likely never be the same. For better and for worse, these experiences and states have molded culture and counterculture, art and music, science and psychiatry, and catalyzed social movements such as those for peace and civil rights. They continue to inspire spiritual practices, to fertilize brain research, and to suggest new understandings of consciousness, creativity, and cults. Millions of Westerners now practice meditation, yoga, and contemplation, and research on altered states flourishes. The transition is still far from complete, as culture wars and drug wars attest, but the balance has shifted, and the Western world seems on its way to becoming a polyphasic culture.

THE POLITICS OF SHAMANIC CONSCIOUSNESS

Shamanic studies reflect this shift and, for several decades, have emphasized the importance of ASCs and ASC-inducing techniques. Yet recently there has been a backlash. A minority movement has emerged to dismiss the importance or even existence of ASCs in shamanism and to expunge words such as "trance" or "ecstasy" from the discussion. Leading this charge has been the French anthropologist, Roberte Hamayon, whose goal is succinctly summarized in her paper titled "To Put an End to the Use of 'Trance' and 'Ecstasy' in the Study of Shamanism."[140]

Hamayon makes three valuable criticisms, but goes too far in her conclusions. Her first critique is that the terms "trance" and "ecstasy" are painfully vague, ill defined, and sloppily used. She is perfectly correct, and neither term recognizes the rich variety of shamanic states nor do they identify precisely the nature of these states. Consequently, in later chapters we will map these states with a new technique that allows far greater precision than previous methods. We will also avoid the term "trance," while retaining for occasional use "ecstasy" where it implies an ASC associated with a subjective out-of-body experience.

Hamayon's second concern is that altered states are not universal in shamanism. Certainly she is correct that some practitioners who have been called shamans do not induce altered states.

Hamayon's third concern is how we determine whether practitioners are actually in altered states, let alone which state they are in. Clearly there are many cases in which we don't have enough information to decide.

But Hamayon goes too far when she concludes that there is no valid reason to refer to a shaman's state of mind at all. Her preference as a social anthropologist is to use nonparticipant observation to focus on objective behavior and roles. Like any method, this one has a selective focus, yields selective findings, and overlooks others.

Every method sets unavoidable limits on knowledge because every perspective both reveals and conceals. In contemporary philosophical terms, each epistemological method reveals or unveils congruent observations, while leaving others latent and invisible.

What is invisible to the objective methods of social anthropology are subjective experiences and states of consciousness. That these are invisible is not a problem per se. However, it becomes a problem when these undetected states and experiences are then denied and reduced to merely objective behavior and physiology. Hamayon's purely objective approach allows her to conclude that states of mind are not "a necessarily relevant question to the study of shamanism in 'traditional' or 'tribal' societies."[141]

Hamayon's denial of the possible role of altered states in shamanism seems to reflect several factors:

- First, some of the groups she worked with may not use them.

- Second, her commitment to objective methods makes it difficult for her to recognize subjective ASCs.

- Third, she makes no reference to the use of psychedelics, whose mind-boggling states can hardly be denied by even the fiercest critic of ASCs.

Finally Hamayon makes no mention of having undertaken shamanic practices herself. Consequently, she may be limited by what Michael Harner calls *cognicentrism,* which "is the counterpart of ethnocentrism between cultures, but in this case it is not the narrowness of someone's cultural experience that is the fundamental issue but the narrowness of someone's conscious experience."[146]

States of consciousness are clearly central to some shamanic practices. Hamayon correctly warns that we need to be careful and precise in naming and discussing these states.

MODIFYING CONSCIOUSNESS

Of course, shamans are not the only ones who have developed techniques for modifying consciousness. Fully 90 percent of the world's cultures have institutionalized ASCs, and in traditional societies these states are usually sacred. This is "a striking finding and suggests that we are, indeed, dealing with a matter of major importance."[30] Clearly humankind has devoted enormous energy and ingenuity to altering consciousness. The physician Andrew Weil, best known for his books on complementary medicine, concluded that the "desire to alter consciousness periodically is an innate normal drive analogous to hunger or the sexual drive."[401]

So shamans are hardly alone in seeking alternate states of mind. Meditators, yogis, contemplatives, and mystics also seek them and claim that it is these states that birth the deepest realizations. Mystical traditions have therefore developed techniques for altering consciousness in systematic ways, and these techniques constitute a *technology of transcendence* and a *technology of the sacred.*

Spiritual traditions serve as road maps for applying this technology. Religious and spiritual traditions are created, and their higher reaches preserved, by people who first open to transcendent states and then provide practices whereby others can also access them. In this way, subsequent generations of practitioners can re-create the founder's insights and states of mind. And the first such tradition was shamanism. However, with its many healing and other techniques, it is also more than only a technology of transcendence.

At its best, the shamanic tradition transmits information and techniques that allow novices to re-create the altered states and abilities of their predecessors. Each generation can then refresh a living, continuously re-created tradition and even add to its accumulated treasure of wisdom and techniques.

Truth Decay: The Ritualization of Religion

But transmission can fail. When this occurs, the technology of transcendence is lost and, with it, transcendent states and direct experience of the sacred. Transformative techniques now give way to mere symbolic rituals, direct experience yields to secondhand belief, and doctrine decays into dogma. This is a process of "truth decay" or "the ritualization of religion" of which the *Tao Te Ching* laments: "Ritual is the husk of true faith."[243]

Examples are widespread throughout the world's religions. In fact, authentic spiritual traditions with effective sacred technologies capable of offering true transcendence are far rarer than conventional institutions offering comforting rituals. In technical terms, transcendence (growth beyond one's current stage) is far rarer than translation (support of one's current stage).[411]

Examples occur in shamanism, and Hamayon describes one herself: "The modern-day successors of shamans in urbanized Siberia confine themselves to such practices as speaking with their patients, laying on of hands, massaging, etc..."[141] Ritualization has also replaced realization in contemporary Japan, where today:

> Trance occurs only rarely. The capacity for this kind of dissociation, and for the visionary journey which goes with it, seems to have diminished in recent centuries, and today the magic journey is most commonly accomplished by symbolic action in full waking consciousness.[25]

Of course, these purely ritualistic practices would not meet the stringent definition of shamanism used in this book. Here the focus is on practitioners who employ an effective technology of transcendence to induce ASCs, journey, and directly experience the sacred.

The survival of authentic spiritual traditions depends on succeeding generations continuing to access the transcendent states from which the tradition was born. Shamanism has been largely successful in this. For thousands of years it has survived as a vibrant tradition that has successfully preserved one of humanity's earliest technologies: a sacred technology of transcendence for inducing specific sacred states of consciousness.

CHAPTER 25

Transforming Consciousness: Contemporary Understandings and Shamanic Methods

It is the quality of your consciousness at this moment that is
the main determinant of what kind of future you will experience.
—*Eckhart Tolle*[369]

How can we induce desirable states of consciousness? This has been a central question animating spiritual traditions for thousands of years. Each tradition has forged its own answer, developed its own practices, and evolved its preferred states. Yet there are general principles at work, and knowing them will enable us to better understand shamanic methods. Charles Tart offers a useful theory involving three stages of induction:

- Destabilization of the initial ordinary state,

- Transition to a new state,

- Stabilization of the new state.[361]

In the first stage, destabilizing forces disrupt usual brain-mind function. Destabilizers can be sensory, social, physiological, or chemical. Examples include sensory input such as intense music and drumming, physiological disturbances such as hunger and sleep deprivation, or chemicals such as psychedelics. Specific mental exercises that can function as destabilizers include contemplative disciplines such as intense concentration or mantra recitation.

When destabilizing forces are sufficiently intense, they disrupt the usual state of consciousness, and transition toward another state begins. The contours of this new state will depend largely on the combination of "patterning forces" operating on it, forces such as beliefs, physiology, drugs, or the environmental setting. These patterning forces impose a specific organization on brain-mind function and thereby induce a corresponding state of consciousness. During the third and final stage, consciousness settles into the new state, which, if sufficiently stable, will endure as a stable state or even trait of consciousness.

Hypnosis provides a good example. A standard hypnotic induction procedure—e.g., relaxation and imagery—destabilizes the usual waking state. However, the nature of the state and experiences that follow can vary dramatically according to the different patterning forces—instructions, expectations, etc.—that the hypnotist employs. When the hypnotic state stabilizes, it may endure until new instructions (patterning forces) are given.

The ability to access altered states is a learnable skill. Entering a specific state for the first time can be difficult but may become easier with practice. For example, a person who first smokes marijuana may be disappointed, but further attempts may be increasingly successful. This is a curious phenomenon known as "reverse tolerance," in which a drug's effects become more powerful with repeated use.[361]

Mature Potentials of Altered States

The fact that the ability to enter alternate states can be developed and refined points to four important implications and potentials. These potentials are greater ease, independence, stabilization, and infusion.

- *Ease* means that practitioners can enter desired states more easily and rapidly.

- *Independence* implies that practitioners may become less dependent on supportive preparations or external aids such as drums or drugs.

- *Stabilization* transforms a fragile, temporary altered state into an increasingly imperturbable and enduring altered trait. Stabilization transforms transient states into enduring stages, peak experiences into plateau experiences, epiphanies into personality, temporary gifts into permanent abilities, and flashes of illumination into abiding

TRANSFORMING CONSCIOUSNESS

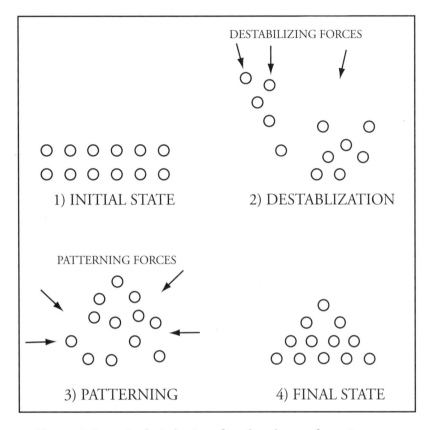

Figure 13. Stages in the induction of an altered state of consciousness.

light. Examples of enduring meditation states include TM's continuous "cosmic consciousness" and Tibetan Buddhism's unceasing "Great Contemplation."[264]

- *Infusion* occurs when qualities and capacities of an ASC begin to permeate the waking state. For example, meditators who master states of calm and concentration will eventually enjoy these qualities throughout the day.

These potentials are evident in shamanism. For example, spirit vision initially requires arduous training, but over time becomes increasingly sensitive and accessible. As Eliade summarized, shamanic training "has as its object transforming the apprentice magician's initial and momentary ecstatic experience…into a permanent condition."[83] This infusion of the sacred into daily experience is one of the great goals of spiritual life.

SHAMANIC TECHNIQUES

Shamans have used these principles for centuries. Their techniques for inducing ASCs span sensory, social, psychological, physiological, and chemical approaches.

Preparatory rituals include periods of solitude and prayer and the creation of the appropriate set and environmental setting. Contemporary psychedelic users are well aware that set and setting are enormously important in determining the quality of psychedelic experiences. Skillful users therefore go to great lengths to optimize expectations and the environment,[132] and shamans do likewise.

Timing is critical. Séances are usually held at night so that the spirits and geography of other worlds can be better seen, presumably because of "perceptual release," the process by which subtle objects become visible as stronger stimuli are withdrawn. For example, house lights mistakenly left on may only become recognizable when night falls. Likewise with subtle shamanic experiences.

Physiological techniques are common. Ascetic preparations may involve a day or more without food, sleep, sex, or even water. Temperature extremes include icy cold winter streams or the searing heat of the sweat lodge. The séance itself may include intense rhythmic stimulation such as dancing and drumming, as well as ingestion of sacred drugs. Any of these techniques can disrupt normal physiology and consciousness; rhythm and psychedelics are particularly potent.

Rhythm

> …we have been making music since the dawn of culture. More than 30,000 years ago early humans were already playing bone flutes, percussive instruments and jaw harps—and all known societies throughout the world have had music.
>
> —*Norman Weinberger*[403]

Mystics the world over have long recognized the power of rhythm—especially music, singing, and dancing—to evoke powerful emotional and sacred states. The Bible relates that over 2,000 years ago, when the prophet Elisha sought inspiration, he requested, "'But now bring me a minstrel.' And when the minstrel played the power of the Lord came upon him." As Evelyn Underhill, author of the classic text *Mysticism,* noted,

> Dancing, music and other exaggerations of natural rhythm have been pressed into the same service by the Greek initiates of Dionysus, by the Gnostics, by innumerable other mystic cults. That these proceedings do effect a remarkable change in the

human consciousness is proved by experience: though how and why they do it is yet little understood.[375]

Shamans also employ rhythm, and drums and rattles are their favored instruments. Drumming probably facilitates shamanic states and journeying in several ways. First, it acts as a concentration device. It continuously reminds the shaman of her purpose, drowns out distracting stimuli, and reduces the mind's incessant tendency to wander. Concentration is a crucial spiritual skill,[392] and shamans discovered a quick and easy way to attain it.

Second, drumming can also destabilize ordinary consciousness. Charles Tart says that in his experience, loud drumming can overwhelm stabilizing forces, making an abrupt change of state very easy. Interestingly, Zen teachers make use of the same principle. Numerous stories relate how they trailed students, crept up behind them, and suddenly yelled at the top of their voice. The ideal result is an instant *satori*.

Drumming is commonly assumed to harmonize neural activity, and two apparently supportive studies have been widely quoted.[253, 254] In both, electroencephalograms (EEGs or brain waves) of subjects listening to drumming seemed to show auditory driving responses. Auditory driving occurs when a repetitive sound evokes or "drives" similar EEG frequencies in the brain. Unfortunately the studies are flawed and give us little reliable information.[3]

We do not know the precise effects of drumming but we do know that music has far-reaching effects on the brain. For example, the sensitivity and even size of the auditory cortex changes, and the brain devotes more neurons to personally important tones.[403] But whatever the mechanisms, anyone who has been entranced by music is well aware of rhythm's potential for affecting states of mind.

When a drum is played at a tempo of some 200 to 220 beats per minute, most Western novices can journey to some extent, even on their first attempt.[146] With greater expertise, shamans can become less dependent on external stimulation[12] as would be expected if accessing altered states is a learnable skill.

OVERVIEW OF SHAMANIC TECHNIQUES

Whatever the precise neural mechanisms involved, it is clear that shamans discovered a wide variety of psychological, physiological, and chemical aids to modify consciousness and welded them into an effective technology of transcendence. The techniques were relatively simple and were probably first discovered accidentally, such as when the tribe faced hunger,

Figure 14. A Koryak woman shaman with drum.

fatigue, and dehydration, or accidentally ate psychedelic plants. Because of their valuable effects, these techniques were likely remembered and repeated. Thus our forebears would discover and rediscover humankind's first technology of transcendence, through which would pour the sacred visions that inspired and sustained humankind for thousands of years.

CHAPTER 26

Psychedelics and Entheogens:
Revealers of the Divine Within?

The observations from psychedelic therapy and other forms of deep experiential work…suggest an even more radical reformulation of the relationship between the human personality and spirituality. According to the new data, spirituality is an intrinsic property of the psyche that emerges quite spontaneously when the process of self-exploration reaches sufficient depth….The individual who connects with these levels of his or her psyche automatically develops a new worldview, within which spirituality represents a natural, essential, and absolutely vital element of existence. In my experience, a transformation of this kind has occurred without exception in a wide range of individuals, including stubborn atheists, skeptics, cynics, Marxist philosophers, and positivistically oriented scientists.

—Stan Grof[309]

THE POLITICS OF DRUG USE

Having an intelligent discussion about psychedelics is hard, so great is the misunderstanding and emotion that surrounds them. As a culture we are remarkably ambivalent about drugs. The aptly titled book *Overdosed America*[2] points out that we are bombarded by drug advertisements and each year gulp down billions of dollars worth of tranquilizers, sacrifice about 500,000 (yes, that's half a million) people to tobacco consumption, and lose another 100,000 to alcohol. Yet we subsidize tobacco growers while imprisoning marijuana growers and make no distinction between socially destructive and sacred drug use.

Yet the use of drugs to induce sacred states of consciousness has flourished through-out human history.[30] Historical examples include the Zoroastrian *haoma*, the Australian aboriginals' *pituri*, Zen's tea, and Hinduism's *soma*, otherwise known as "the food of the gods."[345] In ancient Greece, *kykeon* fueled the Eleusinian mysteries and wine the ecstasies of the Dionysians.

Contemporary examples are also common. They include Native American peyote, Ras-tafarian ganja (marijuana), and the South American shamans' ayahuasca.[145] Clearly there has been widespread agreement across centuries and cultures that psychedelics can induce valuable religious experiences.[18, 125, 126, 307, 348]

However, the story is very different in the West. Psychedelics were all but unknown until the 1960s when they came crashing into a culture utterly unprepared for them. For the first time in its history, a significant portion of Western society experienced power-ful ASCs. Some of these were clearly painful and problematic, while others were appar-ently transcendent and illuminating. Suddenly the question of whether drugs can induce genuine religious and mystical experiences morphed from dry academic debates to pitched political battles.

The very names given to these curious chemicals say it all. For naysayers these drugs are *psychotomimetics* (mimickers of psychosis) or *hallucinogens* (hallucination inducers), while for most people they are *psychedelics* (mind manifesters) and, for some researchers, *entheo-gens* (revealers of the divine within).

Unfortunately, careful analysis and dispassionate discussion were long ago overwhelmed by political posturing and media madness. Misinformation has flourished. All too often, apologists denied the drugs' dangers, while opponents and governments exaggerated them. For example, drug opponents repeatedly misused shaky scientific research to bolster claims of neurotoxicity. This process continues to the present day, especially with MDMA (Ec-stasy),[56] though the actual nature of MDMA-induced neural effects remains moot.[126, 164]

The importance of psychedelics has often been overlooked by anthropologists, possibly because of lack of personal experience. Such was the case with Michael Harner. Only after ingesting yage did he appreciate its impact on the natives' reality and shamanic practices.

> For several hours after drinking the brew, I found myself, although awake, in a world literally beyond my wildest dreams….transported into a trance where the supernatu-ral seemed natural, I realized that anthropologists including myself, had profoundly underestimated the importance of the drug in affecting native ideology.[145]

SHAMANIC USE OF PSYCHEDELICS

The range of drugs employed by shamans is impressive. Some one hundred different plant agents have been identified, and archeological records suggest that drug use may extend back over 3,000 years.[108]

It is Siberian and Latin American shamans who have most often employed psychedelics as boosters for their cosmic travels. In Siberia, the preferred substance has been the mushroom *Amanita muscaria*, or fly agaric, which may be the much-praised *soma* of early Indian religion and a drug of European legends.[350] If so, then its religious and cultural impact has been remarkable.

Curiously, this red mushroom speckled with white is familiar to Western children from drawings in fairy tales. If you watch Disney's movie *Snow White*, you'll see it flourishing.[308] Even more curious, it is famous for being able to inebriate several people with one dose, since it passes unchanged into the users' urine, which Russian peasants would happily line up to drink.[350]

Among the many chemicals used in Latin America, two of the most powerful and popular psychedelics are peyote and yage. Peyote is a distasteful cactus that can make users nauseous, and Indians describe it as "a hard road." The great American philosopher William James, who had powerful experiences with nitrous oxide, was sick for twenty-four hours after eating a single piece. He concluded that he would take the peyote visions on faith rather than personal experience. For those able to keep it down, the effects are much like those of its major active component, mescaline.

Yage, or ayahuasca as it is also known, is an equally nausea-producing psychedelic made from an Amazonian "visionary vine" called banasteriopsis. Yage is chemically complex, but the most important psychoactive ingredient may be harmaline.[350] Of course, shamans attribute the effects not to chemicals but to the spirit that dwells within the plant.

Yage elicits strong visual experiences. Users describe long sequences of dreamlike visions that appear in a spiritually significant progression. Yage is famous for provoking specific images: jungle scenes and visions of dangerous creatures such as tigers, snakes, and naked women.[350] Several Westerners, including Michael Harner, have marveled at the power of the imagery and its consistency with native reports.[145] Of course, much of this consistent imagery may reflect expectations and the jungle setting.

Yage is shamanically interesting because of claims for its healing and telepathic effects. In South America it is known as "the great medicine" that can reveal remedies or produce healing by interceding with the spirits. In contrast to Western medical notions, yage is thought to be curative whether the patient or the healer swallows it.[72]

Yage is also famous for its supposed clairvoyant powers. Native reports abound of yage-empowered journeys and extrasensory perception. One anthropologist reported that "on the day following one Ahayuasca party, six of nine men informed me of seeing the death of my chai, my mother's father. This occurred a few days before I was informed by radio of his death."[350]

Recent reports suggest that Nepalese shamans make extensive use of psychedelics, including over twenty kinds of psychoactive mushrooms. Previous ethnographers apparently overlooked these drugs because they are used secretively.[248] If so, we may have underestimated the use of psychedelics by shamans, in general, and also by other religious practitioners.

In traditional cultures that treat psychedelics as sacraments, addictive or hedonistic misuse is rarely a problem. However, with the encroachment of civilization, these traditional drugs are now being displaced in many areas by tobacco and alcohol, which are less psychedelic and far more addictive. Andrew Weil lamented that in some places alcoholism is replacing the ceremonial use of sacred drugs.[402]

PSYCHEDELICS AND RELIGIOUS EXPERIENCES

In the West there is currently a strong tendency to deny religious significance to any drug experience, and psychedelic use by shamans has led people to dismiss them. Even some firm supporters, such as Eliade, regard drug use as a degenerative form of the tradition.

And yet the question—one of the most important of all concerning these drugs—still remains: Can psychedelics induce genuine mystical experiences? Stanislav Grof, the world's most experienced psychedelic researcher, concluded that "after 30 years of discussion, the question of whether LSD and other psychedelics can induce genuine spiritual experiences is still open."[133]

At the present time, both research and theory suggest an answer to this question. That answer is a very qualified "yes." Yes, psychedelics can induce genuine mystical experiences, but only *some* times, in *some* people, under *some* circumstances. To evaluate this conclusion, let's examine the arguments used against it, recent research, and a theory that may make sense of the research.

Arguments Against the Validity of Drug-Induced Religious Experiences

Five major arguments have been advanced against the idea that drug experiences can be truly religious or mystical.[345, 348]

1) Some drug experiences are clearly anything but mystical and beneficial.

2) The experiences induced by drugs may actually be different from those of genuine mystics.

3) A theological position argues that mystical rapture is a gift of God that can never be brought under mere human control.

4) Drug-induced experiences are too quick and easy and could therefore hardly be identical to those hard-won by years of contemplative discipline.

5) Aftereffects of drug-induced experiences may be different, less beneficial, and less long-lasting than those of contemplatives.

There are possible answers to each of these concerns. Let's consider them in sequence.

1) There is no doubt whatsoever that some, in fact most, drug experiences are anything but mystical. According to Huston Smith:

> There are, of course, innumerable drug experiences that have no religious features; they can be sensual as readily as spiritual, trivial as readily as transforming, capricious as readily as sacramental. If there is one point about which every student agrees, it is that there is no such thing as the drug experience per se....This of course proves that not all drug experiences are religious; it does not prove that no drug experiences are religious.[345]

2) Are drug and natural mystical states experientially the same? Smith concludes that "descriptively drug experiences cannot be distinguished from their natural religious counterparts."[345] In philosophical terms, drug and natural mystical experiences can be phenomenologically (experientially) indistinguishable.

The most dramatic experiment affirming this was the "Harvard Good Friday study," also known as "the miracle of Marsh Chapel." In this study, divinity students and professors were placed in a highly supportive setting—Harvard University's Marsh Chapel during a Good Friday service—and given either the psychedelic psilocybin or a placebo. Several psilocybin subjects reported "mystical experiences" that researchers could not distinguish from those of mystics throughout the centuries.[73]

Perhaps the people best equipped to decide whether drug and contemplatively induced mystical experiences might be the same are those who have had both. Such people are obviously few and far between. However, several spiritual teachers and scholars concluded from their personal experience that they can be identical.[388, 396]

3) The third argument—that mystical rapture is a gift from God that could never be brought under human control—will only seem plausible to people who hold very specific theological beliefs. It would hardly be regarded as valid by religions such as Buddhism, for example, that do not believe in an all-powerful creator god. Nor, presumably, would it appeal to those theists who believe more in the power of good works than of grace.

4) The complaint that drug experiences are too easy to be genuine is readily understandable. After all, it hardly seems fair that a contemplative should labor for decades for a sip of what the drug user may effortlessly swim in for hours. However, unfair or not, if the states are experientially identical, then the fact that they are due to different causes may be irrelevant. Technically, this is called "the principle of causal indifference."[349] Simply stated, this means that subjectively identical experiences can be produced by multiple causes.

5) The final argument against the equivalence of drug and natural mystical states is that they can have different long-term effects. Specifically, drug experiences may result in beneficial transformations of personality and behavior that are less enduring. Once again Huston Smith put the case eloquently: "Drugs appear to induce religious experiences: it is less evident that they can produce religious lives."[345]

Theoretical Understandings

So it seems that drug and natural mystical experiences can be subjectively similar or even identical, yet still differ in their aftereffects. But still the debate continues over whether psychedelically induced mystical experiences are "really genuine."

One reason the debate continues unabated is that there has been no theory of mystical states that could resolve it. What is needed is a theory accounting for the induction of similar or identical states by such different means as LSD and meditation, followed by possible different aftereffects.

Charles Tart's systems model of consciousness is helpful here.[360] Tart suggests that any one state of consciousness is the result of the function and interaction of many psychological and neural processes, such as perception, attention, emotions, and identity. If any one process is changed sufficiently, it may shift the entire mind-brain system and state of consciousness. For example, a yogi might focus unwaveringly on the breath, a Christian contemplative might cultivate the love of God, or a Sufi might recite the name of Allah (*dhikr*).[392] Yet despite their different practices, all might eventually be rewarded with mystical experiences, though not necessarily identical ones.[z]

A specific altered state may be reached in several ways via altering different processes. For example, states of calm may be reached by reducing muscle tension, visualizing restful scenery, repeating a pacifying thought, focusing attention on the breath, or taking a tranquilizer. In each case the brain-mind process used is different, but the resulting state is similar, a convergence that systems theorists call "equifinality."

A similar phenomenon may occur with mystical states. Different techniques might affect different brain-mind processes, yet still result in a similar ASC. A contemplative might finally taste the bliss of mystical unity only after years of cultivating qualities such as concentration, love, and compassion. Yet a psychedelic might affect chemical and neural processes so powerfully as to temporarily induce a similar state.

So Tart's theory of consciousness may provide an explanation for the finding that "chemical mysticism" and natural mysticism can be experientially identical. But what of the claim for differing long-term effects? This claim is also compatible with the theory. But first we need to consider whether the claim that the long-term effects of chemical mysticism are less beneficial and enduring is actually true.

Long-Term Effects

Contrary to common arguments, psychedelic mysticism *can* sometimes have an enduring impact. For example, Huston Smith[348] described just such an impact on himself, as did the psychologist Frances Vaughan,[379] while Sherana Harriette Frances[101] portrayed hers in a series of exquisite drawings. Research studies also suggest possible long-term benefits. Significant numbers of Buddhist retreatants were drawn to spiritual practice following the use of psychedelics.[357] Likewise, the Harvard Good Friday subjects, when interviewed more than twenty years later, reported that their psilocybin experience had contributed to their spiritual lives.[73]

But even if we were to assume that the drugs have relatively little long-term benefit, is this so surprising? Or is it so different from other powerful experiences? After all, the stabilization of transient experiences and insights into enduring change is one of the great challenges facing all transformative disciplines. Psychoanalysts say "insight is not enough," while clinical psychologists speak of breakthroughs, regressions, and the "problem of generalization," i.e., the problem of getting insights on the couch to generalize to daily life. Likewise, learning theorists describe "spontaneous recovery," whereby newly learned behavior fades and old patterns recover.[229] It is true that powerful experiences can *sometimes* induce dramatic, enduring "quantum change."[242] Yet, most people suffer from "false hope syndrome" and underestimate just how hard it is to change ingrained habits.[289]

The same is true of religious disciplines. Profound experiences can *sometimes* effect enduring changes, but all too often these fade unless stabilized by further practice, as Phillip Kapleau made clear for Zen:

> Even the Buddha continued to sit. Without *joriki*, the particular power developed through *zazen* [seated meditation], the vision of oneness attained in enlightenment in time becomes clouded and eventually fades into a pleasant memory instead of remaining an omnipresent reality shaping our daily life. To be able to live in accordance with what the mind's eye has revealed through *satori* requires, like the purification of character and the development of personality, a ripening period of *zazen*.[348]

A single spiritual experience is certainly no guarantee of a spiritual life or an ethical lifestyle.[21, 266] However, long-term practice and multiple experiences can have a cumulative impact.[380, 392] Major enduring change usually requires long-term practice.[211, 222]

So the limited long-term effects of psychedelic mystical experiences are far from unique. Rather, they reflect one of the central problems of psychological and spiritual growth: the "problem of stabilization."[394]

But let's assume the critics' position. Let's assume for the moment that chemical mysticism is less transformative than contemplative mysticism, as well it might be. Why might this be so?

Both psychological and social factors may be involved. Psychedelic users may have dramatic experiences, perhaps the most dramatic of their entire life. However, a single experience, no matter how powerful, may be insufficient to permanently overcome mental and neural habits conditioned for decades to mundane modes of functioning. A shaman or contemplative, on the other hand, may spend decades deliberately working to retrain habits along more spiritual lines. Thus, when the breakthrough finally occurs, it visits a mind already prepared for it. The shaman probably has a belief system to make sense of the experience, a tradition that values it, a discipline to cultivate it, a social group to support it, and an ethic to guide it. As Louis Pasteur said, "Chance favors the prepared mind." The contemplative's mind may be prepared, but there is no guarantee that a drug user's is.

Therefore, different long-term effects of chemical and contemplative experiences could occur, even if the original experiences are identical. Consequently, none of the five common arguments against psychedelic experiences being genuinely mystical seem to hold.

CONCLUSION

In summary, it seems that some drugs can induce genuine mystical experiences in some people on some occasions. However, they may be more likely to do so, and more likely to produce enduring benefits, when used as part of a long-term spiritual practice. This is exactly how shamans use psychedelics, and therefore it is not surprising that many shamans value them as aids to spiritual life and healing work.[aa]

CHAPTER 27

Divination and Diagnosis

Humans respond not to events but to their meanings and can read into any event an endless variety of meanings.

—*Jerome Frank* [103]

The world and life are mysterious. And yet we must choose and act in the face of this inevitable mystery. This is our existential dilemma. What to do?

One obvious solution is to ask those who know. Throughout most of history these have been the gods and spirits or those who could divine their intentions.

Not surprisingly, diviners or oracles have been part of every culture, including our own. Also not surprisingly, the questions people ask have been similar across cultures. [59, 60] People ask about the cause and cure of suffering, the ways to health and happiness, and about relationships and religion.

Shamans were among our earliest diviners, and their many roles as diagnosticians, counselors, and healers demanded many methods. Most often they rely on their spiritual helpers or spiritual vision. [154] Helping spirits may be consulted during a journey or, less commonly, by object divination such as with a randomly selected stone or bone. Spirit vision may be employed to discover spirit intrusions. Other strategies for diagnosis and treatment foreshadow contemporary psychological techniques, and intriguing examples include group confession and the world's first projective test assessing muscle tension.

THE WORLD'S FIRST PROJECTIVE TEST

Projection makes perception. The world you see is what you gave it, nothing more than that….it is the witness to your state of mind, the outside picture of an inward condition. As man thinketh, so does he perceive.

—A Course in Miracles[10]

The shaman's projective test is remarkably similar to clinical psychology's Rorschach test. Both tests make use of the mind's tendency to structure ambiguous scenes into personally meaningful images that symbolize underlying motives and emotions.

The shamanic projective test is deceptively simple. The patient with a question or problem chooses a rock and brings it to the shaman. The shaman then instructs him to hold his question in mind, to view each side of the rock, and report the images seen there. When complete, the patient is asked to describe how each image speaks to his question or concern.[150] The beauty of this technique lies in its simplicity and its ability to reveal unconscious forces at work in the patient's mind.

THE HEAD LIFTING TEST

In a second technique, an Eskimo shaman addresses a series of questions to a patient while lifting the patient's head. Changes in the apparent weight of the head are taken to indicate positive or negative responses. Rasmussen described the procedure as follows:

> The one who is to consult the spirits, lays a person down on the floor, or on the sleeping place, face upwards, the operator's waist belt being often fastened around the subject's head. Various questions are now put to the qila'na: the person through whose head the spirits are to answer. While asking the questions, the operator endeavors to raise the person's head by means of the belt, calling upon the spirit, which is supposed to enter the scene immediately below the body of the qila'na. When the latter's head grows heavy, so heavy that the operator, despite all his efforts, cannot move it in the slightest degree, this means that the spirits are present and answer in the affirmative. If, on the other hand, the head is normal and easily moved, this constitutes a negative answer to the question put….I once wrote down the proceedings in such a case….The object was to ascertain the cause of a particular illness….
>
> "is the illness due to forbidden food?"

The head grows lighter, the shaman lifts it with ease, and the listener answers: "*a'k'agoq*": "No!"

"*isarajannik?*": "Is the illness due to forbidden work?"

The spirit answers:

"Yes!"....

Should the spirit answer yes, then it remains to investigate further, with constant pulls at the line, what breach of taboo has taken place and under what circumstances. So the questioning goes on, letting the spirit answer all the time, until the presumable cause of the sickness has been ascertained.[299]

Changes in the apparent weight of the head presumably reflect variations in muscle tension. Both conscious and unconscious concerns affect muscle tension, and the test therefore allows the patient to communicate and confess these concerns in spite of conscious resistance. Confession may be good for the soul, but it can also be good for the body, especially where psychosomatic illness is involved.

GROUP CONFESSION

Shamans also use group confession. An interesting example occurs after the Eskimo shaman has placated the sea spirit Takánakapsâluk. Having interceded with her on behalf of the tribe, the shaman journeys back from the bottom of the sea to be greeted by cries for information about the success or failure of the journey. But the shaman does not give the information. Rather he hedges, saying, "Words will arise." Then he waits, knowing what will happen. Rasmussen described the scene as follows:

then all in the house must confess any breaches of taboo they have committed.

"It is my fault, perhaps," they cry, all at once, women and men together, in fear of famine and starvation, and all begin telling of the wrong things they have done. All the names of those in the house are mentioned, and all must confess, and thus much comes to light which no one had ever dreamed of; every one learns his neighbors' secrets. But despite all the sins confessed, the shaman may go on talking as one who is unhappy at having made a mistake, and again and again breaks out into such expressions as this:

"I seek my grounds in things which have not happened; I speak as one who knows nothing."

There are still secrets barring the way for full solution of the trouble, and so the women in the house begin to go through all the names, one after another; nearly all women's names; for it was always their breaches of taboo which were most danger-ous. Now and again when a name is mentioned, the shaman exclaims in relief:

"*taina, taina!*"....Thus at last the cause of Takánakapsâluk's anger is explained, and all are filled with joy at having escaped disaster. They are now assured that there will be abundance of game on the following day. And in the end, there may be almost a feeling of thankfulness towards the delinquent. This then was what took place when shamans went down and propitiated the great Spirit of the Sea.[299]

Many elements of contemporary group therapy are evident here. The group as a whole collaborates on a project of common concern. Members confront their shortcomings, and this leads to confession and catharsis. The sharing of intimate secrets creates a sense of trust and group cohesion. The result is a recognition of what psychologists call "universality" as members discover that they are not the only sinners and that their failures are a universal part of the human condition. The resulting sense of relief and closeness can be healing for all concerned. Of course, to the shaman these psychological benefits are minor compared to the importance of identifying breeches of taboo in order to appease the great sea spirit. However, the procedure could clearly be therapeutic for individuals and socially cohesive for the tribe, and in Native American traditions such healing groups are called "medicine wheels."

CONTEMPORARY DIVINERS

It is intriguing to compare these methods and their likely success with contemporary ap-proaches. While some shamanic divination methods were doubtless successful, others were probably ineffective. But so are many recent ones. For example, phrenology was once wildly popular; palmistry remains so. Even some highly respected and lucrative professions do little better. A book aptly titled *The Fortune Sellers: The Big Business of Buying and Sell-ing Predictions*[334] reviews the success rates of several types of forecasting. Its conclusion? Predictions in economics, investing, futurology, technology assessment, and organizational planning do about as well as a coin toss (which was an early form of divination). Political pundits and television "experts" fare no better. In fact they are no more successful at predicting the future than ordinary mortals like us, although they are far better paid.[364] In fact, the better known the expert, the less accurate their political predictions are likely to be.

As yet we have no studies of shamanic diagnostic accuracy. They may not fare as well as modern physicians with their high-tech tools, but they likely do better than some of our most famous forecasters.

CHAPTER 28

How Do They Heal?

I don't know what you learned from books, but the most important thing I learned from my grandfathers was that there is a part of the mind that we really don't know about and it is that part that is most important in whether we become sick or remain well.

—*Thomas Large Whiskers, Navaho Medicine Man*

Shamans are healers. As Sandra Harner summarized: "Oral reports, ethnographic studies, travelers' records, comparative religion studies, and living experience among some indigenous peoples today testify that, worldwide, the shaman works with spirits to cure."[156]

But how do they cure? While the spiritual domain is paramount, as the world's most enduring general practitioners they also draw from the gamut of physical, social, and psychological therapies. Much of their effectiveness may reflect social and psychological factors since, like many healers, they use suggestions and support, skillful psychotherapy techniques, and a variety of rituals, all of which can elicit psychosomatic and placebo effects.

Shamans have often been called our first psychotherapists, which is not surprising, considering the many activities encompassed by the definition:

Psychotherapy is a planned, emotionally charged, confiding interaction between a trained, socially sanctioned healer and a sufferer. During this interaction the healer seeks to relieve the sufferer's distress and disability through symbolic communications, primarily words but also sometimes bodily activities. The healer may or may not involve the patient's relatives and others in the healing rituals. Psychotherapy also often includes helping the patient to accept and endure suffering as an inevitable aspect of life that can be used as an opportunity for personal growth....All psychotherapeutic methods are elaborations and variations of age-old procedures of psychological healing.[104]

BENEFITS OF PSYCHOLOGICAL HEALING

Psychological treatments are surprisingly helpful in a wide array of illnesses for several reasons. First, many patients who complain of physical ills are suffering from psychological or psychosomatic problems. In fact, approximately half the visits to Western general practitioners are motivated by psychological factors. Likewise, a study of native healers in Taiwan found that 90 percent of their patients suffered from psychological disorders and almost half of their physical complaints were traced to psychosomatic causes.[194] This finding is consistent with the shamanic belief that much healing involves treating "soul loss," a condition of being dispirited or disheartened.

Of course the process can also work in the opposite (somatopsychic) direction. Physical illness can produce disabling anxiety or depression that, in turn, may exacerbate the physical symptoms, thus setting up a vicious cycle that psychological help can break.

Social and psychological interventions may be treatments of choice for existential anxiety and guilt, which in tribal cultures can be overwhelming. In such societies "the strain for survival may be intense, the structure of the society may be intricate and frustrating and the fear of the unknown may be terrifying."[311] Life is hedged in by countless taboos, and the least infringement may mean sickness, suffering, and death. No wonder shamans devised an array of rituals and techniques to allay these threats, and no wonder psychological factors play such a major role.

INVITING HEALING:
THE NATURE AND EFFECTS OF RITUALS

Ritual, through its formal properties, can traditionalize or sacrilize anything....Rituals always provide meaning.

—Encyclopedia of Cultural Anthropology[88]

Much shamanic healing occurs within the context of ritual, which is defined as "formal, patterned, and stereotyped public performances."[86] Ritual is part of every society, and just as habit is the flywheel of psychological stability, so ritual is the flywheel of social stability.

Rituals embody and express a people's worldview: their "big picture" understanding of reality. Healing rituals focus on expressing beliefs about the cause and cure of illness.

Healing rituals have both technical and symbolic components. The technical element can be a straightforward intervention such as bone setting or massage, but even a simple technique is often embedded in a symbolic context. The symbolic component seeks to effect change—in the patient, the world, or the spiritual realm—via manipulation of symbols: objects that represent important forces or beings. Both technical and symbolic components can be therapeutic.

Anthropologists often divide the effects of rituals into *manifest* and *latent*. *Manifest* effects are obvious to both participants and observers. However, *latent* effects are subtle, secondary, and may be unsought or even unrecognized by participants. Examples of latent effects of rituals might include social stability and the affirmation of power structures.

An integral approach is helpful in recognizing the many effects of ritual. Ken Wilber's integral theory emphasizes the importance of four domains of reality: collective culture, objective society, individual subjective experience, and individual objective phenomena.[410]

In the collective culture, rituals evoke *communitas:* a sense of shared concern, contribution, and humanity. Importantly, psychotherapy studies find that cohesion is a crucial factor in determining the healing power of groups.

In the objective world of society, rituals can repair relationships, solidify and stabilize social structures, and affirm or challenge authority. In fact, in contemporary anthropology, ritual is increasingly seen as "a symbolic device integral to the communication and construction of power....ritual and ritual symbols are increasingly understood as a complex battleground in the struggle for hegemony..."[88]

Healing rituals transform the inner world of participants, especially of patients. Rituals change experience and expectations, nourish a sense of relationship and support, and encourage reconciliation with the spirits and the sacred. These subjective experiences mediate and evoke objective effects on the body and its disease.

Rituals can exert remarkably wide-ranging effects on the body via "symbolic penetration."[208] Because of their highly charged meaning, the symbolic elements that are used in rituals penetrate into the mind-body system and elicit powerful psychological responses. These in turn can cause a cascade of corresponding biological responses throughout the body. These responses extend across organ systems such as the brain, endocrines, and autonomic nervous system, and across biological levels from organs to physiology to biochemistry and even down to gene expression (the ways in which genes create new cellular building blocks).

The emerging field of *psychosocial genomics* explores how "psychotherapy and related cultural processes and rituals (such as meditation, prayer, and the deeply meaningful humanistic experiences of art, drama, dance, music, poetry, etc.) can modulate alternative gene expression to facilitate health, rehabilitation, and healing."[314] For example, the amount and even type of neurotransmitter enzymes can be thrown out of balance by stress and can presumably be brought back into healthy homeostasis by stress-relieving rituals.[314] The Nobel Laureate Eric Kandel summarized the new understanding:

> Simply stated, the regulation of gene expression by social factors makes all bodily functions, including all functions of the brain, susceptible to social influences.[190]

Because its effects penetrate so widely, an effective healing ritual at its best is simultaneously:

- *Cultural Therapy:* Healing and cohering culture and creating *communitas*
- *Sociotherapy:* Repairing relationships, harmonizing social structures, and stabilizing society
- *Psychosomatic Therapy*: Diminishing disease and its complications
- *Gene Therapy*: Modulation of gene expression
- *Psychotherapy*: Healing the subjective dis-ease of illness
- *Spiritual Therapy*: Relieving a sense of alienation and estrangement from the universe, creating a sense of connection and alignment with the sacred, and fostering a transpersonal/transegoic sense of identity.

This spiritual element, so often overlooked in contemporary medicine, is central to shamanism and probably crucial to thoroughgoing healing. As Abraham Maslow put it: "Without the transcendent and the transpersonal, we get sick, violent, and nihilistic, or else hopeless and apathetic."[225]

At their best, shamanic rituals probably induce this full panoply of healing responses, and they do so through a rich array of technical and symbolic methods.

SHAMANIC RITUALS AND TECHNIQUES

The healing ritual must be preceded by careful preparation, and both preparation and ritual are steeped in faith-inspiring symbolism. In Western medicine, patients are usually treated in privacy, whereas shamans often assemble the family and even the whole tribe. The patient thereby becomes the center of attention and receives considerable community support. Participants may be required to confess their breaches of taboo, resulting in a shared healing catharsis and *communitas*.

Music and song may be central. The recognition that music can heal is an ancient one. In Greece, both Plato and Aristotle ascribed curative power to certain melodies, while Apollo was the god of both medicine and music. "With song, one can open the gates of heaven," claimed a Jewish Hassidic teacher.[162]

Today, music therapy is a valued healing aid, while there has been both enormous excitement and nonsense spawned by research suggesting that music can improve intellectual function. This "Mozart effect," so called because Mozart's music was played in the original research, has been used to sell all kinds of musical snake oil. However, while music can undoubtedly transform mood, enhance well-being, and induce altered states, its cognitive benefits seem limited and brief.[49] In short, despite the breathless media headlines, hold off on buying a new stereo system for your fetal Einstein.

In Latin America, either shaman or patient or both may take yage to obtain a spirit vision that reveals the cause of illness. Once recognized, the shaman corrects the problem by, for example, intervening with troublesome spirits, retrieving the patient's soul, or exorcism to remove spiritual intrusions.

Patients may also have to pay the shaman, make offerings to the spirits, and adhere to rigid rituals, restricting diets, and meticulous taboos. This may increase the effectiveness of treatment, or at least patients' belief in its effectiveness, since due to expectation and cognitive dissonance, the more people pay for something the more they are likely to value it.

Some of these healing rituals are both arduous and time-consuming, and sessions can last through the night. Clearly a shaman who uses these techniques gives enormous time and attention and can see very few patients. The result is that "the more popular a shaman becomes, the less time he is able to devote to any one patient. This results in the paradoxical situation that the elaborate healing rituals described in loving detail by social anthropologists are carried out by those healers who have very few patients."[341]

ASCs in Patients

Shamans enter altered states, and their patients may do likewise[418] in at least three ways: through ritual, music, and psychedelics. Healing suggestions given during their ASC could produce hypnosis, which can have considerable therapeutic benefit.

The neurological basis of hypnosis is only now coming to light. Since similar neural mechanisms may underlie the placebo effect and other therapeutic processes crucial to shamanism, it is worth examining them.

Information first flows in from our sense organs to primary sensory centers in the brain. There it is processed and then forwarded to higher brain centers in a "feedforward" flow of information. At the same time, "feedback" information flows downward from higher centers to filter, modulate, and interpret this data.

The big surprise has been the sheer amount of feedback. There are some ten times as many neural fibers devoted to feedback (running from top to bottom) as feedforward,[26] which means that a remarkable portion of our experience is based on what neuroscientists call "top down processing." This explains why expectations, beliefs, and conditioning are so potent in shaping our experience and why hypnotic and placebo effects can be so far-reaching. Our reality owes as much to creation as reception, and believing that we simply see things the way they really are is exactly what philosophers call it: "naïve realism."

THE PLACEBO EFFECT

A cheerful heart is good medicine, but a crushed spirit dries up the bones.
—Proverbs 17:22

The word *placebo* comes from the Latin meaning "I shall please." It refers to

> a poorly understood process in which psychological factors such as belief and expectation trigger a healing response that can be as powerful as any conventional therapy—be it drugs, surgery or psychotherapy—for a wide range of medical and psychological problems.[170]

Consider, for example, the humble wart. It can be dissolved by hypnosis, incantations, burying a rag at the crossroads under a full moon, in fact by almost any treatment, provided only that patients believe it will work. Yet no one understands how mind and body produce this minor miracle. Many people assume that since the placebo effect relies on something so ethereal as mere belief it must be a weak effect, but consider the following:

> In the 1950s a man dying of advanced cancer was given a highly publicized experimental drug called krebiozen. After a single dose, his huge cancers "melted like snowballs on a hot stove" and he was able to resume normal activities.
>
> Then studies of krebiozen showed it to be ineffective. When the patient learned this, his cancer began spreading again. At this stage his doctor tried an experiment. He announced that there was now a new "improved" krebiozen and proceeded to give it to his patient. Once again the man's tumors shrunk. Yet the doctor had given him only water.[196]

Clearly, placebo effects can be powerful, even lifesaving. They are also widespread, and approximately one-third of people treated with completely inactive placebos improve.[170] Even an effective drug may gain part of its impact from the patients' and doctors' expectations of cure. Indeed, the placebo effect has probably been a major factor in most therapies through human history.

> In the past, various useless agents were believed to be effective against disease: lizard's blood, crushed spiders, putrid meat, crocodile dung, bear fat, fox lungs, eunuch fat, and moss from the skull of a hanged criminal. Likewise, cupping, blistering, plastering and leaching had their day. When *both* physician and patient believed in them, these remedies could indeed have been helpful some of the time.[23]

But beliefs can also be negative and produce negative (*nocebo*) effects, including sickness and death. For example, a common complication of chemotherapy is hair loss, and in one study 31 percent of cancer patients who received only a placebo did in fact lose some of their hair.[95] The nocebo effect is probably the basis for so-called voodoo sickness or voodoo death, which can occur when tribal people are hexed.

Urban dwellers are also at risk. Believers in Chinese astrology, but not disbelievers, die significantly earlier if they contract a disease that their astrological chart considers ill-fated.[286] Expectation is so powerful that believing negative astrological health predictions can actually hasten death.

How the placebo works its remarkable effects is unclear. What is clear is that the process is, as the physician Lewis Thomas put it, "absolutely astonishing." The intelligence directing such a healing process must combine the skills of a world-class cell biologist, immunologist, surgeon, and executive officer. This, says Thomas, points to "a kind of superintelligence that exists in each of us, infinitely smarter and possessed of technical know-how far beyond our present understanding."[367]

Certainly expectations and beliefs are key forces in the placebo response. Beliefs can harm or heal, and native healers seem well aware of this. A Navaho medicine man made the point about as succinctly as anyone could: "If the patient really has confidence in me, then he gets cured. If he has no confidence, then that is his problem."[319]

The patient's confidence is affected by the entire healing context. The personality, status, and beliefs of the therapist as well as the nature of the ritual and audience all play a role. Skillful healers have long recognized this and sought to bolster what Jerome Frank calls "the healing power of expectant faith" through whatever means they could. In light of this, the tricks and sleight of hand so widely used by shamans to impress their patients may actually enhance expectant faith and healing. Clearly the placebo effect has been a powerful healing force throughout history, and shamans were among the first to harness it.

HOW SUCCESSFUL ARE THEY?

Shamans have not always been the world's most humble healers, and some have claimed to be virtually infallible. On the other hand, more modest practitioners see themselves as instruments of the spirits to whom true credit is due.[146]

Just how successful are they? The short answer is "we don't really know." We have virtually no research data, and the only systematic studies have been done not on patients of tribal shamans but on Westerners doing shamanic journeys. These neoshamans reported feeling better after their journeys[156, 204] and had elevated levels of salivary immunoglobulin A (a measure of immune function).[155] However, the studies are preliminary, and the results are difficult to extrapolate to tribal patients. Therefore, the best we can do at present to assess tribal healing is to make estimates drawn from general principles.

One principle we need to keep in mind is the distinction between helping subjective illness and curing objective disease. This distinction is embedded in the medical aspiration "to cure sometimes, but to help always."

There is no question that many patients feel helped. There are ample reports of this, and shamans have managed to stay in business longer than any other healing institution.

Of course, none of these facts prove cure. For hundreds of years, some of both Western and Oriental medicine's most bizarre treatments—such as bloodletting or mercury ingestion—killed thousands of grateful patients.

However, there are several shamanic practices that should produce considerable healing and some cures. These include careful selection of cases, skillful use of social and psychological interventions, hypnosis, the placebo effect, and the harmlessness of interventions.

Shamans try desperately to avoid taking hopeless cases. After all, their livelihood and even their lives depend on success, and in some cultures the shaman who loses a patient may also lose his life.[311] Treating only patients likely to recover certainly bolsters one's success rate.

Importantly, shamanic interventions are relatively harmless. This is no small claim. One of Western medicine's golden rules is "first do no harm." However, this rule was unwittingly broken for centuries by physicians whose well-intended but deadly nostrums sometimes did considerable harm. Even today, side effects from effective drugs kill many thousands of people worldwide, even when used carefully and cautiously. There are no free therapeutic lunches. By comparison, the low-tech and highly spiritual treatments of shamans seem most benign.

Skillful use of the placebo effect would also bolster success rates. Many rituals seem admirably designed to elicit it, since the effect is most likely when therapies are elaborate, time-consuming, expensive, fashionable, or esoteric.[170]

What types of success rates would general principles such as these lead us to predict? Of course this will vary with the disorder being treated. For psychological problems, such as mild anxiety or depression that respond well to psychological interventions and social support, success rates might approach those of contemporary psychotherapies. For other disorders that, according to Western theories, require drugs or surgery, we would expect success rates that approximate placebo rates.

Of course these claims would make little sense to shamans. For them, the pains their patients suffer are primarily spiritual in origin and consequently require spiritual responses. Once again we face a paradigm clash. For the questions of how, and how well, shamanic healing works will be answered very differently by shamans and Western physicians, whose spiritual and mechanistic worldviews are largely meaningless to each other.

The shaman's worldview is far from meaningless to patients who share it. It is this sharing that constitutes a so-called "shared healing myth" or "shared healing story" within which therapy can take place. Because of this shared healing myth, shamans have long been a source of hope and help for problems ranging from physical illness to spiritual crises. For the tribe, the shaman is a guide, a healer, a source of social cohesion, and a keeper of myths. In a world of vast incomprehensible forces, the shaman offers hope that these forces might be mastered and that humans need not be helpless victims of an uncaring universe, but that illness might be healed, guilt assuaged, spirits mollified, and even death robbed of some of its sting. What an extraordinary symbol of hope the shaman must have been for thousands of years.

CHAPTER 29

Healing the Healer:
How Do They Heal Themselves?

Physician, heal thyself.
—*The Bible*

Healing is not a one-way street. What heals the patient can also heal the therapist. Even the desire to help another may benefit both people. This mutual healing may be especially important for those shamans who undergo an initiation crisis. Some of these were the original "wounded healers," healers who had themselves once suffered and were therefore enabled to relieve the suffering of others.

Shamans have often suffered greatly. Their pain may burst upon them in the initiation crisis or be sought deliberately through isolation and asceticism. Learning to shamanize and help others may rescue them from their initial crises. In other cases, "The shaman must first cure himself and his initiatory sickness and only afterwards can cure the other members of the community."[168] If he gives up his calling, he may relapse, and according to the Chuckchee, "While the shaman is in possession of the inspiration, he must practice, and cannot hide his power. Otherwise it will manifest itself in the form of bloody sweat or in a fit of madness similar to epilepsy."[29]

How does self-healing occur? The traditional explanation is through the power and grace of the spirits. However, psychological and cultural processes doubtless play their parts, and these processes can be viewed, according to one's belief system, as either complementing the spiritual factors, mediating them, or accounting for them.

What social and psychological factors contribute to the dramatic reversal from patient to physician and from psychologically disturbed to psychotherapist? Major factors include reinterpretation of their symptoms, the shamanic journey and social role, altered states of consciousness, and the benefits of altruism and service.

REINTERPRETING SYMPTOMS OF THE INITIATION CRISIS

The initiation crisis can begin as a dramatic, even life-shattering disturbance. In our own culture, the patient would likely be seen, and see himself, as sick and disturbed.

In tribal cultures similar symptoms may be viewed very differently. The "patient" would be regarded as a shaman-to-be and the symptoms seen not as a pathology but as a calling, not as an emergency to be suppressed but as an emergence to be guided. This is what Western psychologists call *reattribution* or *reframing*, a powerful technique by which symptoms are reinterpreted from a more healthful perspective. This encourages the patient to value and work with the symptoms as part of an important developmental learning process and as a doorway to a new and valued social role.

THE SHAMAN'S WORK AND ROLE

To love and to work—these were the hallmarks of psychological health for Sigmund Freud. Of shamans' ability to love we know little, but of their ability to do meaningful work we are certain. The shaman's work is crucial for the tribe and likely confers significant status and self-esteem, both of which foster physical and psychological health. Having been healed oneself may also inspire confidence in potential for healing others.

ALTERED STATES OF CONSCIOUSNESS

A defining characteristic of shamans is their ability to enter ASCs, some of which are both psychologically and psychosomatically healing. ASCs can easily slip into self-hypnosis, which can be a powerful aid to healing. Since shamans enter altered states expecting to receive spiritual help, these expectations might produce significant healing, especially when melded with hypnosis. In addition, the music of many rituals could benefit both shamans and their patients.

It has been suggested that the ability to enter hypnotic states was genetically selected, and this played a role in the evolution of shamanism and other religious traditions.[231] However, there are specific problems with this suggestion[137] and general problems with any theory that tries to explain (away) religion purely in terms of underlying psychological or neural mechanisms.[411]

THE SHAMANIC JOURNEY

Experiences during soul flight may also be healing. These experiences may include ecstatic love and compassion,[154] but even terrifying confrontations can be beneficial. Visions of death and destruction may arise, together with malevolent spirits and supernatural forces. Yet the shaman's task is not to quail, but to overcome all that stands in the way of bringing information and healing to the community. Shamans must confront, not flee, whatever horrors arise.

Confronting fears can extinguish them. In "implosive therapy," patients create and confront images of whatever they fear until they become less reactive. The result is a desensitization in which the images, as well as the feared objects or people that the images symbolize, lose their fearful impact.

The similarities of this process to the shamanic journey are obvious. Shamans themselves recognize this desensitizing process and say that "you may see dead persons walking towards you, and you will hear their bones rattle. If you hear and see these things without fear, you will never be frightened of anything."[85]

Spontaneous fearful images can symbolize what Jungians call the *shadow*, those aspects of self and psyche that have been disowned and repressed because we judge them as bad and fearful. Yet when these shadow aspects of ourselves are recognized and accepted, they lose their compulsive terror. Jungians regard a confrontation with the shadow as essential maturation and individuation: the process of becoming a unique, self-actualized individual. Jung himself regarded shamanic imagery as an indication that shamans go through a process of individuation.[260] Identification with spirits or power animals may also play a role.

As yet we have almost no research studies of the effects of journeying on shamans. However, pilot studies of neoshamanic practitioners showed improvements on some measures of the sense of well-being, as well as increased levels of salivary immunoglobulin A (a measure of immune function).[155, 156, 204]

ALTRUISM AND SERVICE

All that one gives to others one gives to one's self.
If this truth is understood, who will not give to others?
—*Ramana Maharshi*[297]

Shamans serve their communities, and such service is the final stage of the hero's journey. Michael Harner points out that shamanism, at its best,

> goes far beyond a self-concerned transcendence of ordinary reality. It is transcendence for a broader purpose, the helping of humankind. The enlightenment of shamanism is the ability to light up what others perceive as darkness and thereby to *see* and to journey on behalf of...humanity.[146]

Of course shamans are not alone in this. Every one of the great religions regards service as a crucial practice and culmination of spiritual life. The true person "never deserts benevolence," claimed Confucius,[207] while the Third Zen Patriarch exclaimed that "for the unified mind in accord with the Way all self-centered striving ceases."[329]

Modern psychology agrees and sees altruism and service as hallmarks of health and maturity.[398] According to Abraham Maslow, "Self-actualizing people are, without one single exception, involved in a cause outside their own skin."[226] Greater psychological health results in greater service.[397] Which is why the psychologist Rollo May claimed that "finding the center of strength within ourselves is in the long run the best contribution we can make to our fellow men."[230]

What has been recently recognized is that the reverse also holds true. Not only does health foster service, but service fosters health. Those who assist others may gain both psychological and physical benefits including a "helper's high," an afterglow of well-being, satisfaction, and self-esteem.

A helper's high may also translate into physical benefits. It may relieve high blood pressure and other stress-related conditions and enhance immune system function. Helping others and helping oneself can fuse into a single process, and as Abraham Maslow wrote: "The best way to become a better 'helper' is to become a better person. But one necessary aspect of becoming a better person is *via* helping other people. So I must and can do both simultaneously."[226]

This is remarkably similar to Michael Harner's observation that "in shamanism there is ultimately no distinction between helping others and helping yourself. By helping others shamanically, one becomes more powerful, self-fulfilled and joyous."[146] Shamans may therefore have been among the earliest humans to discover the truth of Albert Schweitzer's statement:

I don't know what your destiny will be, but one thing I do know:
The only ones among you who will be really happy
are those who will have sought and found how to serve.

CHAPTER 30

Shamans and Psi: What Is the Evidence?

Paranormal data have largely been silently passed over in serious anthropological works....This is deplorable, for whether you accept their reality or not they should be discussed and evaluated.
Ake Hultkrantz

Shamans believe that the primary healing forces they invoke are spiritual. There are two very different and very controversial Western views of this belief. Traditionally, the most common interpretation was to see the belief as a classic example of "primitive" or "magical" thinking. The other interpretation is that shamanic healing reflects, in part, the operation of paranormal, psychic abilities.

THE DEBATE

There are many books on how to win friends and influence people, but surprisingly few on how to make enemies and alienate people. Here is a suggestion to fill the gap. Walk into a group of scientists and announce that you believe in parapsychology.

Three things will quickly become clear. First, most scientists, like most of the public, hold very strong opinions on the topic. Second, despite these strong opinions, they know very little about the relevant research. Third, parapsychology is, to put it mildly, a very controversial and highly charged topic.

Supporters claim that "a vast parapsychological literature exists on a host of rigorous experiments,"[217] while skeptics retort that "not a single individual has been found who can demonstrate ESP to the satisfaction of independent investigators."[143] Proponents point to controlled studies showing that humans are capable of both extrasensory perception (ESP) and of psychokinetic (PK or mind on matter) effects on objects and organisms ranging from electronic circuitry to mice.[174] Of particular relevance to shamanic healing are reports of PK effects on the growth of plants and fungi, on the activity of enzymes, the healing of mice, and the level of blood hemoglobin in humans.[291] Hard-core critics dismiss such findings as miniscule, unreplicable, or due to experimenter incompetence. Consensus is not a common thing in parapsychology.

Despite this, any investigation of shamanic healing, if it is to be intellectually honest, needs to examine whether psi (psychic ability) plays a role. For as William James warned, "There is no source of deception in the investigation of nature which can compare with a fixed belief that certain kinds of phenomena are impossible."[232]

A thorough examination of the possibility of psi in shamanism needs to cover three major areas:

- Claims for psi in other religious and healing traditions.

- Evidence (pro and con) in shamanism. This evidence includes anecdotal reports, experimental studies, and theoretical considerations.

- Experimental studies of psi, evaluating primarily its existence, and secondarily its possible nature.

PSI CLAIMS IN OTHER TRADITIONS

Most religions accept the reality of paranormal abilities such as, for example, the charisms of Catholicism, the *siddhis* of yoga, or the "adornments of the man of light" in Sufism.[250] Some religions offer explicit techniques aimed at cultivating psi, but many techniques require enormous powers of concentration.[37, 333]

However, psychic abilities are often viewed as mixed blessings. While they can supposedly be used for good, they can also seduce practitioners away from more important spiritual goals. "All power corrupts," says the old saying, and psychic power is no exception. Consequently, yoga recommends *moksha* (liberation) before *siddhi* (psychic abilities), some

Catholic saints were supposedly chastised for displaying their gifts,[250] and classical Buddhism "abhors the exhibition of occult forces."[123]

In the West some highly respected physicians and psychiatrists, including such notables as Freud, Jung, and Jerome Frank, have suggested that psi plays a role in therapy. Frank wrote:

> My own hunch, which I mention with some trepidation is that the most gifted therapists may have telepathic, clairvoyant, or other parapsychological abilities....they may, in addition, possess something that is similar to the ability to speed growth.... and that can only be termed healing power. Any researcher who attempts to study such phenomena risks his reputation as a reliable scientist, so that pursuit can be recommended only to the intrepid. The rewards, however, might be great.[104]

In short, some very notable religious and medical authorities have accepted psychic abilities. But proof by authority is one of the weakest of all proofs, so let us turn to evidence. We need to consider three kinds of evidence: anecdotal reports, theoretical considerations, and experimental studies.

Anecdotal Reports

Anecdotes of supposed psychic displays are common. For example, a French missionary claimed that he witnessed clairvoyance in a New Caladonian shaman.

> In the course of a great joyous feast he suddenly plunged himself into despair, announcing that he saw one of his illustrious relatives in Arama (a town several miles away) agonizing. A canoe was speedily sent to Arama, a three hour trip from there. The chief had just died.[20]

An example closer to home involved possible psychokinesis. Stanislav Grof reports that a well-known Huichol Indian shaman, Don Jose, was brought to the Esalen Institute in Northern California during a long severe drought when water supplies were strictly rationed.[134] Don Jose therefore volunteered to perform a rainmaking ceremony. As dawn broke the next day, the bemused participants found themselves dancing in the rain.[134]

But anecdotal reports, no matter how dramatic, are at best suggestive, never conclusive, and can be interpreted in different ways. For example, the anthropologist Bogoras observed a Chuckchee who made one of his "spirits" shout, talk, and whisper directly into my ear, and the illusion was so perfect that involuntarily I put my hand to my ear to catch the "spirit." After that he made the "spirit" enter the ground under me and talk right in between my legs, etc. All the time he is conversing with the "separate voices" the shaman beats his drum without interruption in order to prove that his force and attention are otherwise occupied.

I tried to make a phonographic record of the "separate voices" of the "spirits".... when the light was put out, the "spirits" after some "bashful" hesitation, entered in compliance with commands of the shaman, and even began to talk into the funnel of the graphophone. The records show a very marked difference between the voice of the shaman himself, which sounds from afar, and the voices of the "spirits," who seemed to be talking directly into the funnel.[29]

Bogoras was impressed but he remained convinced that these were ventriloquist tricks.

There can be no doubt, of course that shamans, during their performances, employ deceit in various forms and that they themselves are fully cognizant of the fact. "There are many liars in our calling," Scratching Woman (a Chuckchee shaman) said to me. One will lift up the skin of the sleeping room with his right toe and then assure you that it was done by spirits; another will talk into the bosom of his shirt through his sleeve, making the voice issue from a quite unusual place.[29]

However, other people are just as certain that Bogoras witnessed psychic phenomena. They agree that some shamans are tricksters, but deny that all shamans are only tricksters. From their perspective, the problem is that Bogoras "was never able to break through his scientific training and bias to admit that he had witnessed the miraculous....he explained that everything he witnessed was no doubt due to trickery, though he never offered any hint as to how the feats could have been fraudulently performed."[312]

Another clash of interpretations centers on the practice of fire walking. Long practiced by native peoples, including shamans, fire walking has recently become popular in the West, where the debate over competing explanations has become heated, so to speak. Enthusiasts such as Eliade suggest that the ability, at least among shamans, is due to special skills and training.

Skeptics explain the ability to walk on hot coals in purely physical terms. For example, coal can be very hot, yet the fact that it has a low conductivity and capacitance (heat storage capacity) means that relatively little heat is conducted to the foot. They also emphasize the brief time that the foot is actually in contact with the coal and the so-called "Leiden-frost effect," which suggests that evaporation of sweat on the soles of the feet may provide a micro-layer of insulating water and steam. In between are people like Charles Tart, who argues that physical mechanisms may be supplemented by protective effects of ASCs, which reduce inflammation and blistering.[356]

These conflicting interpretations epitomize a central problem of the debate over parapsychology. Most people decide the issue on the basis of their prior beliefs rather than on a considered evaluation of the research. Actually this problem is not unique to parapsychology; it riddles and ruins debate in many controversial scientific areas.[54] Consequently, for true believers, shamans are "psi masters….veritable early warning systems for their peoples";[404] for skeptics, psi is clearly impossible and shamans must therefore be charlatans. Opinions run very strong in this area, and the opinions are usually based on strong convictions and little evidence.

Let us therefore turn from opinions to data and ask what, if any, evidence beyond anecdotal reports we have of psychic abilities in shamans. Two types of evidence need to be examined: theoretical and experimental.

Theoretical Considerations

Theoretical support comes from a novel reinterpretation. Michael Winkelman points out that the conditions employed in tribal magic rituals—such as ASCs, visualizations, and positive expectations—parallel those supposed to facilitate psi.[415] Conceivably, trial and error led tribal peoples to adopt ritual forms that favor psi. The argument is far from conclusive, but Winkelman deserves credit for having the courage to suggest it, since, of course, he was loudly lambasted by critics.

Experimental Studies

If psi does occur in shamanic practices, it could be of two kinds: a psychokinetic (PK) effect, such as accelerated healing, or an extrasensory ability to acquire information.

There have been two reports of significant PK effects in healers that the researchers called "shamans."[115, 318] However, the healers did not fit the definition of shamanism used here, and the studies did not test PK effects on actual healing. Consequently, the question of whether shamans ever successfully use PK to enhance healing cannot be answered at this time. The best we can do is to examine research on other types of healers. If they can demonstrate PK-enhanced healing, then perhaps shamans can too. As we will see, considerable research has been done.

The other parapsychological ability that might be involved in shamanic healing is extrasensory perception (ESP or clairvoyance). Certainly shamans claim to perceive things unseen by ordinary people. Indeed, the development of spirit vision is central to shamanic training and essential for diagnostic and healing work.

Despite the importance of spirit vision to tribal healers, there have been few experiments on it. Two studies of so-called Afro-Brazilian "shamans"[114, 116] seem to have actually observed mediums who became possessed by spirits, but did not usually engage in soul flight. They were asked to identify unknown objects located at a distance, but showed no evidence of ESP, and in one study they scored significantly worse than the controls.[114, 115]

These negative findings are not surprising since the tests were artificial, and subjects performed in an ordinary state of consciousness. Mediums and shamans usually claim that their psi abilities are enhanced in ASCs, and so it remains possible that true shamans sometimes display psi abilities in ASCs.

Since shamans claim that psychic ability is greater in altered states, it is not surprising that psychedelics are used as diagnostic aids. In Latin America, yage (ayahuasca) is regarded as particularly potent, and shamans use it regularly to assist with diagnosis and journeys.[72] Several anthropologists have reported possible ayahuasca-induced psi, and the plant from which yage is produced is called "the visionary vine."[72, 350]

However, despite such tantalizing stories, no experiments have been done on shamans' psychic abilities after taking psychedelics. To learn more we must turn to research in the West. Stan Grof states that "in my own clinical experience, various phenomena suggesting extrasensory perception are relatively frequent in LSD psychotherapy, particularly in advanced sessions....Every LSD therapist with sufficient clinical experience has collected enough challenging observations to take this problem seriously."[133]

Verifying such clinical observations requires controlled laboratory studies, but the results are largely negative. While occasional subjects scored well, overall there was no significant effect.[133]

Of course, these could be false negatives. Unlike shamans, the experimental subjects were not trained in either ASCs or psi. The negative findings could also reflect the uninteresting nature of the experiment and the enormous difficulties that subjects have concentrating. Psychedelics produce a cavalcade of dramatic images and overpowering emotions, so it is hardly surprising that subjects report great difficulty and little interest in focusing on experiments that, by comparison, seem utterly trivial and boring.

There is also a danger of false positives. Psychedelic experiences can be truly mind boggling and belief shattering. Anyone who doubts this statement is invited to read Stan Grof's books, including *When the Impossible Happens*.[134] In fact, psychedelic experiences can be so powerful, their insights so compelling, and their apparent certainty so convincing, that many a novice has come away convinced of the earth-shattering importance and undeniable validity of their insights. This is one reason why so many spiritual teachers, both indigenous and Western, recommend that psychedelics be used only in the context of an ongoing spiritual discipline and that any insights should be adjudicated by teachers and further spiritual practice.[388, 396]

Not surprisingly, Westerners exploring psychedelic shamanism, yet ignoring these caveats, have come up with some wild theories. After some hefty doses of ayahuasca, Fred Alan Wolf attempted to marry shamanism and quantum physics and claimed to have found, in the words of his book's subtitle, "the scientific truth at the heart of the shamanic world."[420] Likewise, Jeremy Narby speculated that the visions of intertwined serpents found across cultures and fueled by ayahuasca reflect insights into the helical structure of DNA[252] and that the DNA is trying to communicate with us. Maybe, but then again…

Psychedelic insights can be valid and valuable, but they can also be compelling and wrong. Proceed with caution!

Let's summarize the evidence for claims that psychedelics can enhance psi. There are many anecdotal reports of psychedelic enhancement of psi abilities in shamans and clinical subjects, but this is not something that occurs regularly in laboratory situations. Whether it occurs at all, and whether it can be harnessed by shamans, remains to be proven.

PARAPSYCHOLOGY MEETS THE LABORATORY

Anecdotes can be intriguing and field studies fascinating, but the fate of parapsychology will be settled in the laboratory. Only impeccably designed, exquisitely controlled, and reliably repeated experiments will be enough to convince believers or skeptics one way or the other, if anything can. What does laboratory research tell us?

For over a century, parapsychology limped along collecting case reports and doing individual studies of such things as card guessing and influencing the throw of dice. A sizable percentage of studies reported significant findings, but virtually no skeptics were convinced. They routinely complained that the studies were unreliable, poorly designed, statistically flawed, due to experimental fraud, or outright impossible. Then came a revolutionary statistical technique.

Meta-Analysis

Meta-analysis combines and analyzes many studies simultaneously and can therefore discern trends that individual experiments easily overlook. Not surprisingly, meta-analysis is revolutionizing research in many fields, and one of them is parapsychology. What does it reveal?

Experimental Findings

Psychic abilities, if such they be, are usually divided into two major categories: "receptive" telepathy or clairvoyance and "active" psychokinesis (PK). Actually it turns out to be extremely difficult, if not impossible, to distinguish telepathy, in which information is supposedly acquired from another mind, from clairvoyance, in which acquired information is not dependent on another mind.

Studies of clairvoyance have typically used three methods: card tests, remote viewing, and Ganzfeld studies. In card tests, subjects are asked to "guess" which of a set of cards has been selected (these days usually automatically by a computer). Meta-analysis of all studies conducted from 1882 revealed odds against chance of more than a billion trillion to one.[291] Since experimental odds of one hundred to one are usually considered sufficient to establish a phenomenon, these results are obviously astronomically high.

Analyses of remote viewing have also been highly positive. In 1995, the CIA commissioned a review of all remote viewing research that had been sponsored by the U.S. government. Even the skeptic on the review team acknowledged that the results could not be dismissed as mere chance.[291]

The Ganzfeld is an experiment in which receivers first relax in a state of sensory isolation. They are then asked to describe, and subsequently identify from an array of choices, a video played in another room. Several meta-analyses have been conducted. The general consensus seems to be that the phenomenon is not always replicable but that the results remain positive even as the quality of studies has improved over the years.[273, 291]

The results of PK are also positive. Subjects appear able to exert small influences on both falling dice and atomic random number generators (RNGs) and to speed healing. Meta-analyses of RNGs analyzed 597 experimental studies done up to 1987 and produced astronomical odds against chance of over a trillion to one.[291]

In summary, meta-analysis reveals highly significant effects for diverse experiments of both ESP and PK. However, the effects are relatively small, not always reproducible in any single experiment, and they remain the subject of intense debate.[6]

Prayer

"Prayer is good medicine" proclaims the title of a book by the noted physician Larry Dossey.[76] A majority of the population agrees and periodically prays for health benefits. Being prayed for could obviously make a person feel cared for and elicit a placebo effect, but could it have other benefits on disease and mortality?

To the surprise of hardheaded skeptics, a few experiments suggested it could.[41] Needless to say, they excited considerable controversy and much media attention. However, better designed follow-up studies have been less favorable, [14] and health benefits from intercessory prayer remain unproven.[203]

Factors Affecting Psi

Most psi researchers feel that the battle has been won, that psi has been demonstrated, and it is time to move on to more interesting questions. The University of California statistician, Jessica Utts, concluded from a review of formerly secret CIA research:

> The statistical results of the studies examined are far beyond what is expected by chance. Arguments that these results could be due to methodological flaws in the experiments are soundly refuted....It is recommended that future experiments focus on understanding how this phenomenon works, and on how to make it as useful as possible. There is little benefit to continuing experiments designed to offer proof.[291]

So what have researchers learned about how psi works? Three kinds of factors seem to affect it: individual differences between people, subjective psychological factors, and physical environmental factors.

Individual Differences: A consistent finding is the famous "sheep-goat effect." Sheep (those who believe in psi) tend to score positively. However, goats (those who disbelieve in it) tend to score at chance or, most intriguingly, below chance. Those below chance scores suggest that the goats are actually picking up psi cues, but are giving opposite answers so as to unconsciously support their belief that psi does not exist.

A small minority of gifted people consistently score well on psi tests, such as remote viewing, while most people do not. Moreover, gifted subjects seem to be born, not made, and neither practice nor training consistently improves remote viewing ability.

Psychological Factors: In fact, practice can be detrimental. Many parapsychology experiments are long, repetitive, and boring. Not surprisingly, subjects commonly show a "fatigue effect" in which their scores drop off the longer the experiment drones on.

However, two things can help. Receiving immediate feedback—being told how well you are doing—can help maintain interest. Altered states of consciousness—such as relaxation, hypnosis, and meditation—also increase psi scores, and this is obviously relevant to shamans who commonly enter ASCs before making diagnoses.

Physical Factors: Physical factors can also exert an influence. For example, when the earth's magnetic field is particularly active, traffic and industrial accidents rise and psi scores plummet.[291]

Two final physical factors are utterly mysterious. The first is sidereal time: a measure of the earth's rotation relative to the stars. For reasons quite unknown, psi scores vary dramatically according to sidereal time.[66] Second, contrary to all other types of signals, psi scores do not seem to depend on distance from the target. People a thousand miles away may score as well as people in the next room. In short, psi scores seem to vary in systematic ways depending on the individual, his or her state of mind, and aspects of the physical environment, but not with distance.[ab]

Despite many valiant attempts, there are no accepted theories to explain psi.[292] If such a theory does arise, it will probably call many laws of physics, principles of psychology, and understandings of reality into question, which, of course, is why psi is so vehemently opposed by many academics.

The Contrast with Astrology

The fault, dear Brutus is not in our stars, but in our selves.

—*Shakespeare,* Julius Caesar

Hard-core critics who know little about experimentation or statistics might attempt to dismiss the research support for parapsychology by saying that if you look hard enough for anything, you'll find it. But that is simply not so, at least for good research.

For contrast, consider astrology. If simply doing large numbers of experiments was sufficient to produce positive findings, then we would certainly expect them for astrology. Its claims have been put to over five hundred experimental tests, yet the findings are uniformly and devastatingly negative.[66]

But what about meta-analyses? Perhaps, like parapsychology, the findings are so subtle that they escape individual studies. In fact, several meta-analyses have been done, and none have found any support for astrology.

Astrologers seem to carefully ignore these distasteful facts. The usual defense, where there is one, is that science cannot test the dimensions most relevant to astrology. But while science cannot test all astrological claims—some are metaphysical or too vague to be measurable—it can test some of the most crucial, and in every case astrology has failed dramatically.[ac, ad]

This does not mean that astrology is never helpful. Since people can be surprisingly effective at rapidly assessing strangers from all sorts of subtle cues,[112] astrologers can sometimes give impressively insightful readings that appear to validate their charts. They can also use the chart as a projective technique similar to divinatory techniques employed throughout history. Sensitive astrologers can therefore offer valuable care, empathy, and support. This shamans can certainly offer, and since astrology is not an essential element of their practices, its negative findings do not diminish their claims.

Implications of Laboratory Research

Experimental research seems to support the validity of some parapsychology claims and to deny the validity of astrological claims. Both sets of findings meet with considerable resistance, because the real issue underlying such resistance is that in each case the findings jeopardize their opponents' belief system and understanding of reality. As such, they represent a metaphysical and mortal threat. Since we identify with our belief system, a death threat to it is experienced as a death threat to us, and we will therefore fight tooth and nail to preserve our image of the cosmos and of our self.

CONCLUSIONS ABOUT PSI AND SHAMANS

Having surveyed ethnographic, clinical, and laboratory research, what can we conclude about the possibility that shamans employ psi in their diagnostic and healing work? Certainly there are some remarkable anecdotal reports of psi in shamans and other native healers. In addition, the conditions used in tribal magic rituals often correspond to those reported to facilitate psi, and many laboratory studies and meta-analyses seem supportive of psi. However, as yet we have no good experimental studies of shamans. Therefore, for those whose minds remain open, the question of whether psi plays a role in shamanism also remains open.

PART VII

THE SHAMAN'S MIND

One conclusion was forced upon my mind at that time and my impression of its truth has ever since remained unshaken. It is that our normal consciousness, rational consciousness, is but one special type of consciousness whilst all round it, parted from it by the filmiest of screens, there lie potential forms of consciousness entirely different. We may go through life without suspecting their existence, but apply the requisite stimulus, and at a touch they are there in all their completeness, definite types of mentality which probably somewhere have their field of application and adaptation. No account of the universe in its totality can be final which leaves these other forms of consciousness quite disregarded. How to regard them is the question—for they are so discontinuous with ordinary consciousness. Yet they may determine attitudes though they cannot furnish formulas, and open regions though they fail to give a map.

—William James[177]

CHAPTER 31

Shamanic States of Mind

The mind is its own place, and in itself
can make a Heaven of Hell, a Hell of Heaven.
—*John Milton,* Paradise Lost

When research on spiritual states began in the 1960s, it was widely assumed that they were all the same, or at least very similar, and that, for example, diverse meditation practices were just different roads up the same mountain. However, this simple idea was simply wrong, and careful study has revealed dozens of meditative and other spiritual states.[121]

THE VARIETIES OF SHAMANIC STATES

What types of altered states occur in shamanism? Much writing assumes only a single ASC, but shamans employ many techniques, and each may induce its own state.

Here we will focus on states occurring during the shamanic journey, which warrant careful description and mapping for several reasons. First, the journey is a central practice of shamanism. Second, we have many detailed descriptions of it. Third, for so long the journey state has been confused with pathological states and is now being confused with meditative and yogic ones. Witness, for example, claims that "shamans, yogis and Buddhists alike are accessing the same state of consciousness"[75] and that the shaman "experiences existential unity—the Samadhi of the Hindus or what Western spiritualists and mystics call enlightenment, illumination, *unio mystica*."[189] However, these claims are based on superficial similarities. More careful comparisons reveal major differences and show that each tradition fosters its own family of ASCs.

Even to say that there is only a single state of consciousness associated with the journey, let alone shamanism, is an oversimplification. Journeys, experiences, and states vary from one session to another and from one person to another: sometimes deep, sometimes shallow; sometimes murky, sometimes clear. In fact, even the concept of "a state of consciousness" is a static crystallization of what is, in real life, a dynamic flow of experience. However, for the sake of simplicity, we can map key features of the shamanic journey and then refer to a single characteristic journey state. Having done so, we can then compare it to pathological and meditative-yogic ones.

How can we best map shamanic journey states? We cannot use physiological measurements for the simple reason that we have almost none. However, we can use the many experiential descriptions given by shamans.

The careful description of raw experience is known as phenomenology. In the East, traditions such as yoga and Buddhism have used phenomenology to classify states of consciousness for over 2,000 years. Using a similar approach will allow us to classify shamanic states of consciousness (SSCs) and compare them to others much more precisely than in the past. With this precision, we can identify differences—for example, between shamanic and yogic ASCs—that previous researchers overlooked. To do this we need to consider the key dimensions of experience that characterize ASCs.

KEY DIMENSIONS FOR MAPPING STATES
OF CONSCIOUSNESS

1) Degree of control: There are two important types of control.
- The ability to enter and leave the ASC at will
- The ability to control experiences while in the ASC

2) Awareness of the environment: To what extent does the practitioner remain aware of the external environment?

3) Ability to communicate: How well can the subject communicate with other people?

4) Concentration: Important factors here include:
- The intensity of concentration
- Whether attention is either
  a. *fixed* immovably on a single object such as in certain yogic samadhi states, or
  b. *momentary* or *fluid,* meaning it is allowed to shift between selected objects such as in shamanic journeys

5) Degree of energy or arousal.

6) Degree of calm: This refers to more than simply low arousal, since calm also implies low levels of agitation and distractibility.

7) Emotion: The dominant emotion(s) and whether the experience is pleasurable or painful.

8) Sense of identity: This may vary widely, from the usual sense of body-based egoity, to the sense of being a soul detached from the body, to a sense of unity with all things.

9) Out-of-body experience (OOBE): Does the subject experience perceiving from a perspective apparently outside the body?

10) Nature of inner experiences: Important distinctions here include:
- *Degree of organization*. Do the experiences consist of a random array of thoughts and images or of coherent patterns and sequences?
- *Sensory modality*: Are the experiences primarily auditory, visual, or somatic?
- *Intensity*: Are experiences subtle and barely perceptible as in some meditations, or are they intense and even overwhelming as in panic states?

MAPPING SHAMANIC JOURNEY STATES

Having outlined major dimensions, we can map shamanic journey states as follows:

Control

A defining characteristic of shamans is the ability to control their states of consciousness, and masters are able to enter and leave the journey state at will. They also have some ability to control the type of experiences that occur. This control is not complete, since there is some spontaneity to the images and worlds that arise. Thus the shaman may decide to journey to the lower world and voluntarily control the descent. Yet the world that arises to greet her may be quite unexpected. The shaman may choose how to respond to these strange worlds and spirits, but how they respond to her may seem quite outside her control.

A familiar analogue to this is a lucid dream in which we recognize that we are dreaming. Here, too, there is partial control of experiences. Strange worlds seem to arise spontaneously, yet, like shamans, we can usually control our responses to them.[205]

Awareness of the Environment

Awareness of the physical environment is reduced during journeys. This is hardly surprising since the shaman is preoccupied with life and death dramas in other worlds.

Ability to Communicate

In spite of these otherworld adventures, the shaman may be able to split her awareness between those worlds and this one sufficiently to communicate with her audience. In such cases, the listeners may be treated to a blow by blow account of the shaman's interactions with the spirits and other worlds.

Concentration

Shamans are known for their superb concentration.[83] During a journey they must focus for long periods without distraction, but their attention is not fixed immovably on a single object as is a yogi's. Rather, their attention is fluid, moving freely as their journey unfolds.

Energy/Arousal/Calm and Emotion

Since they roam between worlds, battle spirits, and intercede with gods, it is small wonder that shamans may feel energized during their exploits. Though deep peace can occur, calm is not a word that would be applied to many shamanic journeys. The emotions vary with the type of adventure and may range from dread and despair to pleasure and excitement. A similar range of reactions may occur after the journey, ranging from vitality to fatigue and depletion.

SHAMANIC STATES OF MIND

Dimension	Shamanic Journey State
Control • Ability to enter and leave ASC at will	Yes: good control
• Ability to control the content of experience	Partial control
Awareness of environment	↓ Decreased
Ability to communicate	Sometimes
Concentration	↑ Increased, fluid attention
Mental Energy/Arousal	↑ Increased
Calm	↓ Decreased
Emotion	Can be pleasurable and positive (+), or painful and negative (−)
Identity or Self-Sense	Separate self-sense, may be a nonphysical "soul" or "spirit"
Out-of-Body Experience	Yes, controlled ecstasy
Nature of Experience	Organized, coherent imagery consistent with shamanic cosmology and the journey's purpose

Table 1: A map of shamanic journey states.

Sense of Identity and Out-of-Body Experience

An out-of-body experience is a defining characteristic of the shamanic journey, and for this reason it is sometimes described as "ecstatic." During the journey, shamans experience themselves as disembodied spirits able to roam vast distances at great speeds.

While their tribespeople experience themselves as earthbound and body bound, shamans escape this constricting identity and experience themselves as free spirits.

Nature of Inner Experiences

The shaman's experiences are rich, complex, and multisensory. These experiences are coherent and purposeful, reflecting the tribal cosmology and serving the journey's purpose.

Having mapped the shamanic journey state, we can now compare it to other states with which it has often been confused. In doing so, we need to remember that there are many other shamanic states—for example, fasting, sleep deprivation, psychedelic, and dreaming. However, comparing all of these shamanic states with all those of other traditions would require another book or even an encyclopedia. Therefore, our focus will continue to be on the journey.

CHAPTER 32

Comparing States of Mind: Shamans, Yogis, Meditators, and Schizophrenics

If mind is comprehended, all things are comprehended.
—*Buddhism's* Ratnamegha Sutra

Previous comparisons between different states of consciousness have often been imprecise and superficial. For example, many writers have claimed that shamanic, schizophrenic, Buddhist, and yogic states are the same, but with phenomenological mapping, major differences leap into view.

SHAMANIC AND SCHIZOPHRENIC STATES

People who argue that shamanic and schizophrenic states are equivalent seem to assume that there is only one shamanic ASC and one schizophrenic state. Yet we have already seen that there are multiple shamanic states, and the same is true of schizophrenia.[8]

To simplify things, let's focus on the acute schizophrenic episode. This can be one of the most devastating of all human experiences. At its worst, extreme psychological disorganization disrupts thinking, emotions, perception, and identity. Victims can be overwhelmed, plunged into a nightmare of terror, haunted by hallucinations, swept from reality, utterly confused about who they are, and lost in a private, autistic world. In terms of our experiential dimensions we can map a typical episode and compare it to the shamanic state as follows.

Control is lost. The victim cannot halt the process or modify experiences. Awareness of the environment may be distorted by hallucinations, and fragmented thinking can make communication difficult. Concentration is drastically reduced, and the patient becomes highly agitated. Emotional responses are often distorted and bizarre, and the episode is usually extremely unpleasant.

So destructive is the process that the schizophrenic's experience can be utterly disorganized and incoherent. This disorganization extends even to the sense of identity, and the patient may feel that he is disintegrating and dying and be unable to locate his own boundaries. This may occasionally result in a sense of being outside the body or of merging with the universe, but the episode is brief and uncontrolled. The whole experience is an incoherent, fragmented nightmare.

Compared carefully, the acute schizophrenic episode is obviously very different from the shamanic journey. The latter experience is meaningful, coherent, and consistent with the journey's purpose. The shaman has good control, heightened concentration, and a clear sense of identity. He leaves his body and roams at will, and in marked contrast to the schizophrenic's terror, the shaman's journey may be a source of wonder and delight.

There are also major differences in social functioning. Recall that shamans are often outstanding members of the community who display considerable intellectual, artistic, and leadership skills. In stark contrast, such skills and contributions are rare among schizophrenics. Although it is understandable that early researchers sometimes labeled shamans as schizophrenic, it is also clear that this is no longer appropriate.

COMPARISONS WITH OTHER TRADITIONS

Popular writings often equate shamans with masters of other spiritual traditions, especially Buddhism and yoga, and also equate their states of consciousness. Such claims are sadly superficial.

Shamans induce multiple ASCs—for example, journey, mediumship, and drug states—while Buddhism and yoga employ even more. For example, Buddhism has literally dozens of meditation practices, and each meditation may develop through several distinct

Dimension	Shamanism	Schizophrenia
Control • Ability to enter and leave ASC at will	Yes: good control	↓↓ Dramatic reduction of control: inability to halt the process or to control the experience
• Ability to control the content of experience	Partial control	
Awareness of Environment	↓ Decreased	↓ Often decreased and distorted
Ability to Communicate	Sometimes	↓ Decreased; communication usually distorted
Concentration	↑ Increased	↓↓ Great reduction of concentration
Mental Energy/Arousal	↑ Increased	↑↑ Increased; agitation may be extreme
Calm	↓ Decreased	↓ Decreased
Emotion	+ or − (Positive or Negative)	− − Usually very negative, often distorted and inappropriate
Identity or Self-Sense	Separate self sense, may be a nonphysical "soul"	Disintegrated, loss of ego boundaries; inability to distinguish self from others
Out-of-body Experience	Yes, controlled ecstasy	Rarely, uncontrolled
Content of Experience	Organized, coherent imagery determined by shamanic cosmology and purpose of journey	Often disorganized and fragmented

Table 2. Comparison of the shamanic journey state to an acute schizophrenic episode.

states and stages. A Buddhist practitioner may therefore cultivate scores of ASCs during training.[121]

Comparing the states of shamanism and other traditions is therefore a complex business, and careful comparisons reveal major differences. Let us therefore outline central yogic and Buddhist meditations and then compare some of their advanced states with the shamanic journey.

Classical yoga uses a concentration practice that stills the mind until it can be fixed unwaveringly on the breath or a mantra. To do this, the yogi withdraws attention from the body and outer world to focus inward. In the words of the *Bhagavad Gita*, "The tortoise can draw in his legs. The seer can draw in his senses."[290] As a result, outer awareness is largely lost. The yogi can now focus undistractedly on ever more subtle internal objects, until finally only pure, unbounded, blissful consciousness remains.[93, ae] The classical yoga sutras of Patanjali describe this process succinctly and exquisitely:

> *Yoga* is the settling of the mind into silence. When the mind has settled, we are established in our essential nature, which is unbounded Consciousness. Our essential nature is usually overshadowed by the activity of the mind.[333]

Whereas classical yoga is a concentration practice, the classical contemplation of Buddhism, which is called *Vipassana* or insight meditation, is an awareness practice. Whereas yoga withdraws awareness from outer objects, *Vipassana* meditation cultivates fluid attention to all objects. All stimuli, both inner and outer, are examined precisely and minutely. The aim is to investigate the workings of mind and thereby cut through the distortions and misunderstandings that usually cloud awareness. "To see things as they are" is the motto of this practice, and the seeing can become very sensitive indeed.

All three disciplines cultivate self-control. Practitioners can enter and leave their respective states at will, although shamans may require external assistance such as drumming. Both shamans and insight meditators exert partial control, while yogis in *samadhi* have considerable control over mental processes.

There are major differences in perceptual sensitivity to the environment. According to both classical accounts and recent research, Buddhist insight meditators can cultivate perceptual sensitivity to remarkable levels.[33; 34] By contrast, awareness of the environment is usually reduced in the shamanic journey and drastically reduced in yogic *samadhi* states.

Dimension	Shamanism	Buddhist (Vipassana) Insight Meditation	Patanjali's Yoga
Control • Ability to enter and leave ASC at will	Yes	Yes	Yes
• Ability to control the content of experience	↑ Partial	↑ Partial	↑↑ Extreme control in samadhis
Awareness of Environment	↓ Decreased	↑ Increased	↓↓ Greatly reduced sensory and body awareness
Ability to Communicate	Sometimes	Usually	None
Concentration	↑ Increased; fluid	↑ Increased; fluid	↑↑ Greatly increased; fixed
Mental Energy/Arousal	↑ Increased	↓ Usually decreased	↓↓ Greatly decreased
Calm	↓ Decreased	↑ Usually increased	↑↑ Greatly increased; extreme peace
Affect	+ or – Positive or negative	+ or – Positive or negative (positive tends to increase as practice deepens)	+ + Highly positive; ineffable bliss
Identity or Self Sense	Separate self sense, may be a nonphysical "soul"	Self sense is deconstructed into a changing flux: "no self"	Unchanging transcendent Self, or Purusha
Out-of-Body Experience	Yes, controlled ecstasy ("ecstasies")	No	No; loss of body awareness ("enstasis")
Content of experience	Organized, coherent imagery determined by shamanic cosmology and purpose of journey	Deconstruction of complex experiences into their constituent stimuli. Stimuli are further deconstructed into a continuous flux.	Single object ("samadhi with support") or pure consciousness ("samadhi without support")

Table 3. Comparison of the shamanic journey state with advanced yogic and Buddhist meditative states.

Eliade defined *samadhi* as "an invulnerable state in which perception of the external world is absent."[82]

These differences in environmental awareness are reflected in communication. Shamans may communicate with spectators during their journeys.[284] Buddhist meditators can do so if necessary, but for yogis even attempting to speak may break their intense concentration. This fixed, unwavering yogic concentration contrasts with both the shamanic journey and Buddhist insight meditation, where attention moves fluidly between objects.

There are also differences in energy levels. Shamans are usually energized during their journey. However, insight meditators gradually develop greater calm, while in yogic *samadhi*, calm may become so profound that some mental processes, such as thinking, cease temporarily.[32]

The sense of identity differs drastically. The journeying shaman is a free-flying soul or spirit. However, the Buddhist meditator's microscopic awareness becomes so sensitive that it dissects the sense of self into its components. Thus the meditator perceives not a solid unchanging ego but rather a flux of thoughts and images that compose that ego. This is the classic Buddhist insight of "no self," which sees through the illusion of egoity and thereby frees the meditator from egocentricity.[120]

The yogi's experience is different yet again. In the higher reaches of meditation, attention is fixed inwardly and immovably on consciousness. Only consciousness remains in awareness, and this is therefore what the yogi experiences him- or herself to be—pure consciousness, ineffable, blissful, beyond time, space, or any limitation. This is *samadhi*, the highest reach of yoga. And it is this experience—the union of self and Self—that gives yoga, which means union, its name. This blissful union contrasts with the sometimes pleasant, sometimes painful experiences of both the shaman and Buddhist.

Yogis' pure consciousness also contrasts with the shaman's complex journey images. The Buddhist meditator has yet a third type of experience. Here awareness becomes so sensitive that all experiences are eventually broken down into their components, and the meditator perceives a ceaseless flux of microscopic images that arise and pass away with extreme rapidity.[121, af]

Neither the yogi or Buddhist meditator experience the shaman's out-of-body experience (OOBE) or ecstasy. In fact the yogi may lose all awareness of the body and become absorbed in the inner bliss of *samadhi* ("enstasis"). Eliade, whose theoretical knowledge of both shamanism and yoga was probably as extensive as anyone's, emphasized the difference:

Yoga cannot possibly be confused with shamanism or classed among the techniques of ecstasy. The goal of classic yoga remains perfect *autonomy*, enstasis, while shamanism is characterized by its desperate effort to attain the "condition of a spirit," to accomplish ecstatic flight.[84]

In summary, contrary to many claims, shamanic, schizophrenic, Buddhist, and yogic states are clearly distinguishable.

CHAPTER 33

How High Do They Fly?
Levels of Consciousness

> The exploration of the highest reaches of human nature and of its ultimate possibilities and aspirations…has involved for me the continuous destruction of cherished axioms, the perpetual coping with seeming paradoxes, contradictions and vagueness, and the occasional collapse around my ears of long established, firmly believed in, and seemingly unassailable laws of psychology.
>
> —*Abraham Maslow*[225]

Our mapping has so far not included a crucial dimension: time. Individuals develop and groups evolve over time. In both children and adults, certain stages and capacities tend to develop later than others. For example, abstract reasoning invariably appears later in life than less sophisticated magical and mythic forms of thinking, and it apparently also emerged later in human evolution.[410]

It seems that similar sequences occur in training states of consciousness, for example, as the successive stages of Jewish ascent, Buddhist insight, or Christian contemplation.[413] In these practices, states tend to emerge in a fixed order, and later states are regarded as more difficult, more developed, and "higher" or "deeper" (depending on one's metaphor and basis of reference—"higher" into consciousness and the sacred; "deeper" into one's Self).[346]

Can we map states on a developmental scale? Ken Wilber has suggested three possible criteria: sequence, access, and capacities.[413]

1. The sequence of emergence: In general, more developed states tend to emerge later.

2. Access to other states: A person who can access more developed contemplative states can also access earlier ones.

3. Later developmental states require and possess additional capacities not available in earlier ones. For example, more mature states may require greater concentration or perceptual sensitivity.

Using these three criteria we can map states developmentally. Metaphorically, we can now compare spiritual states on both vertical (developmental) and horizontal (phenomenological) dimensions.

THE VARIETIES OF SPIRITUAL STATES

The next question is, are there similar developmental patterns across traditions? This could be a difficult question. After all, different practices obviously induce very different types of experiences.

Yet underlying commonalities can be found. For example, the Christian contemplative and journeying shaman who see angels and spirits, respectively, are both seeing visions of spiritual figures. The Buddhist and Hindu meditators who attain cessation and *nirvikalpa samadhi,* respectively, are both in states in which there is only pure consciousness, and no thoughts, images, or sensations arise. Clearly, there are radical differences between the first and second pair of experiences. Consequently, we can group experiences from different practices and traditions into clusters or families of states according to their underlying deep structures.[413]

The deep structure of a family of experiences is the common form that underlies and molds them. For example, human faces vary so dramatically that we can distinguish almost every person on the planet from the other seven billion. Yet underlying these almost infinite differences in appearance lies the same deep structure comprised of two eyes and ears, a nose, and a mouth.

Wilber suggests that a similar principle underlies spiritual experiences. Beneath the vast array of such experiences lies a finite number of deep structures. For example, Buddhist cessation and Hindu *nirvikalpa samadhi* both spring from the same deep structure: a state of formless, objectless awareness.

Wilber's approach is exciting because it suggests a pattern underlying the extravagant profusion of spiritual experiences. Hidden behind different experiences, names, and interpretations are common characteristics and clusters.

This would be a significant contribution by itself. But Wilber goes further to suggest that states tend to emerge in similar sequences across traditions. Granted, it is possible to have spontaneous, temporary peak, or "peek," experience of many states.[411] However, contemplatives usually access spiritual states in a progressive sequence, and that progression shows similarities across traditions.

Wilber suggests that transpersonal states fall into four major groups. His terms have changed over time, but recently he has named them in order of their emergence: gross, subtle, causal, and nondual.

Gross

Gross states are dominated by sensory experiences. You are reading this in a normal waking state that is one kind of gross state. Spiritual gross states arise when, for example, you do yoga and arouse kundalini energy in the body or gaze at an exquisite sunset and feel at one with the physical universe.

Subtle

Subtle states arise when sensory experiences fade into the background, the usual raucous mental chatter quiets, and you become aware of an inner world so subtle that it was formerly overshadowed. This inner stillness and sensitivity usually require considerable training, yet they are central to spiritual progress and open an inner universe of possibilities. Patanjali's classic text defines yoga as "the settling of the mind into silence,"[333] while the Jewish Torah and Christian Bible say, "Be still and know that I am God."

Subtle states are of two kinds. Formless experiences are comprised of pure light or sound, without thoughts or organized content of any kind. Experiences with form may comprise all manner of images, including vast worlds of extraordinary richness and complexity, as well as archetypal figures such as spirits or angels. Examples of subtle states include shamanic visions, Hinduism's *savikalpa samadhi*, and Christian "illumination."

Causal

Beyond the subtle lies the causal. Here, both sensory experiences and mental experiences drop away. Somatic sensations and mental thoughts or images no longer reach awareness.

"Leave the senses and the workings of the intellect, and all that the sense and intellect can perceive…" urged the great Christian Saint Dionysius.[157] When this is accomplished, only consciousness remains, resting in and recognizing itself as unbounded and ecstatic consciousness, Being, Spirit, Mind, Atman, Tao, or Self. This consciousness is experienced as prior to space and time (which it creates) and therefore as infinite and eternal. In the words of Aurobindo, "Spirit is self-existent being with an infinite power of consciousness and unconditioned delight in its being…"[15] This is the state of Jewish *Ayin*, the Christian "Cloud of Unknowing," Sufi *fana*, Buddhist cessation, yogic *nirvikalpa samadhi,* and the formless Tao.

Nondual

Beyond the causal awaits the nondual. Here sensory and mental experiences again reappear, but they are now spontaneously recognized as projections of consciousness, Spirit, or Mind. Consciousness or Spirit is now seen as expressing itself in and as all the worlds and beings of the universe. This is the realization of Hinduism's *turiya* or *sahaj samadhi* or of Zen's "Big Mind," which encompasses all things. Consciousness, Spirit, or Mind has rediscovered its true nature, returned to its Self as its Self, and recognizes its Self in all things. The spiritual genius Ibn Arabi, known to Sufis as "the Greatest Master," exclaimed:

> By Himself he sees Himself, and by Himself He knows Himself.…His veil, that is phenomenal existence, is a part of His oneness.…there is no other and there is no existence other than He.[382]

And this recognition of the utter nonduality of God and creation, consciousness and matter, sacred and profane is said by several traditions to be the ultimate realization. [411]

Of course, these extremely brief descriptions cannot do justice to what are among the most profound experiences available to a human being. In addition, spiritual masters repeatedly warn about the difficulty of comprehending these states without direct experience.[ag] Indeed, the Buddha forbade his monks to speak about advanced meditative experiences to laypeople because he felt they would almost inevitably be misunderstood.

LOCATING SHAMANIC STATES

The obvious next question is, where do shamanic states fit into this scheme? Primarily into two categories: gross and subtle. Much shamanic work is done while fully aware of the environment—in fact, while making full use of the senses for diagnosis and healing—and if altered states are used, these would be gross states.

The shamanic journey is a different story. The journey is usually performed at night to heighten sensitivity to faint images, complex scenes and worlds arise, and encounters with spiritual figures are common. These are consistent with the experiences of subtle states, and Wilber suggests that shamans were the first to systematically access these.[408] Of course, questions remain. For example, what exactly constitutes subtle experiences, and how can we distinguish them from ordinary fantasy?

At the present time these questions cannot be answered definitively. A tentative suggestion is that both are imaginal creations that differ in systematic ways along a spectrum of intensity, scope, and spiritual significance. Ordinary fantasy is relatively intense and easily recognized. However, subtle experiences are faint and can usually only be recognized in sensitive (subtle) states and supportive environments. The scale of subtle experiences may be vast, and whole worlds or even universes may seem to arise in which the earth appears as a mere speck. Spiritually imbued images and themes, which can seem truly "visionary," abound in subtle states, whereas ordinary fantasies tend to be far more mundane.

No one of these characteristics by itself would necessarily distinguish ordinary fantasy from subtle-level experiences. However, taken together they point to differences between routine fantasies and subtle visions, which, at least to the person having them, can seem vast indeed.

Shamans were the earliest masters of these subtle realms. Their specialty was "soul travel" in which they experienced themselves journeying through these realms as free souls, mastering and placating their inhabitants, and bringing back knowledge and power to their earthbound compatriots.

MYSTICAL UNION

In many religious traditions the sense of being a separate individual may give way to an experience of union with another being or even with the entire universe or with God. Thus in the upper reaches of subtle states, as well as in causal and nondual states, there may occur forms of the *unio mystica* or mystical union so celebrated and sought after by the world's mystics.

Shamans sometimes unite with other spirits, but did they ever experience this full-blown mystical union? I have found no reference to it in the literature, nor apparently have others. Hultkrantz categorically states that "we never find the mystical union with the divinity so typical for the ecstatic experiences in the 'higher' forms of religious mysticism."[169] Consequently he concludes that shamanism can be considered a form of mysticism only "if mysticism is not restricted to mean just the *unio mystica*."[169]

Three lines of evidence suggest that this conclusion might be incorrect. First, shamanism is an oral tradition; second, powerful psychedelics may be used; and third, some Westerners report such experiences.

Since shamanism is an oral tradition, *unio mystica* may occasionally occur, but be lost to subsequent generations and anthropologists. Without writing, there may be no way to adequately preserve a record of a tradition's highest and rarest flowerings.

Although not an essential part of shamanism, psychedelic use is common in some areas. Peyote and ayahuasca, for example, are potent catalysts of apparently mystical breakthroughs. Finally, Westerners trained in core shamanic practices can report unitive experiences.[ah]

Though unitive experiences are not the primary aim of shamanic journeys, they may occur. Do shamans ever reach beyond the subtle to causal and nondual states? Two lines of evidence suggest this possibility. The first is that there is always the possibility of a practitioner leaping into realms of consciousness outside those of her tradition. The second is that psychedelics occasionally elicit the causal or nondual.[133] Though shamans aimed primarily for soul travel in subtle states, some may have also broken through into the causal and nondual and dissolved into the ecstasy of mystical union. But no matter how many explored these realms, shamans were humankind's first transpersonal heroes: the first to develop a technology of transcendence, the first to successfully break their identification with the body and the world, and the first to systematically induce and explore subtle states.

CHAPTER 34

The Evolution of Consciousness

In the history of the collective as in the history of the individual,
everything depends on the development of consciousness.
—Carl Jung[186]

THE BATTLE OVER EVOLUTION

Ninety-nine percent of all the species that have lived on earth have died away, and no stars
will wink out in tribute if we in our folly soon join them.
—Timothy Ferris[91]

Biological Evolution

The nature, in fact the very existence, of evolution is one of the great cultural battlegrounds of our time. Based on a literal reading of religious texts, creationists denounce it and proclaim that God created the world as it is, all at once. "The world was created on 22nd October, 4004 BC at 6 o'clock in the evening," concluded a seventeenth-century bishop.[258] Not so, declared Dr. John Lightfoot, Vice Chancellor of the University of Cambridge, who in 1859 corrected the good bishop and put creation back fifteen hours to 9 AM on the 23rd of October, 4004 BC.[258]

Scientists disagree. Based on a reading of geological, archeological, and biological information, scientists regard evolution as one of their greatest and most triumphant theories. The physician Lewis Thomas called it "our most powerful story."[366]

A further battle turns on the interpretation of evolution. Many scientists argue that it is the result of mere chance, a random mutation and weeding of genes in a vast conflict of natural selection. Humans, concludes Richard Dawkins, are "survival machines—robot vehicles blindly programmed to preserve the selfish molecules known as genes."[63] Though this is often presented as a simple fact, Stan Grof points out:

> The probability that human intelligence developed all the way from the chemical ooze of the primeval ocean solely through sequences of random mechanical processes has been recently aptly compared to the probability of a tornado blowing through a gigantic junkyard and assembling by accident a 747 jumbo jet. This highly improbable assumption is a metaphysical statement that cannot be proved by existing scientific methods. Far from being a scientific piece of information—as its proponents so fiercely maintain—it is, in the present state of knowledge, little more than one of the leading myths of Western science.[130]

Has Consciousness Evolved?

So the nature of biological evolution is fiercely debated. What about the evolution of consciousness, which in some ways is even more complex, being molded by both biology and culture? There are four main views of the evolution of consciousness (both human conscious in general and religious consciousness in particular). Historically, these have usually been considered together, so we can start there.

The first view sees history as a cyclical affair of recurrent ups and downs. The second is a downhill view that sees things as getting worse and consciousness as devolving. The third sees no change in consciousness, or at least religious consciousness, since prehistoric times. The fourth is an upward view of progressivism that sees culture and consciousness as evolving. Let's examine these four more closely.

In many cultures, time was seen as a ceaseless cycle of days and nights, light and dark, creation and destruction, in which humankind and consciousness repetitively regenerate and degenerate. Our current time is often regarded as a degenerate phase, and this merges into the second view, that the human condition and consciousness have devolved. Devolving myths describe a prehistoric golden age and a subsequent fall from grace. In the Western monotheisms, it is the story of the Garden of Eden and our subsequent eviction. In China it is the age of virtue and subsequent decline; and in Hinduism it is the fall from the *satya-yuga*, a golden era of righteousness and wisdom, into our present *kali-yuga*, a time of viciousness and ignorance. Contemporary scholars usually consider such ideas as purely mythological, although a few respected thinkers have considered decline as a possibility.[346]

The third idea holds that there has been no significant change in human consciousness, or at least in religious consciousness. From this perspective, the earliest spiritual practitioners were on a par with the latest, prehistoric realizations were as deep as contemporary ones, and ancient shamans enjoyed the same experiences and states as recent mystics. Such ideas are implied by such notable scholars as Mircea Eliade, Joseph Campbell, and Carl Jung. In Eliade's words, "As for the 'inner light' which plays a part of the first importance in Indian mysticism and metaphysics as well as in Christian mystical theology, it is, as we have seen, already documented in Eskimo shamanism."[83]

This theme is now echoed among popularizers of shamanism. To these people, shamanic experiences are on a par with, or even greater than, those of mystics of later traditions. This represents an example of a popular but questionable view that all spiritual practices lead to the same mystical endpoint: they are all just different roads up the same mountain.

Some of the more sophisticated popularizers of this idea use the language of states of consciousness to claim equivalence. We have already noted claims that "shamans, yogis and Buddhists alike are accessing the same state of consciousness"[75] and that the shaman "experiences existential unity—the *samadhi* of the Hindu's or what Western spiritualists and mystics call enlightenment illumination, *unio mystica*."[189] However, we have also seen that careful comparisons reveal these states to be very different.

EVOLVING CONSCIOUSNESS

The fourth view sees human consciousness as a work in progress. For luminaries such as Hegel, Aurobindo, Teilhard de Chardin, Jean Gebser, and Ken Wilber, human consciousness and religious consciousness have evolved. Fortunately we can focus on the narrower yet still extremely complex area of religious consciousness, and since Ken Wilber has synthesized the ideas of so many thinkers, we can draw especially on his ideas.

Wilber draws a crucial distinction between the "average mode" of religious consciousness and the "leading edge."[408] Leading-edge pioneers break through into new states of consciousness and then leave descriptions and instructions whereby others can follow them.

Wilber's division of spiritual states into four broad classes of gross, subtle, causal, and nondual is helpful. He suggests that just as these tend to emerge sequentially in today's contemplatives, so too did they emerge in history, and a survey of historical religious texts supports him.

Humankind's first gross and subtle spiritual experiences are long lost in the dawn of prehistory. Reliable signs of the causal appeared in the first few centuries before the Common Era and are associated with, for example, the Upanishads, the Buddha, early Taoists, and later with Jesus.[408] Such was the extraordinary impact of this breakthrough and the sages who made it that this era is known as the Axial age. Signs of the nondual appear a few centuries into the Common Era and are associated with, for example, the appearance of tantra and with names such as Plotinus in Rome, Bodhidharma in China, and Padmasambhava in Tibet.

Where do shamans fit in this evolutionary ascent? Wilber places them at the beginning of this vast process and regards them as the first spiritual heroes. Though they may occasionally have broken through into the causal and nondual, both their mythology and technology were clearly aimed at eliciting and utilizing specific gross and subtle states.

For thousands or tens of thousands of years, shamans practiced at the leading edge of human consciousness. For it was only millennia later that technologies emerged to awaken the causal and nondual, and the evolution of religious consciousness is intimately tied to the evolution of the technology of transcendence.[391] There has been an enormous development of transformational techniques since some early human first discovered that hitting a stretched skin created a resounding sound, and hitting it repeatedly produced curious and pleasurable experiences. Shamans presumably remembered and recreated such discoveries, welded them into an effective collection of techniques, and then transmitted them across generations. Millennia later, early sages refined shamanic technology, added their own yogic, contemplative, and tantric techniques, and thereby created technologies that unveiled causal and nondual realizations. Subsequently, religions, philosophies, and psychologies arose to express and analyze these realizations, and their cumulative impact on human culture and consciousness is inestimable.

THE RELATIVE DIFFICULTIES OF DIFFERENT REALIZATIONS

The consciousness of each of us is evolution
looking at itself and reflecting upon itself.
—Teilhard de Chardin[363]

Different states emerge with different ease. Anyone can be graced with a spontaneous taste of any state. However, voluntarily inducing spiritual states is another matter, and stabilizing them is even more so.

A crucial question is, how many practitioners actually attain the realizations aimed for by different traditions? We have some hints but very little firm data. These hints suggest that it may be easier to attain shamanic realization than the goals of later traditions.

For example, Michael Harner reports that in workshops, some 90 percent are able to begin shamanic journeys.[148] Of course, there is a huge difference between initial insights and spiritual mastery. However, in later traditions the general sense is that among, for example, Christian contemplatives, Indian yogis, or Buddhist meditators, significant gains can take considerable time, though of course grace can occur at any time.

Nevertheless, there does seem to be a relationship between a state and its ease of access. In general, the "higher" the state, the later it may emerge both in individuals and in history, the more training it may demand, and the smaller the percentage of practitioners who realize it. Shamanism was the earliest tradition to emerge, and it allows relatively easy access to its altered states, a fact that may partly account for its current popularity in the West. Shamanism continues to offer today what it has offered for hundreds of thousands of yesterdays; namely, a relatively rapid means, and for most of human history perhaps the only means, of controlled transcendence. As such, shamans can be considered as the founders of the "great tradition": the sum total of humankind's religious-spiritual wisdom.[105]

CHAPTER 35

The Shaman's Brain: Neurotheology and Neuromythology

Medical materialism seems indeed a good appellation for the too simple-minded system of thought which we are considering. Medical materialism finishes up Saint Paul by calling his vision on the road to Damascus a discharging lesion of the occipital cortex, he being an epileptic. It snuffs out Saint Teresa as an hysteric, Saint Francis of Assisi as an hereditary degenerate…

—*William James*[177]

As neuroscientists push deeper into the crevices of the brain and unveil the workings of the most complex organ in the universe, religious researchers follow close behind them. The attempt to understand religious experiences in terms of biology and the brain is an old and important one and will doubtless make profound contributions.

But there are also many problems. First, current neural measures are still too gross to really understand the subtleties of an almost inconceivably complex organ. Additionally, very few neuroscientists have personal experience of contemplative practices. Consequently, they are unaware of the subtle yet crucial differences between states of consciousness or of the enduring higher stages and capacities that contemplative disciplines aim to develop.[398]

When there is no deep understanding of the real nature or transpersonal potentials of spiritual practices and experiences, the temptation to interpret profound experiences as nothing but neuronal fireworks is a recurrent risk. "We're a bunch of chemical reactions running around in a bag,"[52] claims Dean Hamer, who in his book titled *The God Gene* claims to have found—well, the God gene.[142] This, by the way, is the same scientist who earlier claimed to have found the "gay gene" underlying homosexuality, a claim that quickly fizzled. To suggest that genes and neuronal activity play crucial roles in religious experiences is fine; to state that they adequately explain these experiences is a matter of pseudoscientific faith and reductionism.

There is a perennial problem in scientific studies of religion. This is the tendency for speculation to outrace data, for elaborate theories to be founded on little evidence, and for medical materialization to rise from the dead to explain religion (away) yet again in terms of the most recently discovered neural process.

Yet none of these concerns have slowed the torrent of books purporting to finally explain God, religion, and ecstasy in neural terms. *Zen and the Brain*,[16] *Why God Won't Go Away*,[256] and more pour off the presses, supposedly creating the fields of "neurotheology" and "theobiology" and showing *Where God Lives in the Human Brain*[5] (in the Big G spot, presumably). Yet when one looks carefully, it is clear that many claims outstrip the data. They offer massive speculation atop little information and also suffer from a plague of logical and philosophical fallacies.[136, 313] In many cases, neurotheology turns out to be neuromythology.

The same is largely true of shamanism. While there is now considerable neuroscience data on some spiritual practices, especially the effects of meditation,[43, 398] we know almost nothing about neural activity during shamanic practices, and some oft-cited studies, such as those on EEG effects of drumming,[253, 254] are badly flawed.[3] Yet this has not stopped enormous speculation, much of it presented as simple fact. Michael Winkleman, who contributed so much to cross-cultural studies, devoted several papers and much of a book to the "neural ecology of shamanism."[418] However, many claims float in air without a solid foundation in actual data. Unfortunately, this has not stopped many other people—who have either not read them or have no background in neuroscience—from citing his claims as fact.

Hopefully, future research will provide such data, but for now we all need some neurohumility.

CHAPTER 36

Shamanism(s) in a Changing World

Indigenous peoples have rich storehouses of information about nature, man and the balanced relationship of the two. From their beliefs about the spiritual world to their traditional knowledge of rain forests, healing and agriculture, these societies provide the opportunity for new interpretations about the world and our selves. Many of these populations face severe discrimination, denial of human rights, loss of cultural and religious freedoms, or in the worst cases, cultural or physical destruction....If current trends in many parts of the world continue the cultural, social and linguistic diversity of humankind will be radically and irrevocably diminished....immense undocumented repositories of ecological, biological and pharmacological knowledge will be lost, as well as an immeasurable wealth of cultural, social, religious, and artistic expression.

—*International Cultural Survival Act of 1988, United States Congress*

GLOBALIZATION

Globalization—the meeting, mixing, and conflict of cultures—is all about us, and the world will never be the same again. The meeting of religions is most loudly discussed as the "clash of civilizations," as Islamic and Christian worlds collide. But all religions are affected, and shamanism is no exception. What will be the future and fate of this ancient tradition?

Traditional Shamanism

In its native homelands there seems to be four main possibilities. The first is that it may simply disappear. Elsewhere, among the rare peoples relatively untouched by the industrialized world, it may remain as a major religious, medical, and cultural resource. In newly industrialized countries, it may survive or even flourish alongside Western medicine and religion.[283] Indeed, in countries such as Korea and Nepal, some wily shamans carefully cull their clientele, retaining likely successes and referring more difficult illnesses to physicians.[282] Other shamans may work in partnership with physicians or even treat clients that physicians have deemed incurable.

A final possibility is revival, and this could occur in several ways. One is the emergence of new forms inspired by spontaneous experiences. Examples of such major movements with shamanic elements include the nineteenth-century North American Indian religious revival, the Ghost Dance, and three twentieth-century Brazilian churches that center on the sacramental use of ayahuasca.[240]

Another possibility for revival is the recreation of practices that languished or were outlawed under cultural repression. This is now occurring in several parts of the world.[153] For example, the Northwest American Salish Indians have successfully revived the shamanically related winter spirit dance, and participants are less susceptible to prevalent problems such as depression and alcoholism.[180]

A third revival possibility is the reintroduction of practices by people outside the culture. The American-based Foundation for Shamanic Studies has been doing this upon request and has had success among the Tuvans of Central Asia, the Caribou Inuit of Canada, and the Buriat of Siberia.[153]

Shamanism in the Western World

How much of the current lively interest in shamanism will endure remains to be seen. Part is doubtless mere curiosity and fad. But some reflects deep and durable spiritual seeking and an interest in native traditions. There is also a desire to honor the earth[351] and respond to the alienation from nature that is so much a part of modern life and that is producing "nature-deficit disorder"[218] in individuals and ecological disaster for our planet.

How will its migration to the West affect both shamanism and the West? Perhaps other religious traditions can offer clues. For 2,500 years, Buddhism has slowly migrated around the world from its Indian birthplace. Each new culture it entered has both transformed it and been transformed by it. Time after time it has incorporated and adapted to indigenous ideas and customs in whatever ways best serve its supreme ethic of the awakening and welfare of all beings. In our own time it is evolving once again as it enters the West and confronts the postmodern world.

Already dramatic shifts are evident. Organizational changes include democratization, feminization, and an emphasis on lay as opposed to monastic life. Other shifts include adoption of Western psychological concepts, openness to investigation by scientists, combination with psychotherapy, and social applications such as "engaged Buddhism."

Similar transformations are already apparent in shamanism. New forms and practices are much in evidence, especially "core" and "neo" shamanism. *Core shamanism* was founded by Michael Harner on the assumption that a common, crucial core of practices underlies diverse cultural variants. *Neoshamanism* refers to a more amorphous family of practices. According to anthropologist Joan Townsend, "It is an invented tradition of practices and beliefs based on a constructed metaphorical, romanticized ideal shaman concept which often differs considerably from traditional shamans."[370] How Western forms of shamanism will continue to evolve and what their impact on the West will be remain some of the intriguing cultural questions of our time. However, the British anthropologist Piers Vitebsky makes a powerful point about today's marketplace of ideas and practices:

> Overall, I suggest that shamanism cannot avoid sharing the fate of any other kind of indigenous knowledge in the industrial world: its full implications are too challenging even for radicals to accommodate….This is not a true marketplace, but a rigged one in which your product will sell only if you pretend that it is something else, far less distinctive and valuable, but also far less trouble to come to terms with, than what it really is.[383]

There is also an important research question. For example, shamanic healing methods are increasingly used for physical and psychological disorders. Careful studies of shamanic healing are essential. For if any shamanic techniques are to take their place alongside Western therapies, they must at some stage be tested experimentally. The capacity for self-deception of both healer and patient is endless, and if believed in by both doctor and patient, the most useless or even harmful technique can seem, at least for a time, nothing short of miraculous. Such is the power of the placebo effect. Therefore, it is not enough that shamanic techniques seem to work. The only way to be certain is to test them experimentally using carefully controlled studies.

THE HUMAN CONSCIOUSNESS PROJECT

Two great mapping projects are underway, both of which could radically affect our future. One is well known and well funded, the other virtually unknown and unfunded. The first is the human genome project to map the genetic code. The other is the human consciousness project to map the varieties of consciousness. This project aims to map the range of states and stages of consciousness, its developmental pathways and potentials, the varieties of practices to heal and enhance it, its biological underpinnings, and its social-cultural correlates. We already have initial maps of states and stages, pathologies and therapies,[413] as well as the central practices found among diverse spiritual traditions.[392] Shamanic studies have crucial contributions to make, without which the project cannot be complete.

Perhaps the most crucial finding of the human consciousness project is the recognition of the overlapping claims in diverse spiritual traditions about the unrecognized limitations of our usual waking state. According to contemplative traditions of both East and West, our usual waking state is distorted, constricted, and deluded, so that we live in what the East calls *avidya, maya,* or illusion. In the West this has been called a shared dream, a consensus trance, or a collective psychosis.[355]

Within our collective illusion we act blindly and all too often destructively, as might be expected of someone whose awareness is distorted and constricted. Our behavior is said to be driven by greed and fear in ways destructive to ourselves, our fellow beings, and our planet.

But a few have awoken from this illusion, recognized their true nature, and then returned to point the way for the remainder of us. These are the spiritual heroes, the master game players, the great saints and sages, and those who escape from and then voluntarily return to Plato's cave. These are the people who have created and refreshed the world's spiritual traditions.

The essence of their message is "Wake up!" Awaken to your true nature, awaken to the fact you are not separate from anyone or anything, awaken to the fact that, as the Confucians say, "Heaven, earth and the ten thousand things form one body." Awaken to the recognition that, as one Zen master put it, "You are more than this puny body or limited mind. Stated negatively, it is the realization that the universe is not external to you. Positively, it is experiencing the universe as yourself."[191]

The person who awakens to this recognition is said to realize that "the I, one's real, most intimate self, pervades the universe and all other beings."[144] These, of course, are expressions of the *unio mystica* so revered by contemplatives of all kinds.

But such descriptions are not the exclusive province of mystics. They have been echoed by philosophers, psychologists, and physicists. "Out of my experience....one final conclusion dogmatically emerges," said William James. "There is a continuum of cosmic consciousness against which our individuality builds but accidental forces, and into which our several minds plunge as into a mother sea."[249] Albert Einstein made the point as beautifully and poetically as only a genius could:

> A human being is part of the whole called by us universe, a part limited in time and space. He experiences himself, his thoughts and feelings as something separated from the rest, a kind of optical delusion of his consciousness. This delusion is a kind of prison for us, restricting us to our personal desires and to affection for a few persons nearest to us. Our task must be to free ourselves from this prison by widening our circle of compassion to embrace all living creatures and the whole of nature in its beauty.[120]

The practical implication of this realization is that when we realize that we are not separate from anyone or anything, we naturally want to treat them, quite literally, as our self. Hence, the biblical injunction to "love thy neighbor as thy self," to which Gandhi added, "and every living being is thy neighbor." In the words of the Buddha:

> See yourself in others.
> Then whom can you hurt?
> What harm can you do?[42]

An ethic such as this, aimed at the welfare and awakening of all, may be crucial to the survival of our species and our planet.

OUR GLOBAL CRISIS

Clearly, our species and planet are at an "evolutionary bottleneck," as Harvard biologist E. O. Wilson calls it, in which our natural resources and human ingenuity will be tested to the limits. The next few decades will doubtless determine our collective fate, as Jared Diamond concluded from a study of failed societies in his book *Collapse*:

> Because we are rapidly advancing along this non-sustainable course, the world's environmental problems will get resolved, in one way or another, within the lifetimes of the children and young adults alive today. The only question is whether they will become resolved in pleasant ways of our own choice, or in unpleasant ways not of our choice, such as warfare, genocide, starvation, disease epidemics, and collapses of societies.[71]

Big-picture thinkers, such as Duane Elgin, situate our current crises within an evolutionary view and see us at a developmental crossroads.[81] We may well consume, pollute, and war our way into social collapse or even species oblivion. Alternatively, we may be able to find our way through our current global crises via a forced collective maturation. To achieve this, however, will require development of our inner world as much as our outer one.

For what is remarkable about this era is not only the awesome scope and urgency of our problems. It is that for the first time in millions of years of evolution, all our major threats are caused by humans. Problems such as overpopulation, pollution, poverty, and nuclear weapons stem directly from our own behavior, and from the fears and fantasies, desires and delusions that power this behavior. The state of the world, in other words, reflects the state of our minds. The conflicts outside us reflect the conflicts inside us, and the insanity without mirrors the insanity within.[389]

What this means is that current threats to human survival and well-being are actually symptoms, symptoms of our individual and collective state of mind. If we are to understand and correct the state of the world, we must understand the source of both our problems and their solutions: ourselves. As Senator William Fulbright said: "Only on the basis of an understanding of our behavior can we hope to control it in such a way as to ensure the survival of the human race."[107]

The challenge is to optimize our individual and collective maturation. How best to do so is no longer an academic question but an evolutionary imperative. We are in a race between consciousness and catastrophe, the outcome remains unsure, and we are all called to contribute. How spiritual practices in general, and shamanic practices and studies in particular, can best contribute is a crucial question of our time.

CONCLUSION

No one approach or perspective can fully encompass shamanism's many facets and dimensions. Yet in this book our psychological explorations have provided insights and understandings that other approaches overlook. Clearly we have much to learn from much that shamans do—the myths they live by, the training they undergo, the techniques they use, the crises they confront, the capacities they develop, the states of consciousness they enter, the understandings they gain, the visions they see, and the cosmic travels they take.

The more we explore shamanism, the more it points to unrecognized potentials of the human body, mind, and spirit. For untold thousands of years the world of shamanism has helped, healed, and taught humankind, and it has still more to offer us.

Endnotes

CHAPTER 4

a. Examples of a neural basis (and bias) underlying cross-cultural experiences are "neuro gnostic structures"—genetically prepared neural pathways primed to process information and shape experience in specific directions.[208]

CHAPTER 5

b. This common end stage via multiple pathways is what systems theorists call "equifinality."

c. This section draws on my paper "Asian Contemplative Traditions" in the *Journal of Transpersonal Psychology 32*(2), 38–108, 1999, and on my book *Essential Spirituality*.

d. There is probably a relationship between practice and maturity that we might formulate as follows: The practice-maturation hypothesis suggests that the amount of practitioners' maturation is a function of the extent to which they do the seven central practices.

CHAPTER 6

e. The process of detribalization is part of the larger process of maturation from conventional to post-conventional and personal to transpersonal stages, and it is reflected in multiple aspects of the personality or "lines of development." For ego development, it is the shift from conformist to individualistic and autonomous stages;[216] for moral development, it reflects conventional to post-conventional maturation;[197] for faith, it is the movement from synthetic-conventional to individuative-reflective and conjunctive stages;[100] for the spiral dynamics of Clare Graves and Don Beck,[409] it is the leap from first-tier (blue and orange) to second-tier (yellow and turquoise) thinking, and in Ken Wilber's[410] wide-ranging synthesis, it is, among other things, a shift in orientation from sociocentric to worldcentric.

f. A fuller discussion of conventionality, and the factors that make the call and post-conventional growth so challenging, is available in my chapter, "Authenticity, Conventionality, and Angst."[393]

CHAPTER 7

g. Moreover, random reinforcement of behavior makes it particularly resistant to unlearning, which explains, in part, the remarkable persistence of many superstitions and taboos.

h. There are, of course, many different explanations of the origins and maintenance of taboos in addition to the primarily psychological ones offered here. For a good, brief review of anthropological explanations, see Slater's "Taboo."[343]

CHAPTER 10

i. In Piagetian terms, the death-rebirth process would be a particularly dramatic—perhaps the most dramatic—example of "accommodation." Piaget suggested that experiences are usually "assimilated" into preexisting psychological structures. However, if the experiences are especially novel or dramatic, the psychological structures may have to change, i.e., accommodate, to encompass and integrate the experiences.[97] During death-rebirth, some structures would not only change, but presumably would collapse and then, guided by the psyche's innate holotropic or equilibrative (Piaget) tendencies, would equilibrate to a new, more functional, accommodated form.

j. This actualizing drive of mind is crucial to understanding much of psychological and spiritual growth in general and of the death-rebirth process in particular. It can be strikingly evident in psychedelic therapy, and in the concluding chapter of *Higher Wisdom: Eminent Elders Explore the Continuing Impact of Psychedelics*, Charles Grob and I summarized relevant discoveries by the early researchers as follows:

A further common conclusion concerned a fundamental capacity and drive of mind. The mind increasingly came to be seen as a self-organizing, self-optimizing system. The researchers concluded that, given supportive conditions, the mind tends to be self-healing, self-integrating, self-individuating, self-actualizing, self-transcending, and self-awakening.

These innate tendencies for the mind to flower, unfold, and develop its potentials had been recognized before in both East and West, psychology and philosophy. Long ago Plato spoke of Eros and Tibetan Buddhism of the self-liberating nature of mind. More recent recognitions include neuroanatomist Kurt Goldstein's "actualization," Carl Rogers' "formative tendency," Carl Jung's "individuation urge," Abraham Maslow's "self-transcendence," Erik Erikson's "self-perfectibility," philosopher Ken Wilber's "eros," and Aldous Huxley's "*moksha* drive."[396]

To these I would also add developmental psychologist Jean Piaget's "equilibration" and the spiritual teacher A. H. Almaas's "optimizing force."

The mind's innate drive to heal and transcend itself may be one of its most important properties and one of the most important contemplative and psychological discoveries.

CHAPTER 11

k. The term *authentic* is being used here in the technical sense suggested by Ken Wilber in *A Sociable God*. Wilber describes a religious-spiritual discipline as *authentic* to the extent to which it aims for higher transpersonal developmental stages and for the ASCs that are their usual precursors. Altered states, when experienced repetitively, tend to stabilize into altered traits and facilitate higher stages.

l. Most researchers agree that ASCs are crucial to shamanism. The venerable Swedish scholar Ake Hultkrantz concluded "...if we want to retain the concept of shamanism as a scholarly instrument we must continue to stress its ecstatic character."

The opposing view has been vociferously championed by the French anthropologist Roberte Hamayon who tellingly titled one of her lectures, "To put an end to the use of 'trance' and 'ecstasy' in the study of shamanism."[141] Hamayon rightly raises concerns about the vagueness of terms such as trance and the methodologically sloppy ways by which it has sometimes been inferred, concerns to which we will return later. However, her commitment to a purely objective social anthropology, and apparent unwillingness to consider verbal reports from shamans, pretty much precludes the possibility of recognizing or studying subjective experiences, including ASCs. But those who have had direct experience of shamanic ASCs report that they can be extremely potent and important. Indeed, it would probably be hard to find a researcher trained in shamanism who would deny the importance of ASCs.

The situation is reminiscent of research on psychedelics. Infatuated with objective measures, many investigators fell into what Abraham Maslow called "means centered" as opposed to "problem centered" research.[226] In their "methodolatry," investigators emphasized the method or means (objective measurement) rather than the problem (understanding what is most central). The result, as Charles Tart famously pointed out, was that if we were to believe the researchers, millions of people were smoking marijuana to increase their heart rate and redden their eyes.[361] When subjective experience is overlooked, so too are meaning and significance.

CHAPTER 12

m. What then are the possible causes of shamanic "fits"? Possible diagnoses include various types of epilepsy, but also hysterical seizures and emotional agitation. Possible types of epilepsy include generalized and temporal lobe varieties.

Generalized or grand mal epilepsy is the classic form of convulsion. Here the patient loses consciousness and falls to the ground. After a few seconds, generalized muscle contractions occur, followed by intense jerking movements of the whole body. The movements gradually become less frequent and finally cease, leaving the patient comatose and flaccid. Consciousness then gradually returns, though the patient often remains confused and drowsy and has no memory of the attack.

Temporal lobe epilepsy is a particularly intriguing possibility because it elicits not only changes in behavior, but also dramatic and unusual experiences. During an attack, patients may experience hallucinations, intense emotions ranging from fear to ecstasy, and feelings of unreality; they may also display unconscious automatic movements.

Both generalized and temporal lobe attacks are forms of organic epilepsy. That is, they are due to underlying brain pathology and as such tend to recur over long periods of time. However, accounts of shamanic "fits" usually imply that attacks occurred only during the initial crises and then disappeared spontaneously. This suggests that the fits were not organic in origin and hence were neither generalized nor temporal lobe epilepsy.

This leaves two other possibilities: hysterical epilepsy or emotional agitation. "Hysterical" epilepsy is an old term for a form of conversion disorder. Here psychological conflict is expressed as, or converted to, behavior that mimics an epileptic attack. Some shamanic fits may well be of this kind. The fact that the fits occur during times of psychological stress, disappear afterward, and are expected of would-be shamans, all suggest a psychological cause. Another possibility is that some "fits" are simply episodes of intense emotional agitation.

n. In fact, the "bible" of psychiatric diagnosis, the *Diagnostic and Statistical Manual of Mental Disorders,* specifically excludes from dissociative trance disorders those trance experiences that are "a normal part of a broadly accepted collective cultural or religious practice."[8] Dissociative trance disorders are a culturally specific subset of "Dissociative Disorders Not Otherwise Specified."

o. It is quite possible that the psychological process of dissociation may play a role in the shamanic journey. However, it is important to distinguish dissociative processes—where certain psychological functions appear to operate autonomously outside awareness and, especially in the case of shamans, where they are deliberately induced for personal and social benefit—from dissociative disorders, which seem involuntary and to lead to dysfunction.

p. If a psychotic episode does occur during the initiation crisis, then there seem to be four possible diagnoses. The first is "Brief Psychotic Disorder." As the name suggests, this is a brief episode lasting from a day to a month, often marked by considerable emotional turmoil, yet with eventual full recovery.[8] It is most common in adolescence or early adulthood, which is consistent with the timing of the initiation crisis.

Other possible diagnoses would be schizophrenia or its short-lived variant, schizophreniform disorder. Current diagnostic practices require continuous signs of psychological disturbances for at least six months before a diagnosis of schizophrenia can be made. Where disturbances are shorter but the clinical picture is still consistent with schizophrenia, then the diagnosis of schizophreniform disorder is made.

The fourth possibility would be "Psychotic Disorder Not Otherwise Specified." This diagnosis is given when a psychotic episode does not meet the diagnostic criteria for specific disorders such as schizophrenia or when there is inadequate information to make a specific diagnosis.

If a psychotic episode does indeed occur during initiation crises, then its differential diagnosis includes these four categories. What is the evidence for and against each of them? Given how limited and unreliable the clinical data is, it will obviously be impossible to make a definitive diagnosis. However, we can consider the possibilities as follows:

The American Psychiatric Association's *Diagnostic and Statistical Manual* suggests that the diagnosis of "psychotic disorder not otherwise specified," should be used for psychosis "…about which there is inadequate information to make a specific diagnosis…"[8] This certainly fits the shamanic situation.

Therefore, either this diagnosis or brief psychotic disorder might be appropriate diagnoses. However, it is schizophrenia that has been the most common diagnosis. This may partly reflect a lack of psychiatric sophistication among researchers. Nonpsychiatrists are often unaware of the many varieties of psychosis and therefore assume that all psychoses are schizophrenia.

In fact, although schizophrenia has been the most common diagnosis, it seems the least likely for several reasons. Many shamans have seemed not at all schizophrenic to anthropologists. Likewise, native peoples often make sharp distinctions between shamanic crises and mental illness. Moreover, the initial crisis is brief, and shamans often seem to end up not only psychologically healthy, but even exceptionally so. This is in marked contrast to schizophrenics, of whom about one-third tend to deteriorate progressively over the years. Indeed, this exceptional psychological well-being of shamans also argues against most of the other diagnoses that have been made, e.g., epilepsy and "hysteria." While some patients may spontaneously recover from any of these, one would hardly expect them to end up as the most able members of society.

CHAPTER 13

q. Limitations of the study include the fact that testing was done under poor conditions, scoring was apparently not blind, and many differences were not significantly different. Other problems with the study are described by Fabrega and Silver.[89]

CHAPTER 16

r. There may be a crucial exception in the case of experiences of pure consciousness such as occur in causal states,[99] but that is not central to shamanism, which does not focus on such experiences.

CHAPTER 18

s. Of the many books on mediumship, three thorough yet readable ones are *Channeling,*[195] *With the Tongues of Men and Angels,*[158] and *The Channeling Zone.*[35]

t. For those who would like to explore *A Course in Miracles,* excellent accounts of it are available in Patrick Miller's *The Complete Story of the Course,*[241] Robert Perry's *Path of Light,*[279] and Robert Skutch's *Journey Without Distance.*[342] Collections of poetic excerpts can be found in the book and CD *Gifts from A Course in Miracles*[381] and on the CD *Choose One Again.*[358]

u. There is a useful division to be made between shallow and deep skeptics.

Shallow skeptics are skeptical about all things that do not fit into their belief system (which itself goes unquestioned).

Deep skeptics are skeptical about all things, *including* their belief system (which they are willing to subject to rigorous questioning).

As Zen says, "Little doubt creates little awakening; great doubt creates great awakening."

CHAPTER 19

v. The principle of *underdetermination of theory by data* is also called "model agnosticism" by physicists. The principle is taken to its logical extreme in the Mach-Duhem-Poincare theorem, which argues that we can create an indefinite number of theories to fit any given set of observations.

w. These are examples of philosophical stances:

1) Reductive materialism holds that each mental event is not only type-identical to a neural event, but is in fact *nothing but* a neural event.

2) Eliminative materialism holds that accounts of mental entities, as usually described, should be eliminated in favor of only neural ones.

x. It is also consistent with a contemporary post-Kantian, post-metaphysical epistemology that acknowledges our inherent epistemological limitations and "the death of metaphysics."[411]

CHAPTER 24

y. I suspect that it will not be long before there is an analogous awakening to the distinction between *multistage* and *unistage* cultures, differentiating those cultures that recognize multiple potential psychological and spiritual stages of adult development and those that do not.

CHAPTER 26

z. Whether different traditions can induce identical internal breakthroughs and in what ways they may differ is a long and complex debate. For arguments that the experiences of different traditions are necessarily different, see Katz.[192] For arguments that they can overlap, see Forman,[98] Walsh and Vaughan,[399] and Wilber.[409] Clearly there are multiple kinds of religiously induced mystical experiences, just as there are multiple kinds of psychedelic experiences. Fortunately we don't need to go into these complexities to investigate whether some psychedelic experiences may overlap some mystical experiences.

aa. This chapter draws from *The Spirit of Shamanism*[390] and from a paper, "Entheogens: True or False?"[395]

CHAPTER 30

ab. Examples of comprehensive, informed reviews of psi can be found in Dean Radin's[291] book *The Conscious Universe* and the special issue "Psi Wars: Parapsychology" of *The Journal of Consciousness Studies, 2003,* 10(6–7). Examples of bad reviews that display an astounding ignorance of the research include Charpak & Broch's *Debunked! ESP, Telekinesis, and Other Pseudo-science,*[51] as well as the review of this book by Freeman Dyson,[78] "One in a Million," which appeared in the *New York Review of Books,* 2004, March 25. A review of theories of psi is available in Dean Radin's *Entangled Minds.*[292]

ac. Researchers have studied several capacities that astrologers claim to possess or that are implied by their claims. All of these capacities are essential if astrology is to be considered legitimate, but astrologers display none of them. Five crucial capacities are:

1) Do astrologers agree when judging the same birth chart? The short answer is "No." *There is virtually no agreement whatsoever between different astrologers' interpretations of the same chart.* Correlations average about 0.1 (when 1.0 is perfect correlation and 0 is no correlation). By contrast, this was marginally worse than for practitioners of palmistry and vastly worse than the 0.8 that is demanded of valid psychological tests. This lack of agreement was a consistent finding across all studies, including those using expert astrologers, those run by astrologers themselves, and those run by astrologers and scientists in collaboration.[193]

This finding is devastating. It destroys any claim for reliability or validity of astrological readings, because it means that there are almost as many astrologies as there are astrologers, and they agree not at all.

2) Astrologers are unable to pick the owners of birth charts.[66]

3) Likewise, subjects of astrological readings are unable to pick their own readings from other people's profiles. In other words, subjects are just as likely to think that another person's—in fact, any person's—profile is as accurate a description of them as their own.

The tendency for people to agree enthusiastically with false personality readings has been named the "Barnum effect," in honor of P. T. Barnum's famous line that "there's a sucker born every minute." One amusing demonstration of the Barnum effect was offered by Michel Gauquelin, who placed an advertisement in a Paris newspaper generously offering a free personal horoscope. Of those who received one, 94 percent subsequently rated it as accurate. Yet each and every person had received the same horoscope: that of Dr. Petiot, one of France's most notorious mass murderers.[251] A similar study in the United States (using a different mass murderer) yielded similarly satisfied customers.[65]

4) Astrological predictions fare no better than chance. In fact, earthquake predictions fared worse than chance.

5) Astrologers' readings show no correlation with well-validated psychological tests of personality. These failures held up even when the astrologers were highly esteemed experts, helped design the study, regarded the study as a good measure of their skills, and felt confident of their readings.[234]

ad. There is, however, one body of research much cited by astrologers: the studies of Michel Gauquelin. Unfortunately, it is clear these astrologers have either not read, or else have not understood, Gauquelin. Closely examined, Gauquelin's findings offer no support for conventional astrological claims.

Gauquelin labored mightily for decades searching for astrological correlations. From his massive statistical database he concluded that "all the results remained negative. There seemed to be no truth in the idea that signs of the zodiac determined anything or that horoscopes could be used to predict the future."[113]

However, to his surprise, analysis did reveal very small but significant correlations between eminence in various professional fields and the position of certain planets at birth. For example, eminent scientists, soldiers, and athletes were likely to have the planets Saturn, Jupiter, and Mars, respectively, just over the horizon or at the zenith of the sky at the time of their birth.

Not surprisingly, these claims met with enormous skepticism. However, independent re-analyses have generally been confirmatory, despite a scandalous attempt by the Committee for the Scientific Investigation of Claims of the Paranormal (CSICOP) to discredit it.[300] CSICOP is, for the most part, a good example of shallow skepticism.

Gauquelin's research deserves further study, even though it is probably an artifact of nine-teenth-century parents changing their children's birth dates to favorable days.[65] However, contrary to claims by astrologers,[353] there are several reasons why it offers no support for traditional astrology. To briefly summarize these reasons:

- Gauquelin's patterns do not fit traditional astrological patterns.

- Gauquelin's findings apply *only* to eminent people: an elite 0.005 percent of the population. People who do not attain eminence show no correlation with planetary birth position. In other words, for 99.995 percent of the population, the vast majority of us, Gauquelin's data offers no support for astrology whatsoever.

- Analysis of Gauquelin's data suggests that the effect may be due to parents' changing the reported time of birth. Most of his subjects were from the nineteenth century when superstitions abounded and when, for example, there was a dramatic deficit of births reported on the thirteenth of each month.[65]

  The effects are *extremely* small, in fact far, far too small to be of any value whatsoever in making astrological predictions.

In summary, Gauquelin's findings are fascinating but offer no support for traditional astrological claims and are of no value in making astrological predictions.

CHAPTER 32

ae. In the technical terms of yoga, this is the practice of *pratyāhāra* (sense withdrawal) and *dhyāna* (meditation) to produce *samādhi* (enstasy). This arises first as *savikalpa samādhi* (samādhi with form) and then as *nirvikalpa samādhi* (samādhi without form), in which only consciousness re-mains as *sac-cid-ananda* (infinite being—consciousness—bliss).

af. This experience of constant flux is most evident in the Vipassana state-stage of "arising and passing away," when the reality of *annica* (the impermanence and unceasing change of all experience) is deeply realized. Given that there are about a dozen major state-stages in Vipassana meditation, the complexities of comparing different practices becomes obvious.

CHAPTER 33

ag. Without direct experience, descriptions remain what Immanuel Kant called "empty," and we may lack *adequatio*: the capacity to comprehend their deeper meaning and "grades of significance."[327] Aldous Huxley[171] summarized this as "knowledge is a function of being."

These limitations on understanding meditative experiences, especially advanced ones, without direct personal experience of them, can be conceived of in several ways. They can be considered in terms of states of consciousness as reflecting the limits of state-specific knowledge and cross-state transfer,[208, 359] developmentally as stage-specific understanding, in classical epistemological terms as the necessity of opening the eye of contemplation, and linguistically as the difficulty of understanding the signifier (word or term) without having known the relevant signified experience.[410]

ah. I have personally heard two accounts of union. These were of union with the universe rather than with a deity. This points to the fact that there are actually different types of mystical union. Union with the physical universe is an example of gross state "nature mysticism."

Union with a deity figure is subtle-state deity or theistic mysticism. Union with formless consciousness or void is causal-state formless mysticism, while union with the phenomena of all states is nondual mysticism.[413]

Quotations Information

PART I: WHO, WHERE, WHEN, AND WHAT IS A SHAMAN?

Reality is more complex…: Rabbi Yannai, in Shapiro, 1993, p. 38.

Chapter 2: *Why* The World of Shamanism?

A new intellectual understanding…: Grof, 1985, p. 341.

Chapter 3: *What Is a Shaman? The Challenge of Definition*

If names be not correct…: Confucius, in Smith, 1958, p. 182.

For more than a century…: Francfort & Hamayon, 2001, p. 4.

the closest thing we have…: Noel, 1999, p. 107.

It is henceforth one of the…: Hadot, 2001, p. 398.

The problems of definition…: Abelson, 1967, p. 314.

philosophy is a battle against…: Wittgenstein, 1969, p. 109.

Existence is beyond the power…: Lao Tzu, in Bynner, 1980, p. 25.

All human thought proceeds…: Smith, 1958, p. 182.

In all Tungus languages this term…: Shirokogoroff, 1935, p. 269.

only defining attribute is that…: Peters & Price-Williams, 1980, p. 408.

A first definition of this complex…: Eliade, 1964, p. 4.

the shaman specializes in a trance…: Eliade, 1964, p. 5.

a man or woman who enters an altered state…: Harner, 1982, p. 25.

shamanism is ultimately only a method…: Harner, 1985, pp. 328–329.

Chapter 4: The When and Where of Shamanism: Origins and Distribution

Man is the being who…: Barrett, 1962, p. 229.

Anthropologists are fond of reminding…: Brown, 2001, p. 251.

insist that sorcerers, when discovered…: Brown, 2001, p. 252.

PART II: THE BIG PICTURE

Each being contains in itself…: Huxley, 1945, p. 5.

Chapter 5: Essential Spirituality: Central Principles and Practices of Spiritual Life

Although there is a great number…: Geshe Kelsang Gyatso, in Gyatso, 1988, p. 103.

every virtue requires other virtues…: Murphy, 1992, p. 558.

which virtue is the most important?…: Palmer, Sherrard, & Ware, 1993, p. 160.

Possessed of courage but devoid of morality…: Confucius, in Lau, 1979, 17:23.

If one plumbs, investigates into…: Lu Shiang-Shan, in Creel, 1953, p. 213.

This Mind is the Buddha: Huang Po, in Blofeld, 1958, p. 29.

Here, in my own soul, the greatest…: Meister Eckhart, in Harvey, 1998, p. 92.

the Self is that one, immutable…: Aurobindo, 1922, p. 115.

Regard your neighbor's gain…: Tai Shang Kon Ying P'ien, in Penner, 1993, p. 43.

Rare are those who understand ethics: Confucius, in Lau, 1979, p. 132.

Whatever you do, you do to yourself: The Buddha, in Byrom, 1976, p. 118.

whatever is…thought to be necessary…: Gampopa, 1971, p. 271.

I could follow the dictates of my own heart…: Confucius, in Waley, 1989, p. 88.

At first, precepts (ethics) are a practice…: Kornfield, 1993, p. 298.

Everything from ruler, minister, husband, wife…: Wang Yang Ming, in Chan, 1963, p. 661.

Emotions of the soul should be watched…: Maimonides, in Hoffman, 1985, p. 85.

All you want is to be happy…: Nisargadatta, 1973, p. 241.

The learning of the great person…: Wang Yang Ming, in Chan, 1963, p. 660.

Control the mind…: Chuang Tzu, in Merton, 1969, p. 121.

No subject occupies a more central…: Schumacher, 1973, p. 67.

Attention cannot be continuously sustained: James, 1962, p. 51.

Be still and know that I am God: The Bible, in Ramana Maharishi, 1984, p. 53.

When, through the practice of yoga…: *Bhagavad Gita*, in Prabhavananda & Isherwood, 1972, p. 66.

When water is still it is like a mirror…: Chuang Tzu, in Giles, 1969, p. 47.

sees what the eyes sees…: Chuang Tzu, in Merton, 1985, p. 149.

mindfulness…is helpful everywhere: The Buddha, in Nyanaponika Thera, 1962, p. 150.

Awareness per se—by and of itself—can be curative: Perls, 1969, p. 16.

Happy are those who find wisdom…: Jewish Torah, in Proverbs 3:13, 17, 4:5.

He who is learned is not wise: Perry, 1981, p. 739.

Knowledge studies others, wisdom is self-known: Lao Tzu, in Bynner, 1980, #33.

All that one gives one gives to oneself…: Maharshi, 1988, p. 8.

Make it your guiding principle…: Confucius, in Lau, 1979, p. 116.

The best way to become…: Maslow, 1970, p. xii.

Be kind to all: Mohammad, in Angha, 1995, p. 19.

Chapter 6: What Is a Hero? Life's Aims and Games

What people really need…: De Ropp, 1968, p. 11.

Life games reflect life aims…: De Ropp, 1968, p. 12.

The kingdom of heaven is within you: Jesus, Luke 17:21 (King James Version).

Those who know themselves know their Lord: Mohammad, in Perry 1981, p. 855.

Atman and Brahman are one: A frequent theme in the Hindu scriptures, the Upanishads.

Look within, you are the Buddha: Buddhist saying.

is that man is asleep…: De Ropp, 1968, p. 19.

It still remains the most…: De Ropp, 1968, p. 21.

The normal adjustment of the average…: Maslow, 1968, p. 14.

Many are called, but few are chosen: Jesus, in Matthew 22:14 (New International Version).

The study of virtue and vice…: Plato, 1961, p. 1591.

The holy man goes to the lone…: Sioux Indian, in Curtis, 1907, pp. 38–39.

accepts the pains and duties in the…: Underhill, 1974, pp. 140, 173.

PART III: THE LIFE OF THE SHAMAN

The words "many are called…: Jung, 1964, p. 173.

Chapter 7: Times of Trial: The Initial Call and the Initiation Crisis

If you bring forth what is within you…: Jesus, in The Gospel of Thomas.

Mother was put on a very strict…: Rasmussen, 1929, pp. 116–118.

Everyone knew precisely what…: Rasmussen, 1929, p. 54.

our fathers have inherited from…: Rasmussen, 1929, p. 56.

evidence does exist that some…: Laughlin, McManus, & d'Aquili, 1992, pp. 186–187.

I had a wonderful dream…: Nepalese shaman, in Ashok & Skafte, 2001, p. 235.

Hear my words…: Jewish Torah, in Numbers 12:16 (Revised Standard Version).

The rejection of the "spirits" is…: Bogoras, 1909, p. 419.

"sicknesses," attacks, dreams, and hallucinations…: Eliade, 1964, p. 35.

For men the preparatory stage…: Bogoras, 1909, p. 420.

When I was 13, I became possessed…: Nepalese shaman, in Peters, 1987, p. 164.

Chapter 8: A Life of Learning: Shamanic Training and Discipline

The greatest of all wonders…: Durant, 1938, p. 360.

First gain control of the body…: Chuang Tzu, in Merton, 1969, p. 121.

If you aim to live by such principles…: Epictetus, 1995, p. 4.

The person who hasn't conquered…: Maslow, 1968, p. 4.

I have inquired, carefully and most…: Eckhart, 1981, p. 285.

Today this trance occurs…: Blacker, 1986, p. 23.

During the first part of the discipline…: Blacker, 1986, p. 88.

To stand under a waterfall…: Blacker, 1986, p. 92.

The power of solitude is great…: Rasmussen, 1929, p. 114.

Then I sought solitude…: Rasmussen, 1929, pp. 118–119.

sudden apparently unprecipitated wide…: Walsh, 1977, p. 161.

man is not even master in…: Freud, 1938, p. 252.

all scriptures without any exception…: Ramana Maharshi, 1955, p. 63.

Strange unknown beings came…: Rasmussen, 1927, pp. 82–84.

The only true wisdom lives…: Ostermann, 1952, p. 99.

when a man has learned…: Yalom, 1980, p. 398.

Chapter 9: The Culmination of the Quest: Shamanic Enlightenment

In order that the mind should…: Plato, 1945, p. 516.

For the rest of my life I want to reflect…: Einstein, in Russell, 1992, p. 155.

Clearly, the 'inner light' that…: Eliade, 1964, p. 420.

a wonderful light arose within…: Boehme, in Metzner, 1998, p. 170.

This was much more than a simple…: Lusseryan, 1998, pp. 16–21.

Those who seek the light are merely…: Anonymous, 1992, p. 357.

the next thing an old shaman has to…: Rasmussen, 1929, pp. 112–113.

And then in the midst of such a fit…: Rasmussen, 1929, p. 119.

Where there is no vision…: Proverbs 29:18 (King James Version).

Chapter 10: The Culmination of the Quest: Death and Rebirth

It is only in the face of death…: St. Augustine, in Yalom, 1980, p. 30.

Let me know how fleeting my life is: Psalms 39:4 (Revised Standard Version).

Death is a good advisor: Mohammad, in Angha, 1995, p. 82.

A confrontation with one's personal death…: Yalom, 1980, p. 30.

the most radical and total transformation…: Metzner, 1998, p. 136.

Before a shaman attains the stage…: Rasmussen, 1929, p. 114.

they are cut up by demons or…: Fabrega & Silver, 1970, p. 203.

Physical and emotional agony culminates…: Grof, 1980, p. 85.

Death is a mirror in which…: Rinpoche, 1992, p. 11.

Powerful experiential sequences of dying…: Grof, 1988, p. 234.

A grain of wheat remains a solitary grain…: John 12:24 (Revised Standard Version).

PART IV: DIAGNOSING THE SHAMAN

Each investigator most readily sees…: Jung, 1953, pp. 40–43.

Chapter 11: Devil, Madman, Saint, or Sage? The Eye of the Beholder

people of evil custom who have…: Thevet, 2001, p. 13.

drink that rude potion of tobacco: Biet, 2001, p. 17.

May not one of them return!…: Petrovich, 2001, p. 19.

the shaman is mentally deranged…: Devereux, 2001, p. 120.

The negative picture of the shaman…: Kakar, 1982, p. 90.

Devoid of the personal experience of…: Noll, 1983, p. 452.

it is as if Freud supplied to us…: Maslow, 1968, p. 5.

virulent influence of Freudian psychoanalytic…: Noll, 1984, p. 192.

the obvious similarities between…: Alexander & Selesnich, 1966, p. 372.

Who are…the greatest benefactors…: Toynbee, 1948, p. 156.

only by those whose intellectual inquiry…: Wilber, 2000, p. 157.

brush aside its dark truths: Brown, 2001, p. 256.

Chapter 12: Primitive Madmen: Assessing Traditional Views of Shamans as Psychologically Disturbed

The most typical picture of hysterical…: Shirokogoroff, 1935, p. 347.

A curious and not fully explored…: Nemiah, 1985, p. 950.

an outright psychotic: Devereux, 1961, p. 285.

grossly non-reality-oriented ideation…: Silverman, 1967, pp. 22–23.

Chapter 13: Putting Shamans to the Test: Measuring Personality and Spiritual Mastery

the masters were enmeshed in their…: Jonte-Pace, 2004, p. 143.

One would almost believe that…: Jonte-Pace, 2004, p. 146, 148.

Chapter 14: Spiritual Emergency and Spiritual Emergence? New Views of Shamans' Health

of external facts we have had enough…: Barrett, 1962, p. 23.

is not only a sick man…: Eliade, 1964, p. 27.

shamanism is not a disease but…: Ackerknecht, 1943, p. 46.

show proof of a more than normal…: Eliade, 1964, p. 29.

our greatest blessings come to us…: Lukoff, 1985, p. 155.

some patients have a mental illness…: Lukoff, 1985, p. 157.

dispels fear, but also blinds: Castaneda, 1969, p. 80.

spirit [is] constantly striving for release…: Perry, 1986, p. 33, 34, 36.

if you deliberately plan to be less…: Maslow, 1971, p. 36.

Among the Sedang Moi, a person who…: Devereux, 1956/2001, p. 119.

Transpersonal crises of this type bear…: Grof & Grof, 1986, pp. 10–11.

Individuals whose spiritual crises follows…: Grof & Grof, 1986, p. 11.

with good support, experiences of this kind…: Grof & Grof, 1986, p. 15.

if a person undergoing this turmoil…: Perry, 1986, p. 35.

Chapter 15: Shamanic Trickery: The Tricks of the Trade

There can be no doubt, of course…: Bogoras, 1909, p. 429.

During our stay at South Hampton Island…: Rasmussen, 1929, p. 147.

If now a shaman desires to injure…: Rasmussen, 1929, p. 122.

I believe I am a better shaman than others…: Rasmussen, 1929, p. 132.

Plainly, the shaman's tricks serve as…: Warner, 1980, p. 43.

he then 'vomits' out this object and…: Harner, 1973, p. 24.

It is difficult for a healer to doubt…: Warner, 1980, p. 49.

PART V: THE SHAMAN'S UNIVERSE

Many of the transpersonal experiences…: Grof, 1985, p. 341.

Chapter 16: Many Worlds

A sensible man prefers the…: Lao Tzu, in Bynner, 1944, p. 31.

The pre-eminently shamanic technique…: Eliade, 1964, p. 259.

The essential schema is always to be…: Eliade, 1964, p. 259.

the mind is being used to gain access…: Harner, 1987, p. 4.

a cosmotheological concept into a….: Eliade, 1964, p. 21.

The shamans did not create the cosmology…: Eliade, 1964, p. 266.

Shamanism ultimately is only a method…: Harner, 1987, pp. 4–5.

Chapter 17: Many Spirits

Glendower: I can call spirits…: Shakespeare, *Henry IV* (Part I, Act III, Scene I).

the extreme importance of 'spirit visions'…: Eliade, 1964, p. 85.

For three days and nights the two men…: Loeb, 1929, p. 60, 84.

fantasize a large part of the time…: Wilson & Barber, 1982, p. 340.

Everyone may educate and regulate his imagination…: Noll, 1987, p. 47.

All this long and tiring ceremony…: Eliade, 1964, pp. 87–88.

a man who has immediate concrete experiences…: Eliade, 1964, pp. 87–88.

they can appear in the form of bears…: Eliade, 1964, p. 89.

most valuable and rewarding phenomena: Grof, 1988, p. 121.

From *sanyama* on the strength: Shearer, 1989, p. 98, 3:24.

During the period of initial contact…: Siikala, 1978, p. 228.

Chapter 18: Mediums: Channels for the Spirits?

opening of the gate of words: Walraven, 2001, p. 346.

After crossing the Halys…: Hastings, 1991, p. 52.

Leah, a sixth density entity from the planet Venus…: Schultz, 1989, p. 56.

whence she returned with colorful descriptions…: Nemiah, 1985, p. 950.

higher intelligences have got to be smarter…: Wilber, 1988, p. 14.

Having no belief in God…: Skutch, 1984, p. 134.

the three books comprise one of…: Skutch, 1984, p. 127.

perhaps the most important writing in the…: Skutch, 1984, p. i.

The *Course* is clearly inspired…: Wilber, 1988, p. 34.

The *Course* is the most systematic spiritual…: Hastings, 1991, p. 24.

consist solely of strings of loosely associated…: Reed, 1989, p. 385, 390, 388.

The unity of consciousness is illusory…: Hilgard, 1986, p. 1.

just the opposite of what one would expect…: Thomason, 1989, p. 393.

Chapter 19: What Is a "Spirit"?

Several volumes would be needed for an…: Eliade, 1964, pp. 5–6.

I saw with my own eyes a large gray blob…: Turner, 2001, p. 260.

for the most part, grossly and transparently fake: Sante, 2006, p. 17.

From my studies with hypnosis I know…: Tart, in Klimo, 1987, p. 223.

suddenly there appeared from the right a winged…: Jung, 1961, pp. 182–183.

a stream of cool water circulating through…: Achterberg, 1985, p. 98.

Tao is beyond words: Merton, 1969, p. 152.

Things keep their secrets: Heraclitus, 2001, p. 9.

Reality is steeped in mystery…: Smith, 1991, p. 389.

stands at the cradle of true art…: Einstein, in Mallove, 1986, p. 12.

Chapter 20: Cosmic Traveling: The Shamanic Journey

We must close our eyes and invoke…: Plotinus, in O'Brien, 1964, p. 42.

Any ecstatic cannot be considered a shaman…: Eliade, 1964, p. 5.

he commands the techniques of ecstasy…: Eliade, 1964, p. 182.

an ineffable joy in what he sees…: Harner, 1982, p. 27.

Entrances into the Lowerworld commonly lead…: Harner, 1982, p. 32.

A shaman about to make this journey…: Rasmussen, 1929, pp. 123–127.

the cause of *Takánakapsâluk*'s anger is explained…: Rasmussen, 1929, p. 129.

Chapter 21: A World of Ecstatics: Journeys in Other Religious Traditions

Divine reality is infinite…: Ramakrishna, in Hixon, 1992, p. 11.

glory be to Him, who carried…: Koran, Surah 17:1–2.

if I would go one step further…: Schimmel, 1975, p. 219.

eyes swayed not, nor swept astray…: Koran, Surah 53:17–18.

He fell to the ground…: Acts 9:4, 8, 9 (New Revised Standard Version).

I will go on to visions and revelations…: 2 Corinthians 12:1–4 (New Revised Standard Version).

Which I had heard speaking,..: Revelation 4:1 (English Standard Version).

moral purity, rabbinic learnedness…: Blumenthal, 1978, p. 90.

when a man is worthy and blessed with certain…: Ariel, 1988, p. 22.

harsh, fearful terrifying… Bolts of lightening…: Blumenthal, 1978, p. 63.

The mystic who in his ecstasy has passed…: Scholem, 1946, p. 56.

For on the day of the New Year of the year…: Baal Shem Tov, in Ullman & Reichenberg-Ullman, 2001, p. 79.

Up to the Cracks of Heaven…: Kohn, 1993, pp. 256–257.

by sinking deep in rapture within the confines…: Robinet, 1989, p. 164.

frolics in the paradise protected by them…: Robinet, 1989, p. 168.

Adepts visualize the pure energy of the…: Kohn, 1993, p. 267.

In all cases, first undertake purifications…: Kohn, 1993, p. 259.

To attain the Tao through ecstatic excursions…: Kohn, 1993, p. 250.

To practice the Tao excursion to the seven…: Kohn, 1993, p. 257-258.

Once the tour of the whole universe…: Robinet, 1989, p. 167.

The greatest of all wonders is not the conqueror…: Durant, 1968, p. 360.

Chapter 22: The Varieties of Journey Experiences: Dream, Out-of-Body, Near-Death, and Abduction Experiences

Maybe you and I are still in a dream…: Chuang Tzu, in Feng & English, 1974, p. 136.

You do not understand even life…: Confucius, in Lau, 1979, XI:12, p. 107.

Visit the graves: Mohammad, in Sayed, 1969, p. 92.

Death is a good adviser: Mohammad, in Angha, 1995, p. 82.

I recommend almost dying…: Sagan. in Kornfield, 2000, p. 38.

The shaman, then, is a master of death…: Kalweit, 1988, p. 15, 11.

We are such stuff…: Shakespeare, in *The Tempest* (IV.1).

a person must control his thoughts…: Ibn El-Arabi, in Shah, 1971, pp. 155–156.

witnessing the process of dreaming…: Shearer, 1989, I:38, p. 64.

Then prayer never stops in a man's soul: Saint Isaac, in Harvey, 1998, p. 63.

It's surprising that more of the neighbors…: Sagan, 1993, p. 5.

Which is more likely—that we're undergoing…: Sagan, 1993, p. 5.

approximately nine out of ten persons…: Harner, 1985, p. 452.

Chapter 23: Interpreting and Researching Journeys

What is this awesome mystery…: Symeon, in McGuckin, 2003, p. 160.

when she takes leave of the body and…: Socrates, in Jowett, 1953, p. 65.

There is no difference between the…: Ramana Maharshi, in Osborne, 1962, p. 193.

PART VI: SHAMANIC TECHNIQUES

This is why it is so difficult to explain…: Satprem, 1968, p. 84.

Chapter 24: The Politics of Consciousness

After hypnotizing a man with a gangrenous leg…: Tart, 1986, p. 80.

a necessarily relevant question to the study...: Hamayon, 1998, p. 177.

is the counterpart of ethnocentrism between…: Harner, 1982, p. xvii.

a striking finding and suggests that we are…: Bourguignon, 1973, p. 11.

desire to alter consciousness periodically…: Weil, 1972, p. 17.

Ritual is the husk of true faith: Tao Te Ching, in Mitchell, 1992, #38.

the modern-day successors of shamans…: Hamayon, 1998, p. 181.

trance occurs only rarely…: Blacker, 1986, p. 23.

Chapter 25: Transforming Consciousness: Contemporary Understandings and Shamanic Methods

It is the quality of your consciousness…: Tolle, 1999, p. 174.

has as its object transforming the apprentice…: Eliade, 1964, pp. 84–85.

we have been making music since the dawn…: Weinberger, 2004, p. 90.

But now bring me a minstrel…: 2 Kings 3:15 (Revised Standard Version).

Dancing, music and other exaggerations…: Underhill, 1974, p. 58.

Chapter 26: Psychedelics and Entheogens: Revealers of the Divine Within?

The observations from psychedelic…: Grof, in Roberts & Hruby, 2002, pp. 76–77.

For several hours after drinking the brew…: Harner, 1973, pp. 16–17.

on the day following one Ahayuasca party…: Stafford, 1992, p. 353.

after 30 years of discussion, the question…: Grof, 2001, p. 270.

There are, of course, innumerable drug…: Smith, 1964, pp. 520, 523.

Descriptively drug experiences cannot be…: Smith, 1964, p. 523.

the principle of causal indifference: Stace, 1988, p. 29.

Drugs appear to induce religious experiences…: Smith, 1964, pp. 528–529.

Even the Buddha continued to sit…: Smith, 2000, p. 31.

Chapter 27: Divination and Diagnosis

Humans respond not to events but to…: Frank, 1982, p. 4.

Projection makes perception…: Anonymous, 1992, p. 248.

The one who is to consult the spirits…: Rasmussen, 1929, pp. 141–142.

then all in the house must confess any breaches…: Rasmussen, 1929, pp. 128–129.

Chapter 28: How Do They Heal?

Oral reports, ethnographic studies, travelers' records…: Harner, 2004, p. 16.

Psychotherapy is a planned, emotionally charged…: Frank, 1985, pp. 49–50.

The strain for survival may be intense…: Rogers, 1982, p. 133.

Ritual, through its formal properties…: Evans, 1996, pp. 1121, 1122.

formal, patterned, and stereotyped public…: Evans, 1996, p. 1121.

a symbolic device integral to the communication…: Evans, 1996, pp. 1121, 1123.

psychotherapy and related cultural processes…: Rossi, 2004, p. 13.

Simply stated, the regulation of gene…: Kandel, 1998, p. 460.

Without the transcendent and the transpersonal…: Maslow, 1968, p. iv.

With song, one can open the gates of heaven: Hoffman, 1981, p. 163.

The more popular a shaman becomes…: Skultans, 1986, p. 262.

A cheerful heart is good medicine…: Proverbs 17:22 (New International Version).

a poorly understood process in which…: Hurley, 1985, p. 4.

a kind of superintelligence that exists…: Thomas, 1980, p. 65.

If the patient really has confidence in me…: Sandner, 1979, pp. 17–18.

Chapter 29: Healing the Healer: How Do They Heal Themselves?

Physician, heal thyself: Luke 4:23 (King James Version).

The shaman must first…: Hoppal, 1987, p. 84.

while the shaman…: Bogoras, 1909, p. 419.

you may see dead persons…: Elkin, 1977, p. 70.

All that one gives…: Ramana Maharshi, 1988, p. 8.

goes far beyond a self-concerned…: Harner, 1982, p. 139.

never deserts benevolence: Confucius, in Lau, 1979, p. 72.

self-actualizing people…: Maslow, 1970, p. 28.

Finding the center of strength…: May, 1953, p. 79.

The best way to become…: Maslow, 1970, p. xii.

In shamanism there is…: Harner, 1982, p. 139.

I don't know what your…: Schweitzer, www.quotationspage.com/collections.html#20thcent.

Chapter 30: Shamans and Psi: What Is the Evidence?

vast parapsychological…: Long, 1982, p. 49

not a single individual…: Hansel, 1980, p. 314.

There is no source…: James, in McDermott, 1977, p. 787.

abhors the exhibition of occult forces: Govinda, 1970, p. 82.

My own hunch…: Frank, 1985, p. 72.

In the course of a great joyous…: Barker, 1980, p. 175.

Made one of his "spirits"…: Bogoras, 1909, p. 436.

There can be no doubt…: Bogoras, 1909, p. 429.

was never able to break…: Rogo, 1987, p. 138.

psi masters….veritable…: Wescott, 1977, p. 340.

in my own clinical experience…: Grof, 2001, pp. 276, 278.

The statistical results of the…: Utts, in Radin, 1997, pp. 4–5.

The fault, dear Brutus is not…: Shakespeare, *Julius Caesar* (I, ii).

PART VII: THE SHAMAN'S MIND

One conclusion was forced…: James, 1958, p. 29.

Chapter 31: Shamanic States of Mind

The mind is its own place…: Milton, in *Paradise Lost,* Book 1, Line 253.

shamans, yogis and Buddhists…: Doore, 1988, p. 223.

experiences existential unity…: Kalweit, 1988, p. 23.

Chapter 32: Comparing States of Mind: Shamans, Yogis, Meditators, and Schizophrenics

If mind is comprehended…: Ratnamegha Sutra, in Nyanaponika, 1962, p. 21.

The tortoise can draw in his legs…. Prabhavananda & Isherwood, 1972, p. 42.

Yoga is the settling of the mind…: Shearer, 1989, p. 49, I: 2–4.

an invulnerable state in which…: Elide, 1958, p. 78.

Yoga cannot possibly be confused…: Eliade, 1969, p. 339.

Chapter 33: How High Do They Fly? Levels of Consciousness

The exploration of the highest...: Maslow, 1968, p. 71.

the settling of the mind into silence...: Shearer, 1989, p. 49, 1–2.

Be still and know that I am God: Psalms 46:10.

Leave the senses...: Saint Dionysius, in Harvey, 1998, p. 50.

Spirit is self-existent...: Aurobindo, 1922, p. 144.

By Himself he sees Himself,...: Ibn Arabi, in Vaughan-Lee, 1995, p. 179.

we never find the mystical union...: Hultkrantz, 1978, p. 42.

if mysticism is not restricted...: Hultkrantz, 1978, p. 28.

Chapter 34: The Evolution of Consciousness

In the history of the collective...: Jung, 1969, p. 272.

Ninety-nine percent of all the species...: Ferris, 1988, p. 389.

The world was created on 22nd October...: Nisker, 1990, p. 141.

Our most powerful story. Thomas, 1974, p. 122.

survival machines...: Dawkins, 1976, p. x.

The probability that human intelligence...: Grof, 1985, p. 23.

As for the 'inner light' which plays...: Eliade, 1964, p. 508.

shamans, yogis and Buddhists...: Doore, 1988, p. 223.

experiences existential unity...: Kalweit, 1988, p. 236.

The consciousness of each of us...: Teilhard de Chardin, 1964, p. 221.

Chapter 35: The Shaman's Brain: Neurotheology and Neuromythology

Medical materialism seems indeed...: James, 1958, p. 29.

Chapter 36: Shamanism(s) in a Changing World

It is an invented tradition...: Townsend, 2004, p. 4.

Overall, I suggest that shamanism...: Vitebsky, 1995/2001, p. 297.

you are more than this puny body...: Kapleau, 1965, p. 143.

the I, one's real, most intimate self...: Harman, 1979, p. 14.

Out of my experience...: James, in Murphy & Ballou, 1960, p. 324.

A human being is part of the whole...: Einstein, in Goldstein, 1983, p. 126.

See yourself in others...: Byrom, 1976, p. 49.

Bibliography

1. Abelson, R. (1967). Definition. In P. Edwards (Ed.), *The encyclopedia of philosophy* (Vol. 2, pp. 314–323). New York: Macmillan Press.

2. Abramson, J. (2004). *Overdosed America: The broken promise of American medicine.* New York: Harper Collins.

3. Achterberg, J. (1985). *Imagery and healing: Shamanism and modern medicine.* Boston: New Science Library.

4. Ackerknecht, E. (1943). Psychopathology, primitive medicine, and primitive culture. *Bulletin of the History of Medicine, 14*, 30–67.

5. Albright, C. & Ashbrook, J. (2001). *Where God lives in the human brain.* Naperville, IL: Sourcebooks.

6. Alcock, J., Burns, J., & Freeman, A. (Eds.). (2003). Psi wars: Parapsychology. *Journal of Consciousness Studies, 10*(6–7).

7. Alexander, F. & Selesnich, S. (1966). *The history of psychiatry.* New York: New American Library.

8. American Psychiatric Association. (1994). *Diagnostic and statistical manual of mental disorders* (4th ed.). Washington, DC: American Psychiatric Association.

9. Angha, N. (Trans.). (1995). *Deliverance: Words from the Prophet Mohammad.* San Rafael, CA: International Association of Sufism.

10. Anonymous. (1992). *A course in miracles* (2nd ed.). Mill Valley, CA: Foundation for Inner Peace.

BIBLIOGRAPHY

11. Ariel, D. (1988). *The mystic quest: An introduction to Jewish mysticism*. New York: Schocken Books.

12. Arrien, A. (1989). Personal communication.

13. Ashok & Skafte, P. (1992/2001). Interview with a killing shaman. In J. Narby & F. Huxley (Eds.), *Shamans through time* (pp. 234–237). New York: Tarcher/Putnam.

14. Astin, J., Harkness, E., & Ernst, E. (2000). The efficacy of "distant healing": A systematic review of randomized trials. *Annals of Internal Medicine, 132*, 903–910.

15. Aurobindo. (1922). *Essays on the Gita*. Pondicherry, India: Sri Aurobindo Ashram Trust.

16. Austin, J. H. (1999). *Zen and the brain: Toward an understanding of meditation and consciousness*. Cambridge, MA: MIT Press.

17. Bachrach, A. (1985). Learning theory. In H. Kaplan & B. Sadock (Eds.), *Comprehensive Textbook of Psychiatry* (4th ed., Vol. 1, pp. 184–198). Baltimore: Williams and Wilkins.

18. Badiner, A. & Grey, A. (Eds.). (2002). *Zig zag zen: Buddhism and psychedelics*. San Francisco: Chronicle Books.

19. Bandura, A. (1986). *Social foundations of thought and action*. Englewood Cliffs, NJ: Prentice-Hall.

20. Barker, D. (1980). Psi information and culture. In B. Shapiro & L. Coly (Eds.), *Communication and parapsychology* (pp. 168–201). New York: Parapsychology Foundation.

21. Barnard, G. W. & Kripal, J. (Eds.). (2002). *Crossing boundaries: Essays on the ethical status of mysticism*. New York: Seven Bridges Press.

22. Barrett, W. (1962). *Irrational man: A study in existential philosophy*. New York: Doubleday/Anchor.

23. Benson, H. (1980). The placebo effect. *Harvard Medical School Health Letter*, August, 3–4.

24. Biet, A. (2001). Evoking the devil: Fasting with tobacco to learn how to cure. In J. Narby & F. Huxley (Eds.), *Shamans through time: 500 years on the path of knowledge* (pp. 16–17). New York: Jeremy P. Tarcher/Penguin. (Original work published 1664)

25. Blacker, C. (1986). *The catalpa bow: A study of shamanistic practices in Japan*. Boston: Allen & Unwin.

26. Blakeslee, S. (2005, November 22). This is your brain under hypnosis. *New York Times*, pp. D1, D4.

27. Blofeld, J. (Trans.). (1958). *The Zen teaching of Huang Po: On the transmission of mind.* New York: Grove Press.

28. Blumenthal, D. (Ed.). (1978). *Understanding Jewish mysticism: The Merkabah tradition and the Zoharic tradition.* New York: Ktav Publishing House.

29. Bogoras, W. (1909). *The Chukchee* (F. Boas, Ed.). Leiden, Netherlands: E. J. Brill.

30. Bourguignon, E. (Ed.). (1973). *Religion, altered states of consciousness, and social change.* Columbus: Ohio State University.

31. Boyer, B., Klopfer, B., Brawer, F., & Kawai, H. (1964). Comparisons of the shamans and pseudoshamans of the Apaches of the Mescalero Indian reservation: A Rorschach study. *Journal of Projective Techniques and Assessment, 28,* 173–180.

32. Brown, D. (2006). The stages of meditation in cross cultural perspective. In K. Wilber, J. Engler, & D. Brown (Eds.), *Transformation of consciousness: Conventional and contemplative perspectives on development* (2nd ed.). Boston: Shambhala.

33. Brown, D., Forte, M., & Dysart, M. (1984). Differences in visual sensitivity among mindfulness meditators and non-meditators. *Perceptual and Motor Skills, 58,* 727–733.

34. Brown, D., Forte, M., & Dysart, M. (1984). Visual sensitivity and mindfulness meditation. *Perceptual and Motor Skills, 58,* 775–784.

35. Brown, M. (1997). *The channeling zone: American spirituality in an anxious age.* Cambridge, MA: Harvard University Press.

36. Brown, M. (2001). Dark side of the shaman. In J. Narby & F. Huxley (Eds.), *Shamans through time: 500 years on the path of knowledge* (pp. 251–256). New York: Jeremy P. Tarcher/Penguin. (Original work published 1989)

37. Buddhagosa. (1975). *The path of purity* (P. M. Tin, Trans.). London: Pali Text Society. (Original work published 1923)

38. Burns, J. (2003). What is beyond the edge of the known world? *Journal of Consciousness Studies, 10*(6–7), 7–28.

39. Bynner, W. (Trans.). (1944). *The way of life according to Lao Tzu.* New York: Perigee/Putnam.

40. Bynner, W. (Trans.). (1980). *The way of life according to Lau Tzu.* New York: Vintage.

41. Byrd, R. (1988). Positive therapeutic effects of intercessory prayer in a coronary care unit population. *Southern Medical Journal, 81,* 826–829.

42. Byrom, T. (Trans.). (1976). *The Dhammapada: The sayings of the Buddha.* New York: Vintage.

43. Cahn, R. & Polich, J. (2006). Meditation states and traits: EEG, ERP, and neuroimaging studies. *Psychological Bulletin, 132,* 180–211.

44. Campbell, J. (1968). *The hero with a thousand faces* (2nd ed.). New York: World.

45. Campbell, J. (1986). *The inner reaches of outer space: Metaphor as myth and as religion.* New York: Alfred van der Marck Editions.

46. Castaneda, C. (1969). *The teachings of Don Juan: A Yaqui way of knowledge.* New York: Ballantine.

47. Castaneda, C. (1971). *A separate reality: Further conversations with Don Juan.* New York: Simon & Schuster.

48. Castaneda, C. (1972). *Journey to Ixtlan: The lessons of Don Juan.* New York: Simon & Schuster.

49. Chabris, C. (1999). Prelude or requiem for the "Mozart effect"? *Nature, 400,* 826–827.

50. Chan, W. (Ed.). (1963). *A sourcebook in Chinese philosophy.* Princeton, NJ: Princeton University Press.

51. Charpak, G. & Broch, H. (2003). *Debunked! ESP, telekinesis, and other pseudoscience.* Baltimore, MD: Johns Hopkins University Press.

52. Chu, G. (2004, October 25). Is God in our genes? *Time, 164*(17), 62–72.

53. Clark, S. & Loftus, E. (1995). The psychological pay-dirt of space alien abduction memories. Review of Mack, J. (1995) *Abduction: Human encounters with aliens. Contemporary Psychology, 40*(9), 861–863.

54. Collins, H. (1985). *Changing order: Replication and induction in scientific practice.* Thousand Oaks, CA: Sage.

55. Collins, J. & Fishbane, M. (Eds.). (1995). *Death, ecstasy, and other worldly journeys.* New York: State University of New York Press.

56. Concar, D. & Ainsworth, C. (2000). E is for evidence. *New Scientist, 174,* 26–33.

57. Creel, H. (1953). *Chinese thought from Confucius to Mao Tse-Tung.* Chicago: University of Chicago Press.

58. Crews, F. (2004, July 15). Out, damned blot! [Review of the book *What's wrong with the Rorschach? Science confronts a controversial inkblot test*]. *New York Review of Books, 51*(12), 22–25.

59. Curnow, T. (2003). Philosophy and divination. *Philosophy Now, 42,* 7–9.

60. Curnow, T. (2003). *The oracles of the ancient world*. London: Gerald Duckworth & Company.

61. Curtis, N. (1907). *The Indian's book*. New York: Harper & Row.

62. Dabrowski, K. (1964). *Positive disintegration*. Boston: Little Brown.

63. Dawkins, R. (1976). *The selfish gene*. Oxford: Oxford University Press.

64. Dean, G. & Kelly, I. (1996). Astrology. In G. Stein (Ed.), *The encyclopedia of the paranormal* (pp. 47–99). Amherst, NY: Prometheus Books.

65. Dean, G. & Kelly, I. (2003). Is astrology relevant to consciousness and psi? *Journal of Consciousness Studies, 10*(6–7), 175–198.

66. DeMille, R. (1976). *Castaneda's journey: The power and the allegory*. Santa Barbara, CA: Capra.

67. DeMille, R. (1980). *The Don Juan papers: Further Castaneda controversies* (R. DeMille, Ed.). Santa Barbara, CA: Ross-Erikson.

68. DeRopp, R. S. (1968). *The master game*. New York: Delta.

69. Devereux, G. (1961). *Mohave ethnopsychiatry and suicide*. Washington DC: U.S. Government Printing Office.

70. Devereux, G. (2001). The shaman is mentally deranged. In J. Narby & F. Huxley (Eds.), *Shamans through time: 500 years on the path of knowledge* (pp. 119–120). New York: Jeremy P. Tarcher/Penguin. (Original work published 1956)

71. Diamond, J. (2005). *Collapse: How societies choose to fail or succeed*. New York: Penguin Group.

72. Dobkin de Rios, M. (1972). *Visionary vine*. San Francisco: Chandler Publishing Co.

73. Doblin, R. (1991). Pahnke's "Good Friday Experiment": A long-term follow up and methodological critique. *Journal of Transpersonal Psychology, 23*, 1–28.

74. Donner, F. (1991). *Being-in-dreaming: An initiation into the sorcerer's world*. San Francisco: Harper San Francisco.

75. Doore, G. (Ed.). (1988). *Shaman's path*. Boston: Shambhala.

76. Dossey, L. (1996). *Prayer is good medicine*. San Francisco: HarperSanFrancisco.

77. Durant, W. (1938). *The story of philosophy*. Garden City, NY: Garden City Publishing Co., Inc.

78. Dyson, F. (2004). One in a million. [Review of the book *Debunked!* by Charpak & Broch, 2003]. *New York Review of Books, March 25*, 4–6.

79. Eckhart, M. (1981). *Meister Eckhart: The essential sermons, commentaries, treatises and defense* (E. Colledge and B. McGinn, Trans.). New York: Paulist Press.

80. Elgin, D. (1998). *Voluntary simplicity* (2nd ed.). New York: William Morrow.

81. Elgin, D. (2000). *Promise ahead: A vision of hope and action for humanity's future.* New York: William Morrow.

82. Eliade, M. (1958). *Yoga: Immortality and freedom* (1st ed.). Princeton, NJ: Princeton University Press.

83. Eliade, M. (1964). *Shamanism: Archaic techniques of ecstasy* (W. Trask, Trans.). Princeton, NJ: Princeton University Press.

84. Eliade, M. (1969). *Yoga: Immortality and freedom* (2nd ed.). Princeton, NJ: Princeton University Press.

85. Elkin, A. (1977). *Aboriginal men of high degree.* New York: St. Martin's Press.

86. Ellenberger, H. (1970). *The discovery of the unconscious.* New York: Basic Books.

87. Epictetus. (1995). *The art of living* (S. Lebell, Ed.). San Francisco: Harper San Francisco.

88. Evans, E. (1996). Ritual. In D. Levinson & M. Ember (Eds.), *Encyclopedia of cultural anthropology* (Vol. 3, pp. 1121–1123). New York: Henry Holt.

89. Fabrega, H. & Silver, D. (1970). Some social and psychological properties of Zinacanteco shamans. *Behavioral Science, 15,* 471–486.

90. Feng, G. & English, J. (Trans.). (1974). *Chuang Tsu: Inner chapters.* New York: Vintage Books.

91. Ferris, T. (1988). *Coming of age in the Milky Way.* New York: Anchor/Doubleday.

92. Ferruci, P. (1982). *What we may be.* Los Angeles: J. Tarcher.

93. Feuerstein, G. (1989). *Yoga: The technology of ecstasy.* Los Angeles: J. Tarcher.

94. Feuerstein, G. (1996). *The Shambhala guide to yoga.* Boston: Shambhala.

95. Fielding, W. (1983). An interim report of a prospective, randomized, controlled study of adjuvant chemotherapy in operable gastric cancer. *World Journal of Surgery, 7,* 390–399.

96. Flach, F. (1988). *Resiliance.* New York: Ballantine.

97. Flanagan, O. (1991). *The science of the mind* (2nd ed.). Cambridge, MA: Bradford/MIT.

98. Forman, R. (Ed.). (1990). *The problem of pure consciousness.* New York: Oxford University Press.

99. Forman, R. (Ed.). (1997). *The problem of pure consciousness: Mysticism and philosophy.* New York: Oxford University Press.

100. Fowler, J. (1981). *Stages of faith: The psychology of human development and the quest for meaning.* New York: Harper Collins.

101. Frances, S. H. (2001). *Drawing it out: Befriending the unconscious.* Sarasota, FL: MAPS.

102. Francfort, H. & Hamayon, R. (Eds.). (2001). *The concept of shamanism: Uses and abuses.* Budapest: Akademiai Kiado.

103. Frank, J. (1982). *Sanity and survival in the nuclear age: Psychological aspects of war and peace.* New York: Random House.

104. Frank, J. (1985). Therapeutic components shared by all psychotherapies. In M. Mahoney & A. Freeman (Eds.), *Cognition and psychotherapy* (pp. 49–79). New York: Plenum.

105. Free John. (1985). *The dawn horse testament.* San Rafael, CA: Dawn Horse Press.

106. Freud, S. (1938). *A general introduction to psychoanalysis* (J. Riviere, Trans.). Garden City, New York: Garden City Publishing. (Original work published 1935)

107. Fulbright, W. (1982). *Sanity and survival in the nuclear age.* New York: Random House.

108. Furst, P. (1987). South American shamanism. In M. Eliade (Ed.), *The encyclopedia of religion* (Vol. 13, pp. 219–223). New York: Macmillan.

109. Gagan, J. (1998). *Journeying: Where shamanism and psychotherapy meet.* Santa Fe, NM: Rio Chana Publication.

110. Gallegos, A. (1987). *The personal totem pole: Animal imagery, the chakras and psycho-therapy.* Santa Fe, NM: Moon Bear Press.

111. Gampopa. (1971). *The jewel ornament of liberation* (H. Guenther, Trans.). Boston: Shambhala.

112. Gaschler, K. (2005). Judging Amy and Andy. *Scientific American Mind, 16*(3), 52–57.

113. Gauquelin, M. (1990). Spheres of influence. In P. Grim (Ed.), *Philosophy of science and the occult* (2nd ed., pp. 37–50). New York: SUNY.

114. Giesler, P. (1985). Differential micro-PK effects among Afro-Brazilian cultists: Three studies using trance significant symbols as targets. *Journal of Parapsychology, 49,* 329–366.

115. Giesler, P. (1985). Parapsychological anthropology II: A multimethod study of psi and psi-related processes in the Umbanda ritual trance consultation. *Journal of the American Society for Psychical Research, 79*, 113–166.

116. Giesler, P. (1986). GESP testing of shamanic cultists: Three studies of an evaluation of dramatic upsets during testing. *Journal of Parapsychology, 50*, 123–153.

117. Giles, H. (Trans.). (1969). *Chuang-tzu, mystic, moralist, and social reformer* (Rev. ed.). Taipei: Ch'eng Wen.

118. Glassé, C. (Ed.). (1991). *The concise encyclopedia of Islam*. San Francisco: Harper San Francisco.

119. Goffman, E. (1959). *The presentation of self in everyday life*. Garden City, NY: Double-day Anchor Books.

120. Goldstein, J. (1983). *The experience of insight*. Boston: Shambhala.

121. Goleman, D. (1988). *The meditative mind*. Los Angeles: J. P. Tarcher.

122. Goleman, D. (1995). *Emotional intelligence*. New York: Bantam.

123. Govinda, A. (1970). *The way of the white clouds*. Boulder, CO: Shambhala.

124. Greeley, A. (1988). Mysticism goes mainstream. In E. Bragdon (Ed.), *A sourcebook for helping people in spiritual emergency* (pp. 228–236). Los Altos, CA: Lightening Up Press.

125. Grinspoon, R. L. & Bakalar, J. (1997). *Psychedelic drugs reconsidered* (2nd ed.). New York: Lindesmith Center.

126. Grob, C. (Ed.). (2002). *Hallucinogens: A reader*. New York: Tarcher/Putnam.

127. Grof, C. & Grof, S. (1986). Spiritual emergency: The understanding and treatment of transpersonal crises. *ReVision, 8*(2), 7–20.

128. Grof, C. & Grof, S. (1990). *The stormy search for self: Understanding spiritual emergence*. Los Angeles: J. Tarcher.

129. Grof, S. (1980). *LSD psychotherapy*. Pomona, CA: Hunter House.

130. Grof, S. (1985). *Beyond the brain*. Albany, NY: SUNY.

131. Grof, S. (1988). *The adventure of self-discovery*. Albany, NY: SUNY.

132. Grof, S. (1993). *Realms of the human unconscious*. London: Souvenir Press.

133. Grof, S. (2001). *LSD psychotherapy*. Sarasota, FL: MAPS.

134. Grof, S. (2006). When the impossible happens: Adventures in non-ordinary realities. Boulder, CO: Sounds True Press.

135. Grof, S. & Grof, C. (Eds.). (1989). *Spiritual emergency: When personal transformation becomes a crisis.* Los Angeles: J. Tarcher.

136. Groopman, J. (2001, September). God on the brain. *The New Yorker,* 166–168.

137. Guthrie, S. (1997). McClenon's "Shamanic healing, human evolution, and the origin of religion": A critique. *Journal for the Scientific Study of Religion, 36,* 355–357.

138. Gyatso, K. (1988). *Universal Compassion.* London: Tharpa.

139. Hadot, P. (2001). Shamanism and Greek philosophy. In H. Francfort & R. Hamayon (Eds.), *The concept of shamanism: Uses and abuses* (pp. 389–402). Budapest: Akademiai Kiado.

140. Hamayon, R. (1995). Pour en finir avec la transe et L extase dans l étude du cha-manisme. *Études Mongoles et Sibériennes, 26,* 155–190.

141. Hamayon, R. (1998). Ecstasy or the west-dreamt shaman. In H. Wautischer (Ed.), *Tribal epistemologies* (pp. 175–187). Burlington, VT: Ashgate Publishing.

142. Hamer, D. (2004). *The God gene: How faith is hardwired into our genes.* New York: Doubleday.

143. Hansel, C. (1980). *ESP and parapsychology: A critical reevaluation.* Buffalo, NY: Prometheus.

144. Harman, W. (1979). An evolving society to fit an evolving consciousness. *Integral View, 1,* 14.

145. Harner, M. (Ed.). (1973). *Hallucinogens and shamanism.* New York: Oxford University Press.

146. Harner, M. (1982). *The way of the shaman: A guide to power and healing.* New York: Bantam Books.

147. Harner, M. (1984). *The Jivaro.* Berkeley: University of California Press.

148. Harner, M. (1985). Comments. *Current Anthropology, 26,* 452.

149. Harner, M. (1987). The ancient wisdom in shamanic cultures. In S. Nicholson (Ed.), *Shamanism* (pp. 3–16). Wheaton, IL: Quest.

150. Harner, M. (1988). Talk given at a workshop. Esalen Institute, Big Sur, CA.

151. Harner, M. (1988). Helping reawaken shamanism among the Sami (Laplanders) of northernmost Europe. *The Foundation for Shamanic Studies Newsletter, 1*(3), 1–2.

152. Harner, M. (1990). *The way of the shaman.* San Francisco: Harper & Row.

153. Harner, M. (2005). The history and work of the foundation for shamanic studies. *Shamanism, 18*(1–2), 5–10.

154. Harner, M. & Harner, S. (2005). Core practices in the shamanic treatment of illness. *Shamanism, 18*(1–2), 122–132.

155. Harner, S. (2003). Shamanic journeying and immune response: Hypothesis testing. *Shamanism, 16*(2), 9–14.

156. Harner, S. (2004). Shamanic journeying and psychological responses: Hypothesis testing. *Shamanism, 17*(2), 16–23.

157. Harvey, A. (Ed.). (1998). *Teachings of the Christian mystics.* Boston: Shambhala.

158. Hastings, A. (1991). *With the tongues of men and angels.* New York: Holt, Rinehart & Winston.

159. Heraclitus. (2001). *Fragments: The collected wisdom of Heraclitus* (B. Haxton, Trans.). New York: Viking.

160. Hilgard, E. (1986). *Divided consciousness: Multiple controls on human thought and action* (2nd ed.). Somerset, NJ: John Wiley & Sons.

161. Hixon, L. (Trans.). (1992). *Great swan: Meetings with Ramakrishna.* Boston: Shambhala.

162. Hoffman, E. (1981). *The way of splendor: Jewish mysticism and modern psychology.* Boston: Shambhala.

163. Hoffman, E. (1985). *The heavenly ladder: A Jewish guide to inner growth.* San Francisco: Harper & Row.

164. Holland, J. (Ed.). (2001). *Ecstasy: The complete guide: A comprehensive look at the risks and benefits of MDMA.* Rochester, VT: Park Street Press.

165. Hooper, J. & Teresi, D. (1985). Lucid dreaming. *New Age Journal,* November, 34–78.

166. Hopkins, J. (1984). *The tantric distinction: An introduction to Tibetan Buddhism.* London: Wisdom.

167. Hoppal, M. (Ed.). (1984). *Shamanism in Eurasia.* Gottingen, Germany: Herodot.

168. Hoppal, M. (1987). Shamanism: An archaic and/or recent belief system. In S. Nicholson (Ed.), *Shamanism: An expanded view of reality* (pp. 76–100). Wheaton, IL: Quest.

169. Hultkrantz, A. (1978). Ecological and phenomenological aspects of shamanism. In V. Dioszegi & M. Hoppal (Eds.), *Shamanism in Siberia* (pp. 27–58). Budapest: Akadamiai Kiado.

170. Hurley, T. (1985). Placebo: The hidden asset in healing. *Investigations, 2*(1).

171. Huxley, A. (1945). *The perennial philosophy.* New York: Harper & Row.

172. Ingerman, S. (1990). *Soul retrieval: Mending the fragmented self.* San Francisco: Harper Collins.

173. Irwin, H. (1985). *Flight of mind: A psychological study of the out-of-body experience.* New York: Scarecrow Press.

174. Jahn, R. & Dunne, B. (1987). *Margins of reality: The role of consciousness in the physical world.* New York: Harcourt Brace Jovanovich.

175. Jahn, R., Mischo, J., Baitl, D., et al (2000). Mind/machine interaction consortium: PortREG replication experiments. *Journal of Scientific Exploration, 14*(4), 499–555.

176. James, W. (1910). *The principles of psychology.* New York: Dover.

177. James, W. (1958). *The varieties of religious experience.* New York: New American Library.

178. James, W. (1962, 1899). *Talks to teachers on psychology and to students on some of life's ideals.* New York: Dover.

179. Jamieson, S. & Mack, J. (2003). Shamanic journeys and UFO encounters. *Shamanism, 16*(1), 16–27.

180. Jilek, W. (1974). *Salish Indian mental health and culture change: Psychohygienic and therapeutic aspects of the guardian spirit.* Toronto: Holt, Rinehart & Winston of Canada.

181. Jonte-Pace, D. (2004). The swami and the Rorschach: Spiritual practice, religious experience and perception. In R. Forman (Ed.), *The innate capacity: Mysticism, psychology and philosophy* (pp. 137–169). New York: Oxford.

182. Jowett, B. (Trans.). (1953). *The dialogues of Plato* (4th ed.). New York: Oxford Clarendon Press.

183. Jung, C. (1953). *Two essays on analytical psychology* (R.F.C. Hull, Trans.). (Collected Works, Vol. 7, Bollingen Series XX.) New York: Pantheon Books.

184. Jung, C. (1961). *Memories, dreams, reflections* (R. Winston & C. Winston, Trans.). New York: Vintage Books.

185. Jung, C. (1964). *The development of personality* (R.F.C. Hull, Trans.). (Collected Works, Vol. 17, Bollingen Series XX.) Princeton, NJ: Princeton University Press.

186. Jung, C. (1969). *Four archetypes* (R.F.C. Hull, Trans.). (Collected Works, Vol. 9, Part I, Bollingen Series XX.) Princeton, NJ: Princeton University Press.

187. Kaelber, W. (1987). Asceticism. In M. Eliade (Ed.), *Encyclopedia of Religion* (Vol. 1, pp. 441–445). New York: MacMillan.

188. Kakar, S. (1982). *Shamans, mystics, and doctors: A psychological inquiry into India and its healing traditions.* New York: Knopf.

189. Kalweit, H. (1988). *Dreamtime and inner space.* Boston: Shambhala.

190. Kandel, E. (1998). A new intellectual framework for psychiatry. *American Journal of Psychiatry, 155,* 457–469.

191. Kapleau, P. (1965). *The three pillars of Zen.* Boston: Beacon Press. (Cited in Smith, 2000, p. 31.).

192. Katz, S. (Ed.). (1983). *Mysticism and religious traditions.* Oxford: Oxford University Press.

193. Kelly, I., Dean, G., & Sakolfske, D. (1990). Astrology: A critical review. In P. Grim (Ed.), *Philosophy of science and the occult* (pp. 51–81). New York: SUNY.

194. Kleinman, A. & Sung, L. (1979). Why do indigenous practitioners successfully heal? *Social Science and Medicine, 13B,* 7–26.

195. Klimo, J. (1987). *Channeling.* Los Angeles: J.P. Tarcher.

196. Klopfer, B. (1957). Psychological variables in human cancer. *Journal of Projective Techniques, 21,* 337–339.

197. Kohlberg, L. (1981). *Essays on moral development: The philosophy of moral development* (Vol. 1). New York: Harper and Row.

198. Kohn, L. (Ed.). (1993). *The Taoist experience: An anthology.* New York: SUNY Press.

199. Kornfield, J. (1993). *A path with heart.* New York: Bantam.

200. Kornfield, J. (2000). *After the ecstasy, the laundry.* New York: Bantam.

201. Krippner, S. (1987). *The psychology of shamanism.* San Francisco: Saybrook Institute.

202. Kristof, N. (2004, July 17). Jesus and Jihad. *New York Times,* Section A, p. 13.

203. Krucoff, M., Crater, S., Gallup, D., et al. (2005). Music, imagery, touch, and prayer as adjuncts to interventional cardiac care: The Monitoring and Actualisation of Noetic Trainings (MANTRA) II randomized study. *The Lancet, 366,* 211–217.

204. Krycka, K. (2000). Shamanic practices and the treatment of life-threatening medical conditions. *Journal of Transpersonal Psychology, 32*(1), 69–88.

205. LaBerge, S. (1985). *Lucid dreaming.* Los Angeles: J.P. Tarcher.

206. Laing, R. (1972). Metanoia: Some experiences at Kingsley Hall, London. In H. Ruitenbeck (Ed.), *Going crazy* (pp. 11–21). New York: Bantam.

207. Lau, D. (Trans.). (1979). *Confucius: The analects.* New York: Penguin.

208. Laughlin, C., McManus, J., & d'Aquili, E. (1992). *Brain, symbol and experience: Toward a neurophenomenology of human consciousness*. New York: Columbia University Press.

209. Laughlin, C., McManus, J., & Shearer, J. (1993). Transpersonal anthropology. In R. Walsh & F. Vaughan (Eds.), *Paths beyond ego: The transpersonal vision* (pp. 190–195). Los Angeles: J. Tarcher.

210. Leighton, A. & Hughes, J. (1961). Cultures as causative of mental disorder. In *Causes of mental disorder: Review of epidemiological knowledge* (pp. 446–470). New York: Milbank Memorial Fund.

211. Leonard, G. & Murphy, M. (1995). *The life we are given*. New York: Tarcher/Putnam.

212. Levi-Strauss, C. (1972). *Structural anthropology* (C. Jacobson and B. Schoepf, Trans.). Middlesex, England: Penguin Books.

213. Levinson, D. (1978). *The seasons of a man's life*. New York: Ballantine.

214. Linley, P. & Joseph, S. (2005). The human capacity for growth through adversity. *American Psychologist, 60*(3), 262–264.

215. Loeb, E. (1929). Shaman and seer. *American Anthropologist, 41*, 60–84.

216. Loevinger, J. (1997). Stages of personality development. In R. Hogan, J. Johnson, & S. Briggs (Eds.), *Handbook of personality psychology* (pp. 199–208). San Diego, CA: Academic Press.

217. Long, J. (1982). Comments. *Current Anthropology, 23*, 49–50.

218. Louve, R. (2005). *Last child in the woods: Saving our children from nature-deficit disorder*. Chapel Hill, NC: Algonquin Books of Chapel Hill.

219. Lukoff, D. (1985). The diagnosis of mystical experiences with psychotic features. *Journal of Transpersonal Psychology, 17*, 155–182.

220. Lusseryan, J. (1998). *And there was light: Autobiography of Jacques Lusseyran, blind hero of the French resistance* (E. Camerbon, Trans.). New York: Parabola.

221. Mack, J. (1994). *Abduction: Human encounters with aliens*. New York: Ballantine Books.

222. Mahoney, M. (1991). *Human change process: The scientific foundations of psychotherapy*. New York: Basic Books.

223. Malkin, S. (1989). Confessions of a former channel. *New Realities, 10*, 25–29.

224. Mallove, E. (1986, April 13). Einstein the religious. *San Francisco Examiner*, p. 12.

225. Maslow, A. (1968). *Toward a psychology of being* (2nd ed.). Princeton: Van Nostrand.

226. Maslow, A. (1970). *Religions, values and peak experiences*. New York: Viking.

227. Maslow, A. (1971). *The farther reaches of human nature*. New York: Viking.

228. Mason, L., Alexander, C., Travis, F., et al. (1997). Electrophysiological correlates of higher states of consciousness during sleep in long term practitioners of the transcendental meditation program. *Sleep, 20*(2), 102–110.

229. Masters, J., Burish, T., Hollon, S., & Rim, D. (1987). *Behavior therapy: Techniques and empirical findings* (2nd ed.). San Diego: Harcourt, Brace, Jovanovich.

230. May, R. (1953). *Man's search for himself*. New York: Dell.

231. McClenon, J. (2002). *Wondrous healing: Shamanism, human evolution and the origin of religion*. DeKalb: Northern Illinois University Press.

232. McDermott, J. (Ed.). (1977). *The writings of William James*. Chicago: University of Chicago Press.

233. McGashan, T. & Carpenter, W. (1981). Does attitude toward psychosis relate to outcome? *American Journal of Psychiatry, 138*, 797–801.

234. McGrew, J. & McFall, R. (1990). A scientific inquiry into the validity of astrology. *Journal of Scientific Exploration, 4*, 75–83.

235. McGuckin, J. (Trans.). (2003). *The book of mystical chapters: Meditations on the soul's ascent from the desert fathers and from other early Christian contemplatives*. Boston: Shambhala.

236. Merton, T. (1969). *The way of Chuang Tzu*. New York: New Directions.

237. Merton, T. (Trans.). (1970). *The wisdom of the desert: Sayings from the desert fathers of the fourth century*. New York: New Directions. (Original work published 1960)

238. Merton, T. (1985). *The hidden ground of love: The letters of Thomas Merton on religious experience and social concerns* (W. Shannon, Ed.). New York: Farrar, Straus, Giroux.

239. Metzner, R. (1998). *The unfolding self: Varieties of transformative experience*. Novato, CA: Origin Press.

240. Metzner, R. (1999). Ayahuasca and the greening of human consciousness. *Shaman's Drum, 53*(17), 27.

241. Miller, D. (1997). *The complete story of the course: The history, the people, and the controversies behind* A Course in Miracles. Berkeley, CA: Fearless Books.

242. Miller, W. & C'de Baca, J. (2001). *Quantum change: When epiphanies and sudden insights transform ordinary lives*. New York: Guilford.

243. Mitchell, S. (Trans.). (1992). *Tao Te Ching*. New York: Harper Perennial.

244. Mitrani, P. (1992). A critical overview of the psychiatric approaches to shamanism. *Diogenes, 158*, 145–164.

245. Monroe, R. (1971). *Journeys out of the body*. New York: Doubleday.

246. Moody, H. & Carroll, D. (1997). *The five stages of the soul*. New York: Anchor/Doubleday.

247. Moody, R. (1988). *The light beyond*. New York: Bantam.

248. Müller-Ebeling, C., Rätsch, C., & Shahi, S. B. (2002). *Shamanism and tantra in the Himalayas*. Rochester, VT: Inner Traditions.

249. Murphy G. & Ballou, R. (Eds.). (1960). *William James on psychological research*. New York: Viking.

250. Murphy, M. (1992). *The future of the body: Explorations into the further evolution of human nature*. New York: Tarcher/Putnam.

251. Myers, D. (1992). *The pursuit of happiness*. New York: Avon.

252. Narby, J. (1999). *The cosmic serpent: DNA and the origins of knowledge*. New York: Tarcher/Putnam.

253. Neher, A. (1961). Auditory driving observed with scalp electrodes in normal subjects. *Electroencephalography and Clinical Neurophysiology, 13*(3), 449–451.

254. Neher, A. (1962). A physiological explanation of unusual behavior in ceremonies involving drums. *Human Biology, 34*, 151–160.

255. Nemiah, J. (1985). Dissociative disorders (hysterical neurosis, dissociative type). In H. Kaplan & B. Sadock (Eds.), *Comprehensive textbook of psychiatry* (4th ed., Vol. 1, pp. 942–957). Baltimore: Williams & Wilkins.

256. Newberg, A., d'Aquili, E., & Rause, V. (2002). *Why God won't go away*. New York: Ballantine Books.

257. Nisargadatta, S. (1973). *I am that: Conversations with Sri Nisargadatta Maharaj, Part II* (M. Friedman, Trans.). Bombay: Cheltana.

258. Nisker, W. (1990). *Crazy wisdom*. Berkeley, CA: Ten Speed Press.

259. Noel, D. (1999). *The soul of shamanism: Western fantasies, imaginal realities*. New York: Continuum.

260. Noll, R. (1983). Shamanism and schizophrenia: A state specific approach to the "schizophrenia metaphor" of shamanic states. *American Ethnologist, 10*, 443–459.

261. Noll, R. (1984). Reply to Lex. *American Ethnologist, 11*, 192.

262. Noll, R. (1985). Mental imagery cultivation as a cultural phenomenon: The role of visions in shamanism. *Current Anthropology, 26*(4), 443–461.

263. Noll, R. (1987). The presence of spirits in magic and madness. In S. Nicholson (Ed.), *Shamanism* (pp. 47–61). Wheaton, IL: Quest.

264. Norbu, N. (1987). *The cycle of day and night* (J. Reynolds, Trans.) (2nd ed.). Barrytown, NY: Station Hill Press.

265. Norbu, N. (1992). *Dream yoga and the practice of natural light* (M. Katz, Ed.). Ithaca, NY: Snow Lion.

266. Novak, P. (1989). Mysticism, enlightenment and morality. *ReVision, 12*(1), 45–49.

267. Nyanaponika Thera. (1962). *The heart of Buddhist meditation.* New York: Samuel Weiser.

268. Nyanaponika Thera. (1976). *Abhidharma Studies.* Kandy, Sri Lanka: Buddhist Publication Society.

269. O'Brien, E. (Trans.). (1964). *The essential Plotinus.* Indianapolis, IN: Hackett.

270. Osborne, A. (Ed.). (1962). *The teachings of Ramana Maharshi.* New York: Samuel Weiser.

271. Ostermann, H. (1952). *The Alaskan Eskimos, as described in the posthumous notes of Dr. Knud Rasmussen* (Report of the Fifth Thule expedition, 1921–24, Vol. X, No. 3). Copenhagen: Nordisk Forlag.

272. Palmer, G., Sherrard, P., & Ware, K. (Trans.). (1993). *Prayer of the heart: Writings from the Philokalia.* Boston: Shambhala.

273. Palmer, J. (2003). ESP in the Ganzfeld: Analysis of a debate. *Journal of Consciousness Studies, 10*(6–7), 51–68.

274. Peck, M. S. (1983). *People of the lie: The hope for healing human evil.* New York: Simon & Schuster.

275. Pelleteir, K. & Garfield, C. (1976). *Consciousness: East and west.* New York: Harper and Row.

276. Penner, S. (1993). *The four dimensions of paradise.* San Diego: Cypress Press.

277. Perls, F. (1969). *Gestalt therapy verbatim.* Lafayette, CA: Real People Press.

278. Perry, J. (1986). Spiritual emergence and renewal. *ReVision, 8*(2), 33–40.

279. Perry, R. (2004). *Path of light: Stepping into peace with* A Course in Miracles. West Sedona, AZ: Circle Publishing.

280. Perry, W. (1981). *The treasury of traditional wisdom.* Pates Middlesex, UK: Perennial Books.

281. Peters, C. (1987). The Tamang shamanism of Nepal. In S. Nicholson (Ed.), *Shamanism* (pp. 161–180). Itasca, IL: Quest.

282. Peters, L. (1981). An experiential study of Napalese shamanism. *Journal of Transpersonal Psychology, 13,* 1–26.

283. Peters, L. (2004). *Trance, initiation and psychotherapy in Nepalese shamanism.* Delhi, India: Nirala.

284. Peters, L. & Price-Williams, D. (1980). Towards an experiential analysis of shamanism. *American Ethnologist, 7,* 397–418.

285. Petrovich, A. (2001). The shaman: A villain of a magician who calls demons. In J. Narby & F. Huxley (Eds.), *Shamans through time: 500 years on the path of knowledge* (pp. 18–22). New York: Jeremy P. Tarcher/Penguin. (Original work published 1672)

286. Phillips, D., Ruth, T., & Wagner, L. (1993). Psychology and survival. *Lancet, 342,* 1142–1145.

287. Plato. (1945). *The Republic* (F. Cornford, Trans.). Oxford: Oxford University Press.

288. Plato. (1961). Seventh letter. In E. Hamilton & H. Cairns (Eds.), *The collected dialogues of Plato* (pp. 1574–1598). Princeton: Princeton University Press.

289. Polivy, J. & Herman, C. (2002). If at first you don't succeed: False hopes and self-change. *American Psychologist, 57,* 677–689.

290. Prabhavananda, S. & Isherwood, C. (Trans.). (1972). *The song of God: Bhagavad Gita* (3rd ed.). Hollywood: Vedanta Society.

291. Radin, D. (1997). *The conscious universe: The scientific truth of psychic phenomena.* New York: HarperEdge.

292. Radin, D. (2006). *Entangled minds: Quantum reality and the reach of the mind.* New York: Simon & Schuster.

293. Ram Dass. (1975). *Association for transpersonal psychology newsletter.* (NP).

294. Ram Dass. (1978). *Journey of awakening: A meditator's guidebook.* New York: Doubleday.

295. Ramana Maharshi. (1984). *Talks with Sri Ramana Maharshi.* Tiruvannamalai, India: T.N. Venkataraman.

296. Ramana Maharshi. (1955). *Who am I?* (T. Venkataraman, Ed.). Tiruvannamalai, India: Sri Ramanasramam. (Original work published 1955)

297. Ramana Maharshi. (1988). *The spiritual teachings of Ramana Maharshi.* Boston: Shambhala.

298. Rasmussen, K. (1927). *Across arctic America.* New York: G.P. Putnam.

299. Rasmussen, K. (1929). *Intellectual culture of the Iglulik Eskimos.* Copenhagen: Gyldendalske Boghandel, Nordisk Forlag.

300. Rawlins, D. (1981). sTARBABY. *Fate, 34*(10), 67–98.

301. Reed, G. (1989). The psychology of channeling. *The Skeptical Inquirer, 13*, 385–390.

302. Reichel-Dolmataoff, G. (1987). *Shamanism and art of the Eastern Tukanoan Indians.* Leiden, Netherlands: E. Brill.

303. Ring, K. (1980). *Life at death.* New York: Coward, McCann & Geoghegan.

304. Ring, K. (1984). *Heading toward omega: In search of the meaning of the near-death experience.* New York: William Morrow.

305. Ring, K. (1992). *The omega project: Near-death experiences, UFO encounters and mind at large.* New York: William Morrow.

306. Rinpoche, S. (1992). *The Tibetan book of living and dying.* San Francisco: HarperCollins.

307. Roberts, T. (Ed.). (2001). *Psychoactive sacramentals: Essays on entheogens and religion.* San Francisco: Council on Spiritual Practices.

308. Roberts, T. (2006). *Psychedelic horizons: Snow White, immune system, multistate mind, enlarging education.* Exeter, UK: Imprint Academic.

309. Roberts, T. & Hruby, P. (2002). Toward an entheogen research agenda. *Journal of Humanistic Psychology, 42*(1), 71–89.

310. Robinet, I. (1989). Visualization and ecstatic flight in Shang Qing Taoism. In L. Kohn (Ed.), *Taoist meditation and longevity techniques* (pp. 159–191). Ann Arbor: University of Michigan Press.

311. Rogers, S. (1982). *The shaman.* Springfield, IL: C.C. Thomas.

312. Rogo, D. (1987). Shamanism, ESP, and the paranormal. In S. Nicholson (Ed.), *Shamanism* (pp. 133–144). Wheaton, IL: Quest.

313. Rosch, E. (1999). Is wisdom in the brain? *Psychological Science, 10*, 222–224.

314. Rossi, E. (2004). Stress-induced alternative gene splicing in mind-body medicine. *Advances in Mind Body Medicine, 20*(2), 12–19.

315. Russell, P. (1992). *The white hole in time.* San Francisco: Harper.

316. Ryan, R. (1999). *The strong eye of shamanism.* Rochester, VT: Inner Traditions.

317. Sagan, C. (1993, March 7). What's really going on? *Parade Magazine,* pp. 4-7.

318. Saklani, A. (1988). Preliminary tests for psi-ability in shamans of Garhwal Himalaya. *Journal of the Society for Psychical Research, 55,* 60–70.

319. Sandner, D. (1979). *Navaho symbols of hearing.* New York: Harcourt Brace Jovanovich.

320. Sante, L. (2006, February). Summoning the spirits. A review of the perfect medium: Photography and the occult. *New York Review of Books,* pp. 17–19.

321. Satprem. (1968). *Sri Aurobindo or the adventure of consciousness* (L. Venet, Trans.). New York: Harper & Row.

322. Sayed, M. H. (Ed.). (1969). *Thus spake Prophet Muhammad.* Madras, India: Sri Ramakrishna Math.

323. Schimmel, A. (1975). *Mystical Dimensions of Islam.* Chapel Hill: University of North Carolina Press.

324. Scholem, G. (1946). *Major trends in Jewish mysticism.* New York: Schocken Books.

325. Schultz, T. (Ed.). (1989). *The fringes of reason.* New York: Harmony.

326. Schumacher, E. (1973). *Small is beautiful: Economics as if people mattered.* New York: Harper and Row.

327. Schumacher, E. (1977). *A guide for the perplexed.* New York: Harper and Row.

328. Schuon, F. (1975). *The transcendent unity of religions.* New York: Harper Touchstone Books.

329. Sengstan. (1975). *Verses on the faith mind* (R. Clarke, Trans.). Sharon Springs, NY: Zen Center.

330. Shah, I. (1971). *The Sufis.* New York: Anchor/Doubleday.

331. Shapiro, A. (1959). The placebo effect in the history of medical treatment: Implications for psychiatry. *American Journal of Psychiatry, 116,* 298–304.

332. Shapiro, R. (Trans.). (1993). *Wisdom of the Jewish sages: A modern reading of Pirke Avot.* New York: Bell Tower.

333. Shearer, P. (Trans.). (1989). *Effortless being: The yoga sutras of Patanjali.* London: Unwin.

334. Sherden, W. (1998). *The fortune sellers: The big business of buying and selling predictions.* New York: Wiley & Sons.

335. Shirokogoroff, S. (1935). *Psychomental complex of the tungus.* London: Kegan Paul, Trench, Trubnor.

336. Shweder, R. (1972). Aspects of cognition in Zinacanteco shamans: Experimental results. In W. Lessa & E. Vogt (Eds.), *Reader in comparative religion: An anthropological approach* (3rd ed., pp. 407–412). New York: Harper & Row.

337. Siikala, A. (1978). *The rite technique of the Siberian shaman.* Helsinki: Suomalainen Tiedeakatemia.

338. Silverman, J. (1967). Shamanism and acute schizophrenia. *American Anthropologist, 69,* 21–31.

339. Sim, S. & Van Loon, B. (2004). *Introducing critical theory.* Thriplow, UK: Icon Books.

340. Skinner, B. F. (1971). *Beyond freedom and dignity.* New York: Knopf.

341. Skultans, V. (1986). On mental imagery and healing. *Current Anthropology, 27,* 262.

342. Skutch, R. (1984). *Journey without distance: The story of* A Course in Miracles. Berkeley, CA: Celestial Arts.

343. Slater, M. (1996). Taboo. In D. Levinson & M. Ember (Eds.), *Encyclopedia of Cultural Anthropology* (Vol. 4, pp. 1279–1285). New York: Henry Holt & Co.

344. Smith, H. (1958). *The religions of man.* New York: Harper and Row.

345. Smith, H. (1964). Do drugs have religious import? *Journal of Philosophy, LXI,* 517–530.

346. Smith, H. (1976). *Forgotten truth: The primordial tradition.* New York: Harper & Row.

347. Smith, H. (1991). *The world's religions.* San Francisco: Harper Collins.

348. Smith, H. (2000). *Cleansing the doors of perception: The religious significance of entheogenic plants and chemicals.* New York: Tarcher/Penguin Putnam.

349. Stace, W. (1988). *Mysticism and philosophy.* Los Angeles: J. Tarcher.

350. Stafford, P. (1992). *Psychedelics encyclopedia* (3rd ed.). Berkeley, CA: Ronin.

351. Stuckrad, K. (2002). Reenchanting nature: Modern western shamanism and nineteenth-century thought. *Journal of the American Academy of Religion, 70*(4), 771–799.

352. Sullivan, L. (1987). Tricksters. In M. Eliade (Ed.), *The encyclopedia of religion,* Vol. 15 (pp. 45–46). New York: MacMillan.

353. Tarnas, R. (2006). *Cosmos and psyche: Intimations of a new world view.* New York: Viking Press.

354. Tart, C. (1977). *Psi: Scientific studies of the psychic realm.* New York: Dutton.

355. Tart, C. (1986). *Waking up: Overcoming the obstacles to human potential.* Boston: New Science Library/Shambhala.

356. Tart, C. (1989). *Open mind: Discriminating mind.* New York: Harper and Row.

357. Tart, C. (1991). Influence of previous psychedelic drug experience on students of Tibetan Buddhism. *Journal of Transpersonal Psychology, 23,* 139–174.

358. Tart, C. (1992). *Choose once again: Selections from* A Course in Miracles. San Bruno, CA: Audio Literature.

369. Tart, C. (Ed.). (1992). *Transpersonal psychologies* (3rd ed.). New York: HarperCollins.

360. Tart, C. (2001). *Mind science.* Novato, CA: Wisdom Editions.

361. Tart, C. (2001). *States of consciousness* (2nd ed.). New York: Backinprint.com.

362. Tedlock, B. (2005). *The woman in the shaman's body.* New York: Bantam.

363. Teilhard de Chardin, P. (1964). *The future of man.* New York: Harper & Row.

364. Tetlock, P. (2005). *Expert political judgment: How good is it? How can we know?* Princeton: Princeton University Press.

365. Thevet, A. (2001). Ministers of the devil who learn about the secrets of nature. In J. Narby & F. Huxley (Eds.), *Shamans through time: 500 years on the path of knowledge* (pp. 13–15). New York: Jeremy P. Tarcher/Penguin. (Original work published 1557)

366. Thomas, L. (1974). *Lives of a cell.* New York: Viking Press.

367. Thomas, L. (1980). *The medusa and the snail.* New York: Bantam Books.

368. Thomason, S. (1989). Entities in the linguistic minefield. *The Skeptical Inquirer, 13,* 391–396.

369. Tolle, E. (1999). *The power of now: A guide to spiritual enlightenment.* Novato, CA: New World Library.

370. Townsend, J. (2004). Individualist religious movements: Core and neo-shamanism. *Anthropology of Consciousness, 15*(1), 1–9.

371. Toynbee, A. (1934). *A study of history.* New York & London: Oxford University Press.

372. Toynbee, A. (1948). *Civilization on trial.* New York: Oxford University Press.

373. Turner, E. (2001). Training to see what the natives see. In J. Narby & F. Huxley (Eds.), *Shamans through time: 500 years on the path of knowledge.* New York: Jeremy P. Tarcher/Putnam.

374. Ullman, R. & Reichenberg-Ullman, J. (Eds.). (2001). *Mystics, masters, saints and sages: Stories of enlightenment.* Berkeley, CA: Conari Press.

375. Underhill, E. (1974). *Mysticism*. New York: New American Library.

376. Van Ommeren, M., Komproe, I., Cardenna, E., et al. (2002, April). *Psychological profile of Bhutanese shamans.* Paper presented at the annual conference of the Society for the Anthropology of Consciousness, Tucson, AZ. (Cited in Krippner, 2002).

377. Van Ommeren, M., Kromproe, I., Cardenna, E., et al. (2004). Mental illness among Bhutanese shamans. *Journal of Nervous & Mental Disease, 192*(4), 313–317.

378. Vaughan, F. (1979). *Awakening intuition*. New York: Doubleday.

379. Vaughan, F. (1983). Perception and knowledge: Reflections on psychological and spiritual learning in the psychedelic experience. In C. Grinspoon & J. Bakalar (Eds.), *Psychedelic reflections* (pp. 108–114). New York: Human Sciences Press.

380. Vaughan, F. (2000). *The inward arc: Healing in psychotherapy and spirituality* (2nd ed.). Lincoln, NC: Backinprint.com.

381. Vaughan, F. & Walsh, R. (Eds.). (1995). *Gifts from* A Course in Miracles. New York: Jeremy P. Tarcher/Putnam.

382. Vaughan-Lee, F. (Ed.). (1995). *Traveling the path of love: Sayings of the Sufi masters.* Inverness, CA: Golden Sufi Center.

383. Vitebsky, P. (1995/2001). Shamanism and the rigged marketplace. In J. Narby & F. Huxley (Eds.), *Shamans through time* (pp. 291–297). New York: Jeremy P. Tarcher/Putnam. (Original work published 1995)

384. Waley, A. (1989). *The analects of Confucius.* New York: Vintage/Random House. (Original work published 1938)

385. Walraven, B. (2001). Opening the gate of writing: Literate shamans in modern Korea. In H. Francfort & R. Hamayon (Eds.), *The concept of shamanism: Uses and abuses* (pp. 331–348). Budapest: Akademiai Kaido.

386. Walsch, N. (1996). *Conversations with God: An uncommon dialogue* (Book 1 ed.). New York: Putnam.

387. Walsh, R. (1977). Initial meditative experiences: Part I. *Journal of Transpersonal Psychology, 9*, 151–192.

388. Walsh, R. (1982). Psychedelics and psychological well-being. *Journal of Humanistic Psychology, 22*, 22–32.

389. Walsh, R. (1984). *Staying alive: The psychology of human survival.* Boston: Shambhala/ New Science Library.

390. Walsh, R. (1990). *The spirit of shamanism.* Los Angeles: Jeremy P. Tarcher.

BIBLIOGRAPHY

391. Walsh, R. (1999). Asian therapies. In R. Corsini & D. Wedding (Eds.), *Current Psychotherapies* (6th ed., pp. 407–444). Itasca, IL: F. E. Peacock.

392. Walsh, R. (1999). *Essential spirituality: The seven central practices.* New York: Wiley & Sons.

393. Walsh, R. (2001). Authenticity, conventionality, and angst. In K. Schneider, J. Bugental, & J. Pierson (Eds.), *The handbook of humanistic psychology* (pp. 609–620). Thousand Oaks, CA: Sage.

394. Walsh, R. (2001). From state to trait: The challenge of transforming transient insights into enduring change. In T. Roberts (Ed.), *Psychoactive sacramentals: Essays on entheogens and religion* (pp. 19–26). San Francisco: Council on Spiritual Practices.

395. Walsh, R. (2003). Entheogens: True or false? *International Journal of Transpersonal Studies, 22,* 1–6.

396. Walsh, R. & Grob, C. (Eds.). (2005). *Higher wisdom: Eminent elders explore the continuing impact of psychedelics.* New York: SUNY.

397. Walsh, R. & Shapiro, D. H. (Eds.). (1983). *Beyond health and normality: Explorations of exceptional psychological wellbeing.* New York: Van Nostrand Reinhold.

398. Walsh, R. & Shapiro, S. (2006). The meeting of meditative disciplines and western psychology: A mutually enriching dialogue. *American Psychologist, 61*(3), 227–239.

399. Walsh, R. & Vaughan, F. (Eds.). (1993). *Paths beyond ego: The transpersonal vision.* New York: Tarcher/Putnam.

400. Warner, R. (1980). Deception and self deception in shamanism and psychiatry. *International Journal of Social Psychiatry, 26,* 41–52.

401. Weil, A. (1972). *The natural mind.* Boston: Houghton Mifflin.

402. Weil, A. (1981). *The marriage of the sun and moon.* New York: Macmillan.

403. Weinberger, N. (2004). Music and the brain. *Scientific American, 291*(5), 88–95.

404. Wescott, R. (1977). Paranthropology. In J. Long (Ed.), *Extrasensory ecology* (pp. 331–346). Metuchen, NJ: Scarecrow Press.

405. Westen, D. & Weinberger, J. (2004). When clinical description becomes statistical prediction. *American Psychologist, 59,* 595–613.

406. Wilber, K. (1988). There is no new age: Baby boomers, narcissism and the 1960s. *Vajradhatu Sun.*

407. Wilber, K. (1999). A sociable god (2nd ed.). In *The collected works of Ken Wilber* (Vol. 3). Boston: Shambhala.

408. Wilber, K. (1999). Up from Eden (2nd ed.). In *The collected works of Ken Wilber* (Vol. 1). Boston: Shambhala.

409. Wilber, K. (2000). *Integral psychology*. Boston: Shambhala.

410. Wilber, K. (2000). *Sex, ecology, spirituality: The spirit of evolution* (2nd ed.). Boston: Shambhala.

411. Wilber, K. (2006). *Integral spirituality*. Boston: Shambhala.

412. Wilber, K. *The many faces of terrorism*. (in preparation). Boston: Shambhala.

413. Wilber, K., Engler, J., & Brown, D. (Eds.). (in preparation). *Transformations of consciousness: Conventional and contemplative perspectives on development* (2nd ed.). Boston: Shambhala.

414. Wilson, S. & Barber, T. (1982). The fantasy-prone personality. In A. Sheikh (Ed.), *Imagery: Current theory, research, and application* (pp. 340–390). New York: Wiley.

415. Winkelman, M. (1982). Magic: A theoretical reassessment. *Current Anthropology, 23,* 37–66.

416. Winkelman, M. (1984). *A crosscultural study of magio-religious practitioners.* Ph.D. dissertation. University of California, Irvine. Ann Arbor: University of Michigan Microfilms.

417. Winkelman, M. (1989). A cross-cultural study of shamanistic healers. *Journal of Psychoactive Drugs, 21,* 17–24.

418. Winkelman, M. (2000). *Shamanism: The neural ecology of consciousness and healing.* Westport, CT: Bergin & Garvey.

419. Wittgenstein, L. (1969). *Philosophical investigations* (G.E.M. Anscombe, Trans.). New York: MacMillan, Blackwell.

420. Wolf, F. A. (1991). *The eagle's quest: A physicist finds the scientific truth at the heart of the shamanic world.* New York: Touchstone.

421. Wong, E. (1997). *The Shambhala guide to Taoism.* Boston: Shambhala.

422. Wood, J., Nezworski, M., Lilienfeld, S., & Garb, H. (2004). *What's wrong with the Rorschach? Science confronts the controversial inkblot test.* San Francisco: Jossey Bass.

423. Yalom, I. (1980). *Existential psychotherapy.* New York: Basic Books.

424. Yap, P. (1951). Mental diseases peculiar to certain cultures: A survey of comparative psychiatry. *Journal of Mental Science,* April, 313–327.

425. Zetzel, E. (1970). *The capacity for emotional growth.* New York: International University Press.

Index

agitation, 95, 112, 239, 245

altered states of consciousness (ASCs), 8,
    14–15, 18, 73, 76, 89–91, 96–97, 145,
    152, 170, 181, 187, 197, 212, 218, 232,
    237–238, 241, 243, 245, 247

altruism, 218, 220

Amanita muscaria, 193

animism, 126

apprentice, 58, 116, 132–133, 187

ascetic, 44, 59–62, 188

astrology, 213, 233

Atman, 32, 40, 254

attention, 28, 31–32, 62, 113, 197, 211, 226,
    231, 239–241, 246, 248

Aua, 49, 51–53, 63, 69–70

awareness, 28, 32–33, 43, 95–96, 102, 128,
    132, 137, 141, 144, 148, 168–169, 240–
    241, 244–248, 252–253, 268

Book of Revelation, 159, 164

Buddha, 3, 28–29, 31, 33–34, 37, 40, 43–44,
    60, 62, 92, 135, 168, 198, 254, 260, 269

Buddhism, 26, 40, 135, 149, 157, 174, 187,
    196, 225, 238, 243–244, 246, 266–267

calm, 9, 26, 29, 32, 91, 162–163, 187, 197,
    239–241, 245, 247–248

Campbell, Joseph, 3, 37–38, 54, 259

Castaneda, Carlos, 6, 109

causal, 52, 196, 253–254, 256, 259–260

channeling, 96, 112, 137–142, 145, 147–148

Chariot Mysticism, 159–160

Chuang Tzu, 31, 33, 57, 165

clairvoyance, 225, 228, 230

cognicentrism, 91, 182

communitas, 209–211

concentration, 9, 18, 27, 31–32, 57, 59, 62,
    68, 72, 91, 107, 186–187, 189, 197, 224,
    239–241, 244–248, 252

confession, 58, 155, 201, 203–204

Confucius, 11–12, 26, 29, 34, 92, 166, 220

consciousness, 4–5, 8–9, 13–16, 18, 28, 39–41,
    47, 59, 61, 71, 73, 76, 89–92, 95, 97, 137,
    141, 145, 148, 163, 168, 170, 174, 176,
    179–190, 192, 197, 218, 228, 232, 235,
    237–239, 243–244, 246–248, 251–252,
    254, 256–261, 263, 268–271

contribution, 41, 45, 209, 220, 253

control, 13, 25, 31–32, 52, 57, 59–60, 63, 95,
    97, 102, 111, 131, 133, 141, 152, 162–163,